Hip

Pressure Cooking

Hip
Pressure Cooking
Fast, Fresh, and Flavorful

Laura D. A. Pazzaglia

St. Martin's Griffin ✹ New York

HIP PRESSURE COOKING. Copyright text and photographs © 2014 by Laura D. A. Pazzaglia. All rights reserved. Printed in U.S.A. For information, address St. Martin's Press, 175 Fifth Avenue, New York, N.Y. 10010.

www.stmartins.com

Design by Ralph Fowler / rlfdesign
Production manager: Adriana Coada

The Library of Congress Cataloging-in-Publication Data is available upon request.

ISBN 978-1-250-02637-8 (paper over board)
ISBN 978-1-4668-5754-4 (e-book)

St. Martin's Griffin books may be purchased for educational, business, or promotional use. For information on bulk purchases, please contact Macmillan Corporate and Premium Sales Department at 1-800-221-7945, extension 5442, or write specialmarkets@macmillan.com.

First Edition: September 2014

10 9 8 7 6 5 4 3 2

TO ALICE,

for passing to me her
passion for cooking
healthy nutritious meals
and her Pyrex collection

Contents

Hip

Pressure Cooking

Introduction

Pressure cookers were invented by Denis Papin in 1689 and were brought into the home kitchen in the early 1900s, a sign of growing industrialization and technology. For more than a hundred years pressure cookers have helped home cooks preserve food and quickly make tasty stews and stocks.

The basic working principle of the pressure cooker remains unchanged since the first: when liquid is heated in a tightly closed container, the steam it produces is trapped and cannot evaporate as it would in an open or loosely covered pot. During the time the contents of a pressure cooker are boiling, the steam increases in volume but, of course, the space in the cooker does not grow. As a result, the pressure inside the cooker raises the boiling point of the contents, which means they cook at a hotter temperature, and thus cook faster.

While the features, power, and safety of pressure cookers have continued to evolve for the better, recipes to use with them have not. Cookbooks and websites are filled with variations of the last century's stews, soups, and beans. Today's pressure cookers obliterate their predecessors in terms of safety, technology, and utility. Most don't even make a peep while under pressure (making those of us used to the old-style cookers wonder if they're even working), while others come with a plug and digital control panel.

I had actually never heard of or seen pressure cooking until I moved to Austria and found myself struggling to get my family fed on a schedule. Then one day an Italian friend whipped up a dinner for six of us in minutes before my very eyes. Tica didn't know it but her dinner was a life-changing moment for me. What was this little noisy thing on her cooktop that so quickly produced an amazing feast? I thought it could be a lifesaver. I had to know more.

Soon after, I had my own old-style pressure cooker pumping steam out like an old locomotive and making potatoes and roasts in minutes. Then my daughter was born. Until she was two, she slept for only 20 minutes, twice a day. As a result, she was cranky and unwell, and, not being particularly well rested myself, the simple act of getting any food on the table (I was cooking mostly one-armed while bouncing my daughter in the other) seemed daunting. The pressure cooker's time-saving properties became even more valuable for me. I started hunting for recipes and was sorely disappointed to only find roast after roast, potato after potato, and bean after bean recipe. In other words: boring, brown, runny food.

How could it be that this amazing kitchen appliance wasn't being used to cook EVERYTHING?!? I began converting my favorite vegetable, rice, and dessert recipes to the pressure cooker and documenting the results on my personal blog (in between the stories of my observations and misadventures living in Austria). I started to get a lot of comments from readers who were excited to find recipes like ricotta-stuffed zucchini prepared in the pressure cooker, tried them, and wanted more.

We moved to Italy, and soon my daughter outgrew her sleep problems, or maybe they were cured by the soft sound of the Mediterranean Sea outside our home, but with a regular sleep schedule for the whole family, I was able to get more organized and think about what to do next. I discovered modern pressure cookers, with their foolproof safety systems, quality materials, and new accessories. I began to contemplate creating a website dedicated to pressure cookery.

The *hip* pressure cooking website was launched in 2010. There were no recipes for boring, brown, runny food. Pressure cooking wasn't going to be fuddy-duddy anymore, it was getting *hip*!

Fellow cooks were not the only ones to notice my new pressure cooker recipes and techniques. Pressure cooker manufacturers invited me to visit them—in Germany, Luxemburg, Seattle, and my old stomping grounds in California—to demonstrate their shiny pressure cookers at cooking schools and high-end national cookware chains.

I went from working on web and *software* projects as an IT Project Director in California's Silicon Valley in my pre-mommy days to being an expert in kitchen *hardware*!

So What Is *Hip* Pressure Cooking?

Hip pressure cooking is about taking advantage of the latest pressure cooker technology and accessories so you are able to preserve the freshness and maximize the nutrients of ingredients without wasting time.

Hip pressure cooking considers the pressure cooker to be a multipurpose culinary tool. Sometimes an entire recipe is cooked under pressure, but often there is a beginning or finishing step that is not. It's to take advantage of all the things a pressure cooker can do to expand your cooking repertoire or make cooking easier.

Hip pressure cooking is NOT about using the pressure cooker just because you have it. There are times pressure cooking doesn't provide a benefit or maybe even produces results that are not satisfactory. If a recipe is not faster or better in a pressure cooker than it is with conventional cooking, I won't publish it. Rubbery pressure cooker frittata that takes twice as long to cook? Using raw onions because it's faster than sautéing? Not here!

Hip pressure cooking features recipes for dishes that look *and* taste good but were never before thought possible with this cooking appliance: How about pasta that absorbs sauce, not water, as it cooks? Hard-boiled eggs with shells that practically fall off? Ribs that look and taste like they just came off the BBQ? Fresh bread cooked without heating the oven? Finger-licking black fudge brownies in minutes? They're all here.

Key Features of *Hip* Pressure Cooking . . .

The pressure cooker really is easy to use. But I've discovered there are many nuances to using it to cook diverse kinds of food well and effectively—so the results are as delicious as they are easy to achieve. Here

are some of the ways I share my insights throughout this book:

The HOW and the WHY. You can't be *hip* if you don't understand what you're doing. The goal of this book is to not just hand you a bunch of new recipes, but explain how certain ingredients react while under pressure. Braising meat, for example, is a completely new experience—under pressure, the cooking liquids actually *increase*, not *decrease*. If you are the sort of cook who likes to experiment, you may find that once you understand why pressure cooking works as it does, you can improvise.

Simple Prep. Also included are shortcuts and tools for making prep easier and faster, for example, coarsely chopping vegetables for soups that will eventually be pureed with an immersion blender.

Logical Ingredient Quantities. The ingredient lists are set up to be shopper-friendly, meaning they specify quantities you can "see" in the market. For example, I don't call for 4 ounces or 2 cups of chopped carrots. How would you know how many carrots to chop and what would you do with a partial leftover carrot? Instead, I specify 3 medium carrots. This reduces waste when cooking and makes it easier to shop, too.

Clean flavors. The aim is to stay true to a recipe's culture or origin without too much meddling. Since not all ingredients are available everywhere substitutions are also mentioned for anything particularly tricky or uncommon.

Accessible Information. The first chapter of this book covers the equipment and the basic pressure cooking process. The remaining chapters feature recipes in a pretty classic cookbook organization. At the beginning of each recipe chapter are *hip* tips that summarize the special challenges or adaptations that need to be made in pressure cookery for that class of ingredients or dishes—the HOW and WHY mentioned earlier. I've incorporated this know-how in all my recipes, so there's no need for you to make accommodations when following them, but the tips can answer questions like "why do *that?*" or help if you decide to create your own dishes.

. . .

I'm excited to share the tools, secrets, and knowledge that can send you and your pressure cooker on a journey of delicious discovery. I hope that I'll convince you to move the majority of your cooking to the pressure cooker to save time and energy while maximizing nutrition and flavor.

If you can boil it, steam it, or braise it . . . you can pressure cook it!

The Basics of Pressure Cooking

Whether you own a pressure cooker or plan to purchase your first one, before you choose a recipe or shop for ingredients or take things out of your refrigerator, take a few minutes to get up to speed on what these machines do for your cooking, how they work, and the accessories that help you make the best use of them. And get *hip*, don't skip—this chapter takes you on a test run of your cooker and explains how the recipes that follow this section address the requirements of different types of cookers.

Benefits of Pressure Cooking

The pressure cooker is one of the few home cooking appliances that can claim to save time, conserve energy, lighten your workload, and preserve flavor—and have *all* of these claims be true!

Pressure Cooking Saves Time

Cooking time can be reduced 60 to 90 percent (depending on the ingredient). This is possible because of the higher temperatures and wet cooking environment. A vegetable stock can be ready in 5 minutes, roasts in 30, legumes (dried beans) in 15, and desserts in just 20 minutes—instead of an hour or more!

Higher temperatures hasten cooking. If you want to cook something faster in the oven, what do you do? You raise the temperature. The pressure cooker does this too—raising the internal temperature from 212°F (which is the highest that can be obtained by boiling food in a conventional pot at maximum heat) to 250°F.

Water is a better conductor of heat than air. If you were to stick your hand into a pot of water at just 120°F you could receive a bad burn (don't try this), but stick it in the oven at 400°F (don't try this, either) and it just feels uncomfortably hot *without* producing a nasty burn. Similarly, wet cooking methods (boiling, braising, and steaming) transfer heat more efficiently to food than dry cooking methods (baking, roasting, or broiling).

Pressure Cooking Preserves Vitamins and Flavor

Pressure cooking can preserve 90 to 95 percent of an ingredient's vitamins; in comparison, steaming without pressure preserves 75 to 90 percent and boiling preserves 40 to 65 percent of these nutrients.

Water-, air-, and light-soluble vitamins are all preserved during pressure cooking. Pressure cooking requires very little liquid compared to boiling and steaming without pressure, so foods retain a larger portion of their water-soluble vitamins. The speed of pressure cooking is another factor in vitamin retention. Because the heat is so high, most vegetables and fruits are flash-cooked and thus retain most of their vitamins, minerals, color, and flavor—much of which would be lost if the food were cooked two to three times as long at a lower temperature, as in conventional cooking.

Pressure Cooking Conserves Water and Energy

Because a pressure cooker is tightly sealed when in use, there is almost no evaporation of whatever liquid it holds. When boiling in an uncovered pot, a cup or more of liquid is lost to evaporation in just 10 minutes, but when boiling in a pressure cooker for the same time, only a tablespoon is lost! Less evaporation translates into recipes that require less water. Consider this: When you boil 5 quarts of water to make pasta conventionally, all that water has to be heated, kept boiling, and then thrown down the drain when it's time to drain the pasta. Pressure cook pasta and you need only about 2 cups of water—most of which is absorbed by the pasta during pressure cooking, so there's no water to drain and no colander to wash—and it takes a lot less time to bring 2 cups of water to a boil, as well!

Once the pressure cooker has reached pressure (more about this later), it needs only a low or very low flame to keep the contents boiling. Add to this the very much faster cooking time described earlier: The resulting energy use is 70 to 90 percent less than that needed for conventional cooking. Yes, that's the *same* savings that energy-efficient fluorescent light bulbs offer over incandescent bulbs! Plus, the pressure cooker's construction—a nice heavy base and thick sides—allows it to absorb heat that can be used to continue the cooking for a while without using *any* additional energy at all! (see Natural Release page 14).

Pressure Cooking Cleanup Is Easy

One thing I really like about pressure cooking is that it is so clean. No more bubbling juices from oven roasts that result in an oven that requires cleaning. No splatter from boiling tomato sauces on the cooktop and backsplash—just the cooker itself to wash.

Heat Source: Stovetop or Electric Pressure Cooker?

Depending on their design, pressure cookers get their heat either from the stove burner—regulated by the cook—or from an internal electric element—regulated by the machine according to options chosen by the cook. Each type has advantages and the decision for whether to purchase a stovetop or electric pressure cooker is really up to the individual cook.

Stovetop pressure cookers have a steeper learning curve, as the cook needs to learn how to regulate the burner heat to maintain pressure: Leave the heat too hot, and the cooker goes into "over-pressure," which causes it to continue venting and thus evaporate most of the liquid, which in turn will eventually cause the contents to burn. Turn the heat too low and the cooker loses pressure and undercooks the contents. The trial period while you learn to

recognize the "sweet spot" that maintains the pressure can make for a frustrating start to a promising pressure cooking partnership. However, once you surmount this initial hump (usually after several trials) pressure cooking with a stovetop pressure cooker becomes relatively easy.

Electric pressure cookers regulate heat automatically, so the cook need only select a cooking program (or pressure cooking time) and press "start." Some electric cookers have advanced features that also turn them into rice cookers and slow cookers.

The difference between the two pressure cooker types becomes more evident when digging into the details—electric pressure cookers often do not meet the conventional pressure standard (13 to 15 psi) and, worse, they are all over the map in their operating pressure, which may range from 9 to 11 psi. Also, durability is an issue: Though there are some good brands there are also bad, flimsy cookers which stop working in less than three years. Additionally, the mechanics of electric pressure cookers (a heating element repeatedly turning on and off as opposed to a constant low flame) are not ideal for some advanced *hip* pressure cooking techniques (such as cooking pasta and sauce together); in fact, recipes cooked with these techniques are likely to end up scorched in an electric cooker. This is because electric pressure cookers generally require about 2 cups of liquid to maintain pressure while many stovetop cookers need 1 cup or less (check your manual). This difference is fine for most recipes, but that extra cup of liquid added to an electric pressure cooker (plus the liquids released by the foods themselves) can turn a braise into a stew or soup. However, using less liquid (such as the amount used for a stovetop cooker) can result in a scorched dish in an electric cooker.

Though electric pressure cookers can reach pressure at the same speed as stovetop models, the often-used Natural Release opening method takes longer (see pages 14–15 to learn about the release methods). This is both because the heating element cannot be removed and the double-walled construction (an outer plastic shell with a removable inner metal cooking pot) acts as a thermos, conserving a fair amount of heat.

The bottom line: Electric and stovetop pressure cookers have similar time-saving, vitamin-conserving, and energy-saving benefits compared to cooking without pressure. The choice between the convenience of the electric models and the fine control possible with the stovetop models is really a matter of individual preference.

How Big Is It, Anyway?!?

Although the volume of 1 liter is not exactly equal to 1 quart, European manufacturers often label their pressure cookers with the same volume in the two systems so as not to confuse consumers. It's a lot easier to describe the volume as 6L/6qt than as 6L/6.34qts. American-manufactured, 6-quart pressure cookers *really* hold 6 quarts while European-manufactured pressure cookers labeled that way *actually* hold 6.34 quarts. So keep this in mind when comparing prices and sizes.

Pressure Cooker Shapes and Sizes

Whether you're new to pressure cooking or looking to upgrade or expand your pressure cooker collection, you have quite a few options for which cooker to choose and use. Especially among stovetop models, there are assorted sizes and shapes, each designed for slightly different use; options among electric models are limited almost entirely to stockpot styles. Plus there are many brands, of both U.S. and European manufacture. All of the recipes in this book can be made with the most common, stockpot-type pressure cooker, but if it happens that another type is particularly suitable, this is mentioned in the recipe headnote.

The various shapes and sizes are suitable for different quantities of ingredients and different techniques, too. Some have one long handle, called a helper handle, while others may have two short handles. Here are the most common and their uses.

Pressure Pan

Small Pressure Pan (1 to 2 quarts). This small, shallow pressure cooker reaches pressure faster than the larger styles but, of course, it holds less food. It is a good size for making sauces and can cook about ½ cup of dry beans or 1 cup of dry rice or almost 3 cups of soup (about 2 servings). This pan is often included as part of a set with a pressure stockpot.

Large Pressure Pan (3 to 4 quarts). A wide, very shallow pressure cooker, this is great for cooking small amounts of meat because its large interior surface means there is more direct contact between ingredients and heat. This size can cook about 1 cup of dry beans or 2 cups of dry rice or almost 8 cups of soup (about 4 servings)—though I don't recommend pressure cooking soup in this shape pressure cooker.

Pressure Braiser

Pressure Braiser (5 to 8 quarts). A wide, medium-depth pressure cooker that is also known as a large pressure pan, pressure fry pan, or pressure sauté pan. Because the broad interior surface width offers a lot of direct contact between ingredients and heat, this pressure cooker is ideal for braising vegetables and larger cuts of meat. Another plus for this width: after you've pressure cooked your food, you can use the pan, uncovered, to quickly reduce the cooking liquid. In comparison to a pressure stockpot, it is very easy to manipulate the contents in a braiser because of its lower sides. This size can cook about 2 cups of dry beans or 3 cups of dry rice or almost 12 cups of soup (6 to 8 servings).

Pressure Stockpot

Pressure Stockpot (6 to 8 quarts). The 6-quart stockpot is the size I recommend most for beginners. It's great for stews,

Hip Purchasing Recommendations

My advice to anyone who is just starting out pressure cooking is to go with a 6-quart/liter or 8-quart/liter stockpot-type pressure cooker. This size can accommodate meals for 2 to 8 people and it has the vertical space to handle some of the advanced pressure cooking techniques in this book (one-pot meals, steaming, and bain-marie). Some manufacturers offer a set that pairs a single pressure cooking lid with both a stockpot base and a small pressure pan base; I recommend going for such a set if your budget can stretch that far.

Additionally, choose a model that features at least two pressure levels (high and low—sometimes indicated with numbers) as well as the newer spring valve, which makes almost no noise during operation.

As more and more of your cooking moves to the pressure cooker, and for advanced pressure cooks, I recommend adding a second (or third if you have a set) pressure cooker. Investing in a shallow wide pressure cooker with a larger cooking surface, such as a braiser, facilitates preparation of recipes that start off with a sauté or browning step.

The *Hip* Pressure Cooking website (www.hippressurecooking.com) includes detailed reviews of the latest pressure cooker models. Be sure to visit!

soups, chili, etc. Any of the models in this range is a manageable size, often with a dishwasher-safe base. Accessories such as a steamer basket can easily fit in this cooker and be stacked several deep. This size can cook about 3 cups of dry beans or 4 cups of dry rice or almost 16 cups of soup (6 to 8 servings).

Large Pressure Stockpot (10 quarts or larger). Because of their larger size, these cookers take much longer to reach pressure and, since the food is cooking while this is underway, recipes need slight time adjustments. The large size of these cookers makes them bulky to store and difficult to wash—they may not fit under the faucet, or even in the sink, much less in a dishwasher! Besides, they're awfully heavy.

These large stockpot cookers are often labeled as pressure cooker/canners by their manufacturer. They accommodate four 1-quart canning jars and satisfy the USDA recommended processing criteria, which were not tested on any cookers smaller than this.

Pressure Cooker Accessories

The addition of a few simple accessories—whether supplied by the manufacturer, or cobbled together from items found in your kitchen—can expand the repertoire of pressure cooking techniques, allowing you to create more diverse recipes. In the descriptions that follow, you can see that each accessory is represented by an icon; when you read the recipes, these icons will quickly clue you to which accessories you'll need—and in what sequence to insert them into the cooker.

Steamer Basket

A steamer basket is used to hold food you want to cook by steam in the cooker. It should be made of heat-proof material and have feet so the food is not submerged in the cooking liquid. For pressure cookers with a nonstick coated interior, purchase a silicone steamer basket if the manufacturer did not supply one, to ensure that the feet do not damage the coating.

For some recipes you may need more than one steamer basket, especially when using "foil packets" (see page 12) or steam juicing (see page 264). You can stack them!

Many of today's pressure cookers come with a steamer basket, but often it lacks feet. When this is the case, the manufacturer also supplies a trivet to elevate the basket above the liquid. For simplicity, when this book calls for a "steamer basket," it is assumed you'll use the supplied trivet if your basket does not have feet (and if the icons don't show a trivet).

Besides supporting a steamer basket, a trivet can be used to keep items like bowls or pans from touching the bottom of the pressure cooker. They can also be used to lift a roast, chicken, or similar food off the bottom of the cooker and out of the cooking liquid. Similarly, you can set a trivet in a sauce at the bottom of the cooker, place a bowl containing another food on the trivet, and cook both items at once. If your cooker did not come with a steamer basket and trivet, you can use any steamer basket that fits in the cooker to elevate a roast or bowl.

Foil Sling

Lowering a bowl of ingredients into a pressure cooker with your hands isn't so easy, and lifting it out of the hot steamy pot after cooking is even trickier. Containers designed for use in a pressure cooker generally have handles, but when using those that don't, a sling fashioned from aluminum foil is invaluable. These slings are easy to make: Just tear off a long piece of heavy-duty foil (long enough to cradle your bowl and extend above it by several inches on each side) and then fold it vertically in thirds to make a strong strap that's wide enough to support a bowl.

To use the sling, simply center the bowl on it and grasp an end in each hand, close to the bowl. Lift the sling to raise the bowl and transfer it to the cooker. Fold the foil handles down. Cook the food; then, when the cooker is open, fold up the handles again and gently lift out the bowl. A firm grip near the edge of the bowl ensures that everything moves together.

Heat-proof Bowl

A heat-proof bowl or similar container can be used for cooking foods that can't be placed directly in a steamer basket because they are either too fine or contain liquid, such as a batter or custard. The bowl will be placed on the steamer basket for cooking, so it will sit above the cooking liquid and not be in contact with the bottom of the cooker. Ideally, this bowl will have handles so it can easily be lifted in and out of the cooker, but any heat-proof bowl that fits in the pressure cooker without touching the sides can be used in conjunction with a foil sling. This includes bowls made of Pyrex, heat-proof glass, ceramic, stainless steel, aluminum, and silicone. A straight-sided, flat-bottomed bowl (think soufflé mold) will hold the most food in the least amount of space.

For some recipes and techniques you'll need to cover a bowl used this way. The cover should be heat-proof, too. You don't want a cover that fits so tightly as to form a hermetic seal: When a sealed container is pressure cooked, its contents could be pressurized and it would not be safe to open until completely cool. The best option is a square of aluminum foil, laid over the bowl and folded down onto its sides.

Ramekins

Ramekins are useful for cooking individual portions. Like the larger heat-proof bowls, they can be made of ovenproof glass, ceramic, stainless steel, aluminum, or silicone. You can use ceramic teacups and glass custard molds as ramekins. Ramekins are used in conjunction with a steamer basket, which can easily accommodate 4 to 6 depending on the size. If your steamer basket does not have handles (or if you've got a pyramid of ramekins) use long tongs or your glove-covered hand to remove ramekins from the cooker.

Foil Packets

Some foods cook faster than others. If you wish to cook foods that have assorted cooking times together, wrap the faster-cooking ones in aluminum foil, folding it into small packets. Do not substitute parchment paper as it can become saturated and tear apart or unfold in the pressure cooker and thus block a safety valve. Specific uses and some recipes for foil packets are in the One-Pot Meals chapter, page 209.

Getting Started

It is very important to read your pressure cooker's manual so you understand how your specific model works. Here is the information you should glean from the manual: the operating pressure, the type of pressure signal, how to release the pressure when cooking time is up, how to remove

the pressure valve for cleaning. At some point of course, you'll want to also read the maintenance info.

Operating Pressure

The "operating pressure" is the pressure at which the cooker will cook food. The pressure may be measured in psi (pounds per square inch), kpa (kilopascals), or bar (the European standard for defining pressure—it matches exactly to atmospheric pressure at sea level). Once you know this measurement (for instance, 15 psi), you'll be able to determine whether or not your cooker functions at a standard pressure setting. Though there is no "official" standard setting, there are pressure conventions for which cookbooks and timing charts are written. Compare the numbers you find in your pressure cooker manual to the ones in the table below to determine whether the cooker falls within the generally accepted pressure cooker standards.

Measure	Low Pressure	High Pressure
psi	6 to 8	13 to 15
kpa	40 to 55	90 to 100
bar	.4 to .55	.9 to 1

If the instruction manual does not include this information, look at the base of a stovetop cooker or contact the manufacturer. Electric pressure cookers have the "maximum safety pressure" written under the removable pressure valve on the lid. It is often written in very small type right on the plastic or metal part of the valve. The "operating pressure" for the electric cooker is generally 2 to 4 psi less than the pressure written on the valve.

This book is written for pressure cookers that do not meet the standard as well as for those that do, so don't worry if yours does not. You can find information on judging cooking times for nonstandard cookers in the "Cooking Times" section of this chapter (pages 18–22).

Most modern cookers have two pressure levels. Generally "High Pressure" (which is 15 psi) means that most foods will cook *three* times faster at that pressure setting than in conventional cooking, and "Low Pressure" means that most foods will cook *twice* as fast. Most recipes call for high pressure—and though most cookers have two settings, very few recipes have been written for the low pressure setting. In my cooking trials and experiments I've found that this more delicate pressure setting is great for using with quick-cooking foods such as some vegetables, eggs, fish, and pasta.

Pressure Signal

Every pressure cooker must be heated until it reaches the pressure level required for it to cook food. You need to know how your

Get *Hip* About the Pressure

Recipes for pressure cooking indicate whether they are to be cooked at high or low pressure. In this book, the pressure cooking step is written like this:

"Close and lock the lid of the pressure cooker. Cook at high pressure for 7 minutes/stovetop or 8 to 10 minutes/electric (or nonstandard stovetop.)"

Although the way pressure is achieved and maintained differs for stovetop and electric pressure cookers, the meaning is the same for both: Once you lock the cover on the cooker, you select a pressure level, heat the cooker until it signals the selected pressure has been reached, and *then* you start counting the cooking time; electric cookers do some of this for you. When you come to the pressure cooking step in the recipes, bring the cooker to pressure in the manner appropriate for its type. Here's the process for each type, in a nutshell.

For Stovetop Pressure Cookers

1. Add ingredients and liquid to the pressure cooker and select high or low pressure. Put the cooker on the stove burner.
2. Turn the burner heat to high and leave it there until the cooker signals pressure is reached.
3. Turn the burner heat down to the minimum required to maintain the pressure and begin counting the cooking time.
4. Release pressure and serve!

For Electric Pressure Cookers

1. Add ingredients and liquid to the pressure cooker and select a cooking program or set the pressure cooking time.
2. Press start and then wait for the beep that signals the end of cooking.
3. Release pressure and serve!

cooker will alert you that it has "reached pressure" because once it does, the cooking time begins. If you're using a stovetop cooker, you'll have to turn down the heat and begin counting the cooking time. Each model has its own way of alerting the cook, so read the manual carefully to understand yours. Here are the most common ways a pressure cooker will signal it has reached pressure:

Electric pressure cookers (also known as third generation) usually "beep" and their display automatically begins to count down the cooking time—nothing for you to do here.

Modern spring-valve pressure cookers (also known as second generation) will signal they have reached pressure with a physical indicator—usually by raising a rod, bar, or similar device; they may have an auditory signal as well. As soon as the indicator is in place, start counting the pressure cooking time.

Jiggler-valve pressure cookers have a valve on the lid that will "rock and jiggle," at first slowly and then vivaciously, as steam begins to escape through it in order to regulate the pressure inside the cooker. The vivacious jiggle, which is a bit of an ongoing rattle, is your prompt to begin counting the pressure cooking time.

A first-generation pressure cooker, one with a weight-modified valve, will "whistle"—but it doesn't sound like an *actual* whistle such as you might hear at a sporting event. Instead, this cooker makes more of a hissing or *"ssssssshhhhhck"* sound, like that of a steam engine releasing vapor—and this is no coincidence because the steam engines used to power locomotives and steamboats were inspired by Denis Papin's seventeenth-century pressure cooker design. As soon as you hear the first whistle, start counting the pressure cooking time.

Pressure Release Methods

How to release the pressure and in which direction the steam will go as it's being expelled are two things you should know *before* you even take the pressure cooker on a test run. There are several methods for releasing the pressure; each takes a different time and benefits specific cooking techniques. When the pressure is released, some cookers wisely expel the steam straight up and into the exhaust hood over your stove, others may shoot it horizontally onto the backsplash, or in two, or even *three*, different directions. Make sure no one is standing where the steam will go when the pressure is released.

Every recipe in this book indicates which release method to use. Because the release method affects the overall cooking time, and especially while you are becoming familiar with pressure cooking, it makes sense to understand which method is specified before you begin to cook. Here are the details:

Natural Release. Just turn off the heat and wait for the pressure signal to indicate there is no pressure; this usually takes 10 to 15 minutes for a stovetop cooker, 20 to 30 for an electric cooker. "Turn off the heat" means turn off the burner under a stovetop cooker, or unplug or push the "off" button on an electric cooker. The actual release time will be longer for a cooker that's filled to its max, and shorter for one that is less full, that's why there is a range given here. During the Natural Release, the food in the cooker will continue to cook using only the residual pressure, heat, and steam contained in the cooker. This release method is recommended when you are cooking foods such as grains and legumes, which tend to generate a lot of foam that could shoot out of the valve during a Normal Release (see below), and also for meats, to allow them (and their juices) to cool before you take them out of the pressure cooker. One more thing: The time for the pressure to come down will be less if the cooking was done at low pressure.

Normal Release. Sometimes called "Manual" and, confusingly, "Automatic," Normal Release is done by pushing a button, twisting a lever, or turning the valve to immediately release the pressure and expel the steam until the pressure signal to indicate there is no pressure (check your manual to see exactly how to do this for your pressure cooker). The pressure cooker may "sigh" and the top will drop down slightly when all of the pressure is released (this takes about 2 minutes). This is the most frequently used opening method.

Slow Normal Release. There are times when Natural Release isn't practical because it takes too long but Normal Release would cause foam or food to spray through the valve. When this is the case, you can use Slow Normal Release: Use whichever mechanism (button, lever, etc.) is appropriate for your cooker. If it allows you to release pressure at variable speeds, do so slowly. If, instead, the mechanism can only go full throttle, activate it in short bursts, waiting a few seconds between them. For any type of mechanism, if anything other than steam comes out of the valve (like foam) wait 10 seconds until the next burst.

10-Minute Natural Release. There are also instances where Natural Release may take too long but you want the benefit of its continued cooking time. When this is the case, turn off the heat and wait 10 minutes;

Hip Timer Trick

For electric pressure cookers only: The cooking time on an electric pressure cooker is regulated automatically, with a digital display that "counts down" to show the time remaining. When the cooking time is finished, some cookers automatically switch to "keep warm" mode and the digital display begins to "count up." You can use this keep-warm timer to keep track of the time lapsed during any of the release methods; it's especially useful for a 10-Minute Natural Release that will be followed by a Normal Release.

then, if the cooker hasn't opened, release any remaining pressure using Normal Release. If the pressure comes down before the 10 minutes are up, which may be the case for a stovetop cooker, wait the full time before opening the cooker. This 10-Minute Natural Release technique is especially useful for rice and other grains, which benefit from the extra 10 minutes in the cooker's steam. (If the cooking was done at low pressure, the recipe will instruct you to use this procedure but count only 5 minutes.)

Cold Water Quick Release. Take the pressure cooker to the kitchen sink and run cold water on the lid, tilting the cooker slightly so as not to wet any of the pressure release or safety valves (usually takes 20 seconds or less). This method generally is used to stop the cooking instantly and so you can immediately open the cooker. It can also be used to hasten the pressure release for foamy foods (mentioned previously) instead of a Natural Release. However one has to be careful carrying a cooker across the kitchen to the sink and ensure that no children, pets, or spouses are underfoot and the sink is empty. This method cannot be used with electric pressure cookers for obvious reasons. I don't specify it for any of the recipes here; you may be the judge of whether to use it when Normal Release is indicated or at any time you want to open the cooker quickly.

Pressure Valve Removal

The pressure regulator valve should always be clean and free of debris. It is the primary safety release on a cooker and not maintaining it properly could damage the cooker or injure the cook! Most pressure cooker manufacturers want to make this task easy for the cook so generally these valves can be removed without tools.

Stovetop pressure cookers will likely have something that can be unscrewed by hand on the underside of the lid to release the valve. Cookers with a pressure selection dial on the lid may indicate a valve removal option (usually following the pressure release option).

Electric pressure cookers have a floating weighted valve that can be pulled off the lid with a quick vertical yank. Some also have valve covers on the underside of the lid that need to be unscrewed and cleaned.

Maintenance and Replacement Parts

The rubber and silicone parts of the pressure cooker will need occasional replacement. In particular, the gasket, the small parts of the primary valve (for instance a small ring around the metal rod), and the safety stopper may need to be replaced every 18 months or so depending on the use. But be aware, these parts age with time as well as use, so even if it's never been used, a brand-new cooker that has been in the box for a few years may *already* need these parts replaced. The manual should include information about where to get replacement parts.

Sometimes, you can feel the gasket becoming less supple and stiffer. Rarely, you may see a crack or damage in the part. More often, you'll know that these parts need to be replaced because the pressure cooker takes more time than usual to reach pressure or is unable to reach or maintain it.

Keep the manufacturer's contact information in case your cooker should need maintenance or replacement parts in the future.

4 Rules of Pressure Cooker Safety

1. Read the instruction manual that comes with your cooker.

2. Never exceed the maximum capacity (that's half full for legumes, grains, and fruits, and two-thirds full for everything else).

3. Tilt the lid away from you when you open the pressure cooker to direct hot steam away from your face.

4. Keep the pressure regulator valve clean.

Discrepancies between your Manual and this Book

If there is ever a discrepancy between the recommendations in this book and your pressure cooker manual (for example, for not cooking a specific kind of food or not using a particular opening method) always heed the manual. Pressure cooker models and technologies change and each manufacturer will know the limitations of its specific models.

Test Run

Now that you've read the manual and are familiar with your pressure cooker's pressure signal, release options, and valve, it's time to see all of these things in action—by boiling some water. This test allows you to observe the amount of evaporation too.

1. Add 4 cups of water to the pressure cooker base (use a 4-cup heat-proof measure—you'll see why later).

2. Close and lock the lid. Double-check that the valve in the lid, or pressure selector, is not at the "exhaust" or "pressure release" position.

3. Select the pressure level: For an electric pressure cooker, choose a high pressure cooking program. For a stovetop cooker with a dial on the lid, turn the dial to "2" or "high." If the lid has a rod with rings on it to indicate pressure, you don't need to do this step; the rings will rise out of the cooker after step 9.

4. Turn the burner to high if using a stovetop cooker or press "start" if using an electric cooker.

5. In about 8 to 10 minutes, the water inside the cooker will begin to boil—place your hand on the handle to feel the vibrations of the water moving inside.

6. You'll see what looks like vapor exiting the valve. This is just the steam pushing oxygen out of the cooker. More and more will exit until there is a crescendo of steam and a small click.

7. No more steam.

8. The lid has sealed shut and the cooker is starting to build pressure. The cooker *has not* reached *full* pressure yet! You'll see the pressure signal on a stovetop cooker begin to rise, dance, or move, but it is not in its final position yet.

9. The pressure signal alerts you that pressure has been reached (by moving firmly into place, whistling, beeping, etc.) and a small stream of vapor comes out of the valve again. For the rod-type pressure signal, the ring indicating high pressure is fully visible.

10. If using a stovetop pressure cooker, turn down the heat to the minimum the cooker needs to maintain pressure—too low and the signal will begin to fall and the cooker will slowly lose pressure, too high and too much steam will leave the valve. It's just right if no more vibrations can be felt when you put your hand on the handle. At this point the pressure inside the cooker has stabilized and is preventing the air bubbles in the boiling contents from breaking to the surface. It will take a few tries to find the exact heat setting for

your particular cooker and cooktop combination.

11. Begin counting the cooking time for 10 minutes using a digital timer, microwave, or cell phone app (the countdown begins automatically in electric cookers once they have reached pressure).

12. When the time is up, release the pressure using either the Normal Release (push a button, lever, or valve as indicated in your manual) or Natural Release (turn off the heat source, or unplug the electric cooker, and don't do anything else).

13. Unlock the pressure cooker and remove the lid, tilting it to direct the remaining steam away from your face. When you first try pressure cooking, you will be tempted to bend down to take a peek at what has happened inside: *don't*. Always wait until the lid is fully removed and the steam has dissipated before peeking.

14. Now you have a chance to see and measure *exactly* how little of the water has actually evaporated from your cooker. Once open, quickly and carefully pour the water from the pressure cooker back into the heat-proof 4-cup measuring cup (liquid evaporates quickly once the lid is off, so move fast).

15. You're done!

Cooking Times

The recipes in this book can be created using both stovetop and electric pressure cookers. The cooking times specified are for standard stovetop cookers with a pressure of 13 to 15 psi and electric cookers with a pressure of 9 to 11.6 psi (see the chart on page 12). For some recipes, particularly those with dense ingredients such as meat, whole grains, a few vegetables, and beans, a slightly longer cooking time is needed when an electric pressure cooker is used. When this is the case, the recipes specify the cooking time first for standard stovetop cookers and then for electric cookers and nonstandard stovetop cookers, which require the electric cooker time. For example, a recipe might instruct you to: Cook for 5 minutes/stovetop or 6 to 7 minutes/electric (or nonstandard stovetop).

What's that range about? If your electric cooker has an operating pressure of 9 psi, use the longer cooking time in the range given. If it has an operating pressure of 11.6, use the shorter cooking time. If you are not sure whether your stovetop cooker is standard or not, begin with the standard time and if the food is undercooked, simply close the lid and pressure cook for a few more minutes—and then use the nonstandard time in the future. Likewise for an electric cooker, if you're not sure where it falls in the pressure range, begin with the shorter cooking time and adjust from there. As you become familiar with your cooker, you'll learn whether your recipes tend to be undercooked, overcooked, or just right, and find you are then automatically choosing the appropriate cooking time.

When the Cooker Has Only One Pressure Level

Some pressure cookers have only one pressure level; when this is the case, it's usually high pressure. But these cookers can be used for recipes that specify cooking at low pressure: simply cut the cooking time in half. The only exception to this is for hard-boiled eggs (page 55), where high pressure for any length of time will crack the shells.

Some old-style European pressure cookers have low pressure only. If you happen to have one of these and want to use a recipe that calls for high pressure, just follow the longest cooking time specified for electric and nonstandard pressure cookers.

Compensating for an Electric Cooktop

The burners on electric stoves do not adjust their temperature quickly, so with them there is no timely way to "turn the heat down to the lowest setting that maintains pressure." To compensate for this, do the "switcharoo": When using a stovetop pressure cooker on an electric cooktop, bring the cooker to pressure on a large burner, and at the same time, preheat a smaller burner on low heat. When the cooker has reached pressure, delicately move it to the lower-temperature burner to maintain pressure for the rest of the cooking time—and be sure to turn off the large burner. Note: The larger burner should not exceed the width of your cooker's base, but the smaller burner can be smaller than the base—the heavy

Get *Hip* About the Timing

When you read a pressure cooking recipe, naturally you want to get an idea of how long it will take to make, especially since pressure cooking is faster than conventional cooking. But you can't just scan and note the cooking times indicated! This is because pressure cooker recipe cooking times do not include the time it takes for the cooker to reach pressure—the time given is only for the time to cook *after* pressure is reached. (Conventional recipes don't tell you how long it will take for the water to reach a boil or the oven to heat, either, so this isn't really any different.) And don't forget, it takes time for the pressure to come down when the cooking is finished, too, so be sure you understand which release method is required (see Pressure Release Methods, pages 14–16).

Rule of thumb: If a recipe begins with a sauté step and thus the cooker is already warm, most cookers will reach high pressure in 5 to 8 minutes. If the recipe begins with a "cold" cooker, most cookers will reach high pressure in 10 to 15 minutes. The time to reach pressure will be longer if the cooker is very full or the contents are very cold or frozen. Your cooker will reach low pressure in about half these times.

There is little or no difference in the time it takes for a specific quantity of liquid to boil in a closed pressure cooker and in a covered pot. But pressure cooker recipes use less liquid than conventional recipes, and this smaller quantity of liquid takes less time to reach a boil. So there is time-saving in this step, too, just not as great as in the pressure cooking itself.

aluminum disk in the base of your cooker will distribute the heat evenly.

Compensating for an Induction Cooktop

Do not bring the cooker up to pressure on the highest setting of the induction burner; this can make the cooker reach pressure too quickly (in about 4 minutes) and not force out all of the air inside the cooker, making the internal cooking temperature lower than that in a properly pressurized cooker, which takes about 10 minutes. Also, bringing a cooker up to pressure at maximum heat on induction will burn and char the food that is in contact with the base. Instead, bring the cooker to pressure on the medium-high setting. For example, if the induction burner has 10 heat settings, bring it to pressure on setting 7.

Compensating for High Altitudes

The general rule of thumb is to increase cooking time by 5 percent for every 1,000 feet above sea level, but seriously, who is going to calculate 15 percent of 8 minutes? There's an easier way. Using a pressure cooker at high altitudes is just like using a nonstandard pressure cooker. A 15 psi pressure cooker at sea level will only operate at 12 psi at 5,000 feet because of the decreased external atmospheric pressure. Translation: just follow the longer cooking times noted for "electric (or nonstandard stovetop)" pressure cookers.

The Pressure Cooker Boils, Steams, and More!

Yes, the pressure cooker will quickly boil and steam all manner of food, but it can be used for several other cooking methods, too. Here's a quick look at the possibilities.

All the recipes in this book are set up for success with whichever techniques are required, but it's useful to understand the ways these techniques differ for pressure cooking and conventional cooking.

Bain-marie

Unlike a bain-marie in an oven (a process in which a filled baking dish or ramekin is partially submerged in a pan of water and used for baking cheesecakes, custards, and similar dishes), pressure cooker bain-marie actually steams the food because the baking dish sits in a steamer basket above (not immersed in) water. Though the cooking temperatures of oven and pressure cooker bain-maries are vastly different, the effect is the same: even and uniform heating of the container and its contents.

Baine-marie

Boiling and Stewing

Boiling and stewing are really no different in the pressure cooker than in conventional cooking. However, since there is almost no evaporation, and the cooker cannot be more than half full (for legumes, grains, and fruit) or two-thirds full for everything

Boiling and Stewing

else, adjustments to the liquid portion of a recipe need to be made. Generally, just covering the ingredients with liquid is sufficient; once under pressure they'll boil and be coaxed to contribute their own juices to the pot.

Braising

Braising under pressure requires a lot of restraint with the liquid ingredients. The goal in the pressure cooker, just as for an oven-cooked braise, is NOT to submerge and boil the ingredients but to provide just enough liquid to boil a small portion near the base and lightly steam the rest. To achieve this in the pressure cooker VERY LITTLE liquid is needed. I recommend using the minimum amount required by the pressure cooker (generally 1 to 1½ cups). This will ensure that the flavors are not diluted and that the ingredients are cooked in their own juices.

Braising

Juice Extraction

It's quite easy to extract the juice from fruit by steaming it in a pressure cooker. You need to use several pressure cooker accessories, but otherwise this is fairly

simple to do: just steam the fruit until its cells burst and the juices are released. This technique is more fully explained in chapter 12, page 249.

Sautéing

You can sauté in the pressure cooker, but not quite the way as you do in conventional cooking. Instead of stirring constantly or at intervals until the food is cooked through, with the pressure cooker the process is only *started* this way. Once the ingredients take on a little color, you add a liquid, lock the lid, and pressure cook briefly, as specified in your recipe, thus finishing with a "faux sauté." This is a terrific way to quickly cook vegetables and meat with some seasoning—they'll be ready in a fraction of the usual time. No more stirring constantly and vegetables retain more of their flavor and vitamins. You can also give meat dishes a sautéed start.

Sautéing

Steaming

The only real difference between steaming in the pressure cooker and in a conventional saucepan is the cooking time. Simply add the minimum amount of liquid required by your pressure cooker

Juice Extraction

Steaming

(usually 1 to 1½ cups) to the base, insert the steamer basket and food, and cook under pressure as indicated by your recipe or on the Pressure Cooking Timetables in the Appendix, pages 269–281.

Cooking Individual Ingredients

You may not always want to follow a recipe: Pressure cooking offers a great alternative to basic steaming, braising, or boiling, or, in some cases, even roasting. The Pressure Cooking Timetables in the Appendix at the end of this book (see pages 269–281) includes charts that give the cooking times and release methods for a variety of individual ingredients, as well as the ratio of water to add and other essential information. Check them out—you'll find what you need to know to prepare your choice of vegetables, grains, and beans, as well as fish, fruit, meats, and nuts.

Browning via Broiler

One thing that really sets a *hip* recipe apart is that it doesn't LOOK like it came out of the pressure cooker. To achieve this—and better flavor, too—some recipes require a quick finish under a broiler. The goal is to crisp and caramelize the top of the food; this can be achieved with an oven broiler, toaster oven, kitchen blowtorch, and even a halogen oven light.

Halving or Doubling Pressure Cooker Recipes

Each recipe in this book includes a note about what to do, if anything, should you want to double the yield or make only half as much. One thing never changes: The cooking time is the same, regardless of the yield. However, the fuller the cooker is, the longer it will take to reach pressure. Here are the rules of thumb that guide any changes to the ingredients quantities:

- For steaming, the amount of liquid stays the same regardless of the yield.

- For boiling or braising, use at least 1 cup of liquid, or your pressure cooker's minimum liquid requirement, whichever is greater. When you cut a recipe in half, don't cut the liquid to less than this amount—regardless of the original quantity. For instance, 1½ cups in the original cannot be halved to ¾ cup; it must not be cut to less than 1 cup or your cooker's minimum liquid requirement.

- For grains, legumes, and fruits, or any food that will expand or cause excessive foaming, do not fill the pressure cooker more than half full, including the cooking liquid.

- To cook foods other than grains, legumes, and fruits, make sure the pressure cooker is no more than two-thirds full.

Adapting a Recipe to the Pressure Cooker

Adapting conventional recipes to the pressure cooker can be tricky. Before you try this, I highly recommend making several recipes designed for pressure cooking so you can learn the little nuances of your cooker and the process in general. Once you feel confident of these, go ahead and undertake a conversion! But here's a suggestion: The easiest way to adapt a conventional recipe to the pressure cooker is to find a similar pressure cooker recipe, and then adjust the ingredients to more closely resemble those in the recipe you want to adapt. Each chapter in this book includes a "Get *hip*" sidebar explaining the principles of pressure cooking the food featured in that chapter; these are helpful for times when your creativity urges you to adapt or develop a recipe.

Here are tips to bear in mind when adapting recipes:

Reduce the Liquid

With the exception of soups and boiled meats, reduce the liquid to the minimum required by your pressure cooker (usually 1 to 2 cups). The minimum is all you'll need, even for recipes such as a braised roast, which in a conventional oven would be covered halfway with liquid.

Wine Correctly

Because there is almost no evaporation during pressure cooking, wine does not boil away as it does in conventional cooking. Instead, it comes out of the cooker lending an unpleasant taste to the food. My solution: If 1 cup or less of wine is added, cook uncovered to evaporate it almost completely before the pressure cooking step. If more is called for—for example in long-cooking stews—cooking the wine uncovered long enough to reduce it by about half before pressure cooking ensures that the dish will not have a raw acidic edge.

Add Thickeners After Pressure Cooking

Does the original recipe start with a butter-and-flour mixture? Involve potato flakes or cornstarch? Because these thicken the cooking liquid and prevent it from boiling, they may prevent the cooker from reaching pressure; to make sure this doesn't happen, add them *after* pressure cooking the recipe. You can prepare the butter-and-flour mixture in a small saucepan in the usual way while the pressure cooker is cooking, and then stir the mixture into the dish when you open the cooker.

Beans: Use Dried Instead of Canned

Dried beans are so quick to prepare in the pressure cooker, and to my taste have superior flavor to canned. If you wish, you can substitute soaked dried beans for canned beans when adapting a conventional recipe. When doing this, add liquid equivalent to one-and-one-half times the volume of the beans before they were soaked. For instance, if you began with 1 cup dried beans, add 1½ cups liquid to the soaked beans when you place them in the pressure cooker. See chapter 5 for more about soaking and pressure cooking dried beans.

Time It for the Longest-Cooking Ingredient

Turn to the Appendix (pages 269–281) and look up the cooking time for the main ingredient on the pertinent Pressure Cooking Timetable, and time your adaptation accordingly. For example, Chicken Cacciatora should be cooked for the time required by bone-in chicken pieces: 10 minutes. Do not improvise on pressure cooking times—food is easily overcooked.

Soups and Stocks

Soups, and the stocks that form their base, are quick and absolutely delicious prepared in the pressure cooker. There are a couple of fundamental differences between making soups in the pressure cooker and in a conventional stockpot that may not be readily apparent to a beginner.

There is almost no evaporation in the pressure cooker, so there's no need to fill the pot to the tippy-top to keep it from running dry. A recipe that feeds six people may only call for 2 cups of stock but have even *more* liquid after pressure cooking. This is because the higher pressure squeezes juice from the vegetable ingredients into the soup and then plumps them up again with hot steam—providing more flavor than conventionally cooked soup. Couple the extracted juices with the minimal evaporation, and the result is intense color and flavor in what only *appears* to be nearly magical quantities.

Don't chop, chop, chop! For creamy soups, coarsely chop the vegetables: they will be pureed anyway. For stocks, just snap the veggies in half so they are small enough to fit in the pressure cooker: the stock will be full of veggie juice and free of the pulp that would ordinarily break off from smaller pieces and turn a stock cloudy.

Caramelize first. To add another dimension of flavor, sauté the aromatics and caramelize the meat and veggies: beginning with a quick browning in the uncovered pressure cooker base will use less energy than oven roasting, and capture the food's precious juice for the recipe!

Cold-start meat stocks. Start meat and poultry stocks with cold water to extract a specific protein, called albumin, that cannot be extracted with hot water. If the name sounds familiar, it's because it is the same protein found in eggs.

Acidify. Just a touch of acid can really make a ho-hum stock more interesting. Use tomatoes or tomato paste (these also add color), lemon, or even a dash of vinegar (white or red depending on whether the resulting stock should remain white). Another acid that can be used is white wine, particularly in poultry and seafood stocks. Don't mix your acids, and *please*, no hard liquor, which will cause a pressure cooker to start shooting flames.

Thicken after, not before. Thick, creamy soups usually begin with a roux of butter and flour, or some other thickener. But when heated under pressure, this thickened paste will not create enough steam, resulting in a cooker that does not reach pressure or a soup that is scorched on the bottom. To make sure your creamy soups cook properly, thicken them *after* the pressure cooking step.

Delay the dairy. Milk, cream, and cheeses don't do well in the super-heated environment inside the pressure cooker; they can foam, scorch, or curdle. Wait to add them until after pressure cooking is finished and you've popped open the lid. A few extra minutes of simmering, uncovered, are enough to infuse their flavor and creaminess into the whole soup.

"Phase" it in. The phased *cooking* method, where the pressure cooker is opened at intervals to add or subtract ingredients, enables ingredients with different cooking times to be used together! For example, the phases of Classic Pasta and Legume Minestrone, page 39, are as follows: pressure cook the legumes, open the cooker, add the pasta and pressure cook again, open and serve!

Reduce it. If you've made a large batch of stock and storage space in the fridge or freezer is a problem, simply simmer the stock, uncovered, until it has reduced by half. You can dilute this concentrated stock to return it to its normal strength later, when you're ready to use it.

Salt or commercialize it. The stocks in this book contain no salt and the recipes calling for stock assume this. If using commercial stock to make one of my recipes, reduce the salt accordingly. Or, if you want to give one of the homemade stocks the salinity of a commercial stock, simply add half a teaspoon of salt per cup of stock (that's assuming the stock is normal strength, not reduced to a concentrate). Of course, salt preference is immensely personal—the amount to use is up to you!

Thicken It

There are myriad ways to thicken soups, and each has its own personality and flavor. Here are some common thickening additives:

All-purpose flour. After the pressure cooking step is finished, sprinkle 1 to 2 tablespoons of flour into the cooker and then bring the soup to a boil, uncovered. Reduce the heat and simmer gently for a few minutes. If a thicker result is desired, add more flour, 1 tablespoon at a time, until the desired consistency is achieved. Avoid lumps by sprinkling the flour through a sifter or fine-mesh strainer.

Rice. Add ½ to ⅓ cup of unrinsed white rice to the cooker along with the other recipe ingredients before pressure cooking. When the rice and soup are fully cooked, puree everything together.

Potato. Cut 1 large potato into large dice (peeled or unpeeled according to taste), and add to the cooker along with the other recipe ingredients before pressure cooking. When the soup has finished cooking and is still in the cooker, either smash the potatoes with a wooden spoon or puree the soup with an immersion blender. A soup can also be thickened with leftover mashed potatoes after the pressure cooking is done: Bring the soup to a boil and stir in the potatoes 1 tablespoonful at a time.

Eggs. Both raw and hard-boiled eggs will thicken soup; add them after pressure cooking, while the soup is still in the cooker: to use a hard-boiled egg, simply crumble the yolk and stir it into the hot soup. To use a raw egg, first beat the whole egg (or just the white or yolk if you prefer) in a small bowl. Slowly drizzle ½ cup of the hot soup into the egg, stirring constantly. Then, drizzle and stir the mixture into the piping hot soup in the cooker. The egg will cook immediately. This is a tricky technique because shocking the egg with too much heat can cause it to scramble rather than emulsify and thicken the soup.

Bread Crumbs. After the pressure cooking step is finished, sprinkle 1 to 2 tablespoons of plain dry bread crumbs into the soup and puree the mixture. This is a particularly good technique for soups that will be served cold.

Cornstarch. After the pressure cooking step is finished, whisk together 1 tablespoon cornstarch and 1 tablespoon of the soup in a small cup. Whisk this slurry mixture into the soup in the cooker, and bring the soup to a boil, uncovered. Boil for a few minutes until the soup has thickened.

Evaporate! After the pressure cooking step is finished, open the cooker as instructed in your recipe and then simmer the soup, uncovered, to evaporate some of the liquid. Continue to simmer until the soup has reduced to the thickness desired.

Creamy Soups

Creamy soups are creamy for a *reason*; their ingredients include a thickener of some sort and they are almost always pureed. Thickening, which is usually done at the *beginning* of a recipe, needs to happen *last* in pressure cooking. The starches that bind *to* the liquid to thicken it can make it too thick to freely boil and generate the steam the pressure cooker needs to reach and maintain pressure.

Carrot, Potato, and Leek Soup

Serves 4 to 6

Potage Crécy, the French name of this soup, refers to the town, Crécy, in France that is famous for growing the *best* carrots in the world. You can use a large yellow onion instead of a leek if you wish.

Note: This recipe can be either halved or doubled provided the total volume of the ingredients does not exceed two-thirds of the pressure cooker's capacity.

> 1 tablespoon olive oil
> 2 tablespoons unsalted butter
> 1 medium leek, white and pale green parts only, coarsely chopped
> 2 teaspoons salt
> 1 pound carrots, coarsely chopped
> 1 large potato, peeled and coarsely chopped
> 4 cups salt-free Chicken Stock (page 48)
> Freshly ground black pepper
> 1 bouquet garni (parsley sprigs, bay leaf, sprig of thyme, tied tightly with string or in cheesecloth)

> ¼ cup heavy cream
> ⅛ teaspoon freshly grated nutmeg
> Fresh thyme sprigs or chopped fresh chives, for serving

1. Heat the pressure cooker base on medium heat, add the oil and butter, and cook until the butter has melted. Stir in the chopped leeks and salt and sauté, stirring infrequently, until the leeks have softened, about 5 minutes. Add the carrots, and cook, stirring infrequently, until they are golden on one side, about 5 more minutes. Add the potato, stock, pepper to taste, and the bouquet garni.

2. Close and lock the lid of the pressure cooker. Cook at high pressure (see "Get *Hip* About the Pressure," page 13) for 7 minutes/stovetop or 8 to 10 minutes/electric (or nonstandard stovetop.) When the time is up, open the cooker with the Normal Release method (see page 15).

3. Fish out and discard the bouquet garni. Using an immersion blender, puree the soup in the cooker. Stir in the cream and nutmeg. Ladle into bowls and dot each serving with a thyme sprig or a few chopped chives.

Carrot, Potato, and Leek Soup

Creamy Potato and Leek Soup

Serves 4 to 6

In France it is called *Potage Parmentier*, but it's more commonly known as *vichyssoise*. In either case, the classic recipe calls for peeled potatoes and heavy cream, but I like to leave the skins on the potatoes for added protein and to use plain whole-milk yogurt for a more tangy flavor and less fat. Serve chilled in the summer, as is the custom in France, or piping hot in the winter.

Note: This recipe can be either halved or doubled provided the total volume of the ingredients does not exceed two-thirds of the pressure cooker's capacity.

1 tablespoon vegetable oil
1 tablespoon unsalted butter
3 leeks, white and pale green parts only, sliced crosswise
1½ teaspoons salt
4 medium unpeeled potatoes, coarsely chopped
4 cups salt-free Chicken or Vegetable Stock (pages 48–49)
½ teaspoon ground white pepper, plus more if desired
½ cup plain whole-milk yogurt
2 tablespoons chopped fresh chives, for serving

1. Heat the pressure cooker base on medium heat, add the oil and butter, and cook until the butter has melted. Stir in the leeks and salt and sauté until the leeks have softened, stirring infrequently, about 5 minutes. Add the potatoes, stock, and pepper.

2. Close and lock the lid of the pressure cooker. Cook at high pressure (see "Get *Hip* About the Pressure," page 13) for 7 minutes/stovetop or 8 to 9 minutes/electric (or nonstandard stovetop). When the time is up, open the cooker with the Normal Release method (see page 15).

3. Using an immersion blender, puree the soup in the cooker. If you wish to serve the soup cold, transfer it to a bowl, cover, and refrigerate. Whether serving it hot or cold, stir in the yogurt just before serving. Taste and season with more pepper if you wish. Sprinkle each serving with a few chopped chives.

Summer Cucumber and Spearmint Soup

Serves 4 to 6

This recipe calls for only 2 cups of stock—not to worry: the rest of the liquid comes from the cucumbers, which are more than 95 percent water. Half the liquid comes from them! You can use any fresh mint you like; my favorite for this recipe is spearmint. Since this soup is served cold, it needs to be a little saltier than you might expect.

Note: This recipe can be either halved or doubled provided the total volume of the ingredients does not exceed two-thirds of the pressure cooker's capacity.

2 cups salt-free Vegetable Stock
(page 49)

4 medium unpeeled potatoes, coarsely
chopped

½ cup blanched almonds

1 pound cucumbers, coarsely chopped

2 fresh mint stems and leaves (reserve a
few leaves for garnish)

1 cup whole milk

2 teaspoons salt

½ teaspoon ground white pepper, plus
more as desired

Extra-virgin olive oil, for serving

1. Add the stock, potatoes, and almonds
to the pressure cooker base.

2. Close and lock the lid of the pressure
cooker. Cook at high pressure (see "Get
Hip About the Pressure," page 13) for
7 minutes/stovetop or 8 to 9 minutes/
electric (or nonstandard stovetop). When
the time is up, open the cooker with the
Normal Release method (see page 15).

3. Add the cucumbers, spearmint, milk,
salt, and pepper to the soup and, using an
immersion blender, puree the soup in the
cooker until very smooth. Transfer to a
bowl, cover, and refrigerate until chilled.
Taste and season with more pepper if you
wish. Ladle into bowls and drizzle each
serving with oil and garnish with a few of
the reserved mint leaves.

Cream of Asparagus Soup

Serves 4 to 6

The thickener for this soup is a blond roux,
a mix of butter and flour that is cooked
just long enough for the flour to be lightly
toasted, which adds a little extra nuttiness
to the flavor.

Note: This recipe can be either halved or
doubled provided the total volume of the
ingredients does not exceed two-thirds of
the pressure cooker's capacity.

1 tablespoon olive oil

3 green onions, sliced crosswise into
¼-inch pieces

1 pound asparagus, tough ends removed,
cut into 1-inch pieces

4 cups salt-free Chicken Stock (page 48)

1 tablespoon unsalted butter

1 tablespoon all-purpose flour

2 teaspoons salt

1 teaspoon ground white pepper, plus
more as needed

½ cup heavy cream

1. Heat the pressure cooker base on
medium heat and add the oil, green onions,
and a pinch of salt. Sauté the green onions
for a few minutes, then add the asparagus
and stock.

2. Close and lock the lid of the pressure
cooker. Cook at high pressure (see "Get
Hip About the Pressure," page 13) for
5 minutes/all cooker types.

3. Meanwhile, make a blond roux: In a
small saucepan over low heat, mix together

the butter and flour and cook, stirring constantly, until the butter has melted and the mixture foams and begins to turn golden beige. Remove from the heat.

4. When the time is up, open the cooker with the Normal Release method (see page 15). Add the roux, salt, and pepper to the soup and puree with an immersion blender until smooth. Taste and season with more pepper if you wish. Swirl in the cream just before serving.

Variations

Cream of Wild Mushroom Soup

Follow the Cream of Asparagus Soup recipe, substituting 1 coarsely chopped yellow onion for the green onions and 1 pound coarsely chopped wild mushrooms for the asparagus. Before adding the stock, push the onion to the side, add the mushrooms, and sauté just until the mushrooms begin to brown at the edges, about 7 minutes. Mix in 1 tablespoon of dark rum just before serving.

Don't have access to fresh, wild mushrooms? Use 1 pound white button mushrooms plus ½ cup reconstituted dried mushrooms (porcini, oyster, etc.).

Cream of Cauliflower and Fennel Soup

Follow the Cream of Asparagus Soup recipe, substituting 1 chopped small fennel bulb for the green onions and 1 pound coarsely chopped cauliflower for the asparagus. Swirl in ½ cup plain whole-milk yogurt just before serving.

Classic Cream of Tomato Soup

Serves 4 to 6

Many classic cream soups are traditionally made with a béchamel base: milk thickened with butter and flour, and this one is no exception. But of course, for the pressure cooker version, you add the flour and milk after the pressure cooking is done. I love to serve this soup with whole wheat, grilled-cheese sandwich triangles.

Note: This recipe can be either halved or doubled provided the total volume of the ingredients does not exceed two-thirds of the pressure cooker's capacity.

1 tablespoon olive oil
1 tablespoon unsalted butter
1 medium yellow onion, chopped
2 celery stalks, coarsely chopped
6 ripe tomatoes, coarsely chopped, with their juice
2 tablespoons tomato paste
1 cup salt-free Vegetable Stock (page 49)
2 fresh oregano sprigs
1 tablespoon all-purpose flour
2 cups whole milk
2 teaspoons salt, or more if desired
½ teaspoon freshly ground black pepper, plus more if desired
Whole wheat, grilled-cheese sandwich triangles, for serving (optional)

1. Heat the pressure cooker base on medium heat, add the oil and butter, and cook until the butter has melted. Add the onion and sauté until it becomes translucent, about 5 minutes. Add the celery, tomatoes, tomato paste, and stock and stir well. Place the oregano sprigs on top.

2. Close and lock the lid of the pressure cooker. Cook at high pressure (see "Get *Hip* About the Pressure," page 13) for 5 minutes/all cooker types. When the time is up, open the cooker with the Normal Release method (see page 15).

3. Fish out and discard the oregano sprigs. Sprinkle the flour over the soup. Using an immersion blender, puree the soup. When the mixture is nearly smooth, pour in the milk and blend for 20 seconds more. Stir in the salt and pepper; taste and adjust the seasoning if you wish. Return the uncovered cooker base to medium heat and simmer the soup, stirring frequently, until it reaches the desired thickness.

Chowders

Chowders are a combination of chunky pieces of vegetables (or seafood) with a hearty base. Some chowders are creamy; when this is the case, just like the creamy soups they must be thickened *after* pressure cooking. Unlike the creamy soups, chowders are not pureed, they stay nice and chunky and chewy.

Corn Chowder

Serves 4 to 6

Use fresh or thawed frozen corn kernels for this recipe. For a richer soup, substitute cream for the milk. To crisp the prosciutto for the garnish, either sauté it in a dry pan or lay the slices on a parchment paper–covered baking sheet and place in a hot oven (400°F) for a few minutes.

Note: This recipe can be either halved or doubled provided the total volume of the ingredients does not exceed two-thirds of the pressure cooker's capacity.

1 tablespoon olive oil
1 medium yellow onion, diced
1 medium red bell pepper, stemmed, seeded, and diced
1 medium green bell pepper, stemmed, seeded, and diced
4 cups salt-free Vegetable Stock (page 49)
3 small unpeeled red potatoes, cubed
4 cups fresh or thawed frozen corn kernels
3 tablespoons unsalted butter
3 tablespoons all-purpose flour
1 cup whole milk

3 teaspoons salt
½ teaspoon freshly ground black pepper, plus more if desired
6 slices crisp-cooked prosciutto, for serving (see headnote)

1. Heat the pressure cooker base on medium heat, add the oil, onion, and red and green bell peppers and sauté, stirring infrequently, until the onion is translucent, about 5 minutes. Stir in the stock, potatoes, and corn.

2. Close and lock the lid of the pressure cooker. Cook at high pressure (see "Get *Hip* About the Pressure," page 13 for 5 minutes/stovetop or 6 to 7 minutes/electric (or nonstandard stovetop).

3. Meanwhile, make a blond roux. In a small saucepan over low heat, mix together the butter and flour and cook, stirring constantly, until the butter has melted and the mixture foams and forms a thick paste. Remove from the heat.

4. When the time is up, open the cooker with the Normal Release method (see page 15). Stir the roux, milk, salt, and black pepper into the chowder. Return the uncovered cooker base to medium heat and simmer the soup, stirring occasionally, until it reaches the desired thickness. Serve with a crispy slice of prosciutto in each bowl.

Veggie Chowder

Follow the Corn Chowder recipe but omit the peppers and use only 2 cups corn kernels. Add 2 whole ripe tomatoes (yes, just put the tomatoes in the pressure cooker whole—they will fall apart during cooking), 1 cup fresh green beans that have been cut into 1-inch pieces, and a sprig of fresh basil to the cooker along with the stock. For a garnish, reserve and fry a few of the corn kernels in a little butter or vegetable oil until golden.

Manhattan Clam Chowder

Serves 4 to 6

One of two classic clam chowders, this recipe is made with tomatoes and is not thickened. Read "Clam Up!" below before beginning, and if you don't get enough juice when you drain the clams, make up the difference with water, or use Seafood

Clam Up!

Here are some tricks for preparing clams for chowder. You wouldn't want to lose any of that delicious juice! If you open or drain them correctly, you may have enough juice for your recipe.

For Live Clams. Prepare the pressure cooker by putting in 1 cup water and a steamer basket. Scrub the clams and then place them in the steamer basket. Cook at low pressure (see "Get *Hip* About the Pressure," page 13) for 5 minutes/all cooker types; then open the cooker using Normal Release (see page 15). Discard any unopened clams. Shake the open shells over the cooker to drain any lingering juice into the bottom, and slide the clam meat out into a bowl. Use the liquid in the pressure cooker for the clam juice listed as a recipe ingredient.

Frozen Clams. Put a strainer over a bowl. If the clams are frozen cooked and in their open shells, empty the package into the strainer; then hold each clam over the bowl while you remove the meat from the shell to the strainer. If the clams are frozen shucked, first let them defrost in the refrigerator overnight or immediately in the sink by running cold water over the unopened package. Then empty the package into the strainer and let the clams drain. Use the liquid in the bowl for the clam juice listed as a recipe ingredient.

Canned or Jarred Clams. Put a strainer over a bowl, pour the contents of the can or jar into the strainer to drain. Use the liquid in the bowl for the clam juice listed as a recipe ingredient.

Stock (page 50). It's traditional to serve this with crackers on the side.

Note: This recipe can be either halved or doubled provided the total volume of the ingredients does not exceed two-thirds of the pressure cooker's capacity.

1 cup coarsely chopped smoked and cured bacon or pancetta
1 medium yellow onion, chopped
2 celery stalks, chopped
2 medium carrots, chopped
1½ cups chopped tomatoes (if using fresh tomatoes, add 2 tablespoons tomato paste)
2 medium unpeeled potatoes, cubed
2 cups clam juice
1 bay leaf
1 fresh thyme sprig
Pinch cayenne pepper, or crushed red pepper flakes
11 ounces frozen or canned clams, drained
Crackers, for serving (optional)

1. Place the pressure cooker base on low heat (keep warm setting for electric cookers) and add the bacon. Cook until the bacon releases its fat and begins to sizzle. Stir in the onion, celery, and carrots, raise the heat to medium, and sauté until the onion has softened, about 5 minutes. Add the tomatoes and scrape all of the delicious brown bits off the bottom of the pan to incorporate into the mixture. Stir in the clam juice, potatoes, bay leaf, thyme, and cayenne.

2. Close and lock the lid of the pressure cooker. Cook at high pressure (see "Get *Hip* About the Pressure," page 3) for 5 minutes/stovetop or 6 to 7 minutes/electric (or nonstandard stovetop). When the time is up, open the cooker using the Normal Release method (see page 15).

3. Add the clams to the cooker base and then return it to medium heat; simmer the chowder, uncovered, for a few minutes to warm through.

Variation

New England Clam Chowder

Follow the recipe for Manhattan Clam Chowder, but omit the tomatoes. While pressure cooking the potatoes and vegetables, mix 1 tablespoon butter and 1 tablespoon all-purpose flour in a saucepan over low heat until they form a roux; it should be a thick paste. When the pressure cooker has been opened, stir the roux, 1 cup whole milk, 1 cup heavy cream, and the clams into the chowder. Return the uncovered cooker base to medium heat and simmer the chowder until it has thickened, about 5 minutes. Serve the chowder in a bread bowl—in San Francisco they serve this East Coast soup in a tangy sourdough bread bowl. Yum!

Just Chunky Soups or . . . Minestroni!

What distinguishes this class of soups from their predecessors in this chapter is that *minestroni* contain a bit of everything: vegetables, legumes, meat, and a grain. These components have different pressure cooking times, so when pressure cooking minestrone, it's best to "phase" the ingredients into the cooker. This just means interrupting the pressure cooking and adding ingredients with shorter cooking times later in the process. Opening and bringing the pressure cooker up to pressure multiple times might sound laborious, but once the contents are already hot and boiling it only takes a minute or two to bring the cooker up to pressure again.

Most people outside of Italy are familiar with minestrone that includes pasta, but in Italy the starch could be rice, barley, and even farro! Many minestrone recipes include dried beans, which should be soaked overnight. If you forget to do this, see page 101 for the quick-soak method. Here is a selection of the *minestroni* most popular in Italy to enjoy—and to inspire you to try your own combinations.

Summer Rice Minestrone

Serves 4 to 6

The Italians know this as *Minestrone alla Milanese*. It can be served hot or, in the summer, at room temperature. When fresh, ripe tomatoes are not available, they can be replaced with the same quantity of drained canned whole tomatoes. The cabbage can be left out completely—my mother, who learned to cook a stone's throw from Milano (in Pavia), never added cabbage to hers. Read "Get *Hip* About Soaking," pages 100–101, to prep the beans.

Note: This recipe can be either halved or doubled provided the total volume of the ingredients does not exceed two-thirds of the pressure cooker's capacity (the amount of beans is small, so don't worry about them expanding greatly).

3 tablespoons unsalted butter (or lard or bacon fat)

1 medium yellow onion, chopped

1 garlic clove, crushed

3 or 4 flat-leaf parsley sprigs (stems and leaves), chopped

3 cups water

½ cup dried borlotti beans or red kidney beans, soaked, rinsed, and drained

1 bay leaf

2 whole medium ripe tomatoes, stem ends removed

2 small unpeeled waxy potatoes (such as red potatoes), diced

1 medium carrot, diced

1 celery stalk, finely diced

Classic Pasta and
Legume Minestrone

2 medium zucchini, diced

2 teaspoons salt

½ cup Roma rice (or any short-grain rice)

⅓ small head Savoy cabbage, sliced
   into strips

Extra-virgin olive oil, for serving

Grated Grana Padano cheese (or any
   grated hard cheese), for serving

1. Heat the pressure cooker base on medium heat, add the butter, and cook until the butter has melted. Add the onion and sauté until it is translucent, about 5 minutes. Stir in the garlic and parsley and continue to sauté for another minute or two until the garlic is golden on both sides. Add the water, beans, and bay leaf.

3. Close and lock the lid of the pressure cooker. Cook at high pressure (see "Get *Hip* About the Pressure," page 13) for 7 minutes/stovetop or 8 to 9 minutes/electric (or nonstandard stovetop). When the time is up, open the cooker with the Slow Normal Release method (in intermittent bursts, page 15).

4. Fish out and discard the bay leaf. Add the tomatoes, potatoes, carrot, celery, and zucchini. Close and lock the lid; cook at high pressure for 5 minutes/stovetop or 6 to 7 minutes/electric (or nonstandard stovetop).

5. When the time is up, open the cooker as before and add the salt and rice. Close and lock the lid; cook at high pressure for 5 minutes/all cooker types. When the time is up, open the cooker again, as before.

6. Stir the cabbage into the soup. Return the uncovered cooker base to medium heat and simmer the soup until the cabbage is tender (just a few minutes). Lightly crush the tomatoes with a soup ladle and, if you prefer, remove the tomato skins, using tongs, and discard. Ladle into bowls, add a swirl of oil to each serving, and dust with grated cheese.

Variation

Winter Rice Minestrone

Follow the recipe for Summer Rice Minestrone, replacing the butter with pancetta (or bacon) and its fat, the zucchini with winter squash, and the parsley with sage. The onion can be replaced with shallots or garlic. Instead of borlotti beans, use any dried beans you like, making sure to adjust the cooking time as indicated on the Pressure Cooking Timetable on page 270.

Classic Pasta and Legume Minestrone

Serves 4 to 6

This is the minestrone recipe that most of the world associates with Italy. It's stuffed with a dizzying array of seasonal vegetables, legumes, and pasta. You can replace the borlotti beans with cannellini beans or red kidney beans without changing the pressure cooking time; read "Get *Hip* About Soaking," pages 100–101, to prep the beans. And add any vegetable that has been spending a little too much time in the veggie drawer in your refrigerator.

Note: This recipe can be either halved or doubled provided the total volume of the ingredients does not exceed half the pressure cooker's capacity.

1 fresh sage sprig

1 tablespoon olive oil

1 yellow onion, chopped

1 carrot, chopped

1 celery stalk, chopped

1 fresh rosemary sprig

1 bay leaf

4 cups salt-free Vegetable Stock (page 49)

1½ cups chopped ripe tomatoes (or one 14.5-ounce can)

1 cup dried borlotti beans, soaked, rinsed, and drained

1 cup ditalini pasta (or other very small-shape pasta)

2 teaspoons salt, plus more if desired

½ teaspoon freshly ground black pepper, plus more if desired

Extra-virgin olive oil, for serving

Grated Parmigiano-Reggiano cheese (or any hard grating cheese), for serving

1. Remove a few leaves from the sage sprig and set them aside. Heat the pressure cooker base on medium heat, add the olive oil, and heat briefly. Stir in the onion, carrot, celery, rosemary, sage sprig, and bay leaf. Sauté, stirring infrequently, until the onion has begun to soften, about 5 minutes. Pour in the stock, tomatoes, and beans.

2. Close and lock the lid of the pressure cooker. Cook at high pressure (see "Get *Hip* About the Pressure," page 3) for 15 minutes/stovetop or 16 to 20 minutes/ electric (or nonstandard stovetop). When the time is up, open the cooker with the 10-Minute Natural Release method (see page 15).

3. Return the uncovered cooker base to high heat and bring the minestrone to a boil again. Add the pasta and cook, uncovered, for the time recommended on the package. Stir in the salt and pepper; taste and adjust the seasoning if you wish.

Chop the reserved sage leaves. Ladle the soup into bowls, add a swirl of extra-virgin olive oil to each serving, sprinkle with the sage, and dust with grated cheese.

Barley and Smoked Prosciutto Minestrone

Serves 4 to 6

Minestrone alla Trentina hails from the snowy Alps in the northeastern area of Italy that used to belong to Austria. A specialty of the region is a particularly delicious pepper-crusted smoked prosciutto called *speck*, which is actually the word for "prosciutto" in German. It's not the easiest cured meat to find outside Italy, but good substitutions are bacon and smoked pancetta. A few mushrooms would also be a great addition to this hearty minestrone. Read "Get *Hip* About Soaking," pages 100–101, to prep the beans.

Note: This recipe can be either halved or doubled provided the total volume of the ingredients does not exceed half the pressure cooker's capacity.

3 thick slices speck (or 5 bacon strips or 3½ ounces smoked pancetta), coarsely chopped

1 medium yellow onion, chopped

2 medium carrots, chopped

1 celery stalk, chopped

1 fresh rosemary sprig (or 1 teaspoon dried rosemary)

1 fresh sage sprig (or ½ teaspoon dried sage)
1 cup pearled barley
6 cups salt-free Meat Stock (page 47)
1 medium unpeeled potato, diced
1 tablespoon unsalted butter
Grated Grana Padano cheese (or any hard grating cheese), for serving

1. Place the pressure cooker base on low heat ("keep warm" setting for electric pressure cookers) and add the speck. Cook until the speck releases its fat and begins to sizzle. Stir in the onion, carrots, celery, rosemary, and sage, raise the heat to medium, and sauté until the onion has softened. Add the barley and stock and scrape all of the delicious brown bits off the bottom of the pan and incorporate into the mixture.

2. Close and lock the lid of the pressure cooker. Cook at high pressure (see "Get *Hip* About the Pressure," page 13) for 15 minutes/stovetop or 16 to 18 minutes/electric (or nonstandard stovetop). When the time is up, open the cooker with the Normal Release method (see page 15). If foam begins to spurt from the valve, stop releasing pressure, wait a moment, and begin again in soft, short bursts.

3. Fish out and discard the herb stems, and add the potato. Close and lock the lid; cook at high pressure for 5 minutes/all cooker types. When the time is up, open the cooker with the 10-Minute Natural Release method (see page 15). Add the butter and stir into the minestrone until it has melted. Ladle the soup into bowls and dust the top of each serving with grated cheese.

Farro and Cannellini Minestrone

Serves 4 to 6

Minestrone alla Toscana is traditionally made with whole farro. However, the easy availability of semipearled farro (or *perlato*), which has been scuffed to speed cooking, makes this version faster. The cooking time of the pearled farro matches *exactly* the cooking time of all the other ingredients, including the soaked cannellini beans, so this minestrone is ready in just one phase! Read "Get *Hip* About Soaking," pages 100–101, to prep the beans.

Note: This recipe can be either halved or doubled provided the total volume of the ingredients does not exceed half the pressure cooker's capacity.

3 thick slices of speck (or 5 bacon strips or 3½ ounces smoked pancetta), coarsely chopped
1 medium red onion, chopped
1 medium celery stalk, chopped
1 medium carrot, chopped
1 fresh rosemary sprig (or 1 teaspoon dried rosemary)
6 cups salt-free Vegetable Stock (page 49)
1 cup dried cannellini beans, soaked, rinsed, and drained
2 cups semipearled farro (farro perlato)
2 tablespoons tomato paste
2 teaspoons salt, plus more if desired
1 tablespoon extra-virgin olive oil

1. Place the pressure cooker base on low heat ("keep warm" setting for electric pressure cookers) and add the speck. Cook until the speck releases its fat and begins to sizzle. Stir in the onion, celery, carrot, and rosemary, raise the heat to medium, and sauté until the onion has softened, about 5 minutes. Add the vegetable stock and scrape all of the delicious brown bits off the bottom of the pan and incorporate into the mixture. Stir in the beans, farro, and tomato paste.

2. Close and lock the lid of the pressure cooker. Cook at high pressure (see "Get *Hip* About the Pressure," page 13) for 7 minutes/stovetop or 8 to 9 minutes/electric (or nonstandard stovetop). When the time is up, open the cooker with the 10-Minute Natural Release method (see page 15).

3. Stir in the salt; taste and adjust the seasoning if you wish. Ladle the soup into bowls and add a swirl of olive oil to each serving.

Brothy Soups

A flavorful stock is the main ingredient in this last category of soups. A few garnishes and adornments make each one unique. Recipes for the Foundation Stocks begin on page 47. Remember, if you use a commercial stock instead, cut down on the amount of salt you add when making these brothy soups.

French Onion Soup

Serves 4 to 6

This is my adaptation of the famous soup from the grande dame who is responsible for teaching Americans how to cook like the French: Julia Child. The roux in this recipe adds body but there isn't enough of it to make the soup thick, which it is not intended to be. Read the recipe all the way through before starting to see how the steps overlap.

Note: This recipe can be either halved or doubled provided the total volume of the ingredients does not exceed two-thirds of the pressure cooker's capacity.

1 tablespoon vegetable oil
3 tablespoons unsalted butter
1½ pounds yellow onions (about 5), thinly sliced (if you wish, reserve a small wedge of onion to grate into the cooked soup)
2 teaspoons salt, plus more if desired
1 teaspoon balsamic vinegar
2 tablespoons all-purpose flour
½ cup dry white wine
6 cups salt-free Meat Stock (page 47)

12 to 24 slices French baguette, sliced about 1 inch thick)
Olive oil
Freshly ground black pepper
3 tablespoons Cognac (optional)
½ cup (about 2 ounces) Gruyère or Swiss cheese shavings (cut using a vegetable peeler)
1 cup (4 ounces) shredded Gruyère or Swiss cheese (shredded on the large holes on a box grater)

1. Heat the pressure cooker base on medium-low heat. Add the vegetable oil and 1 tablespoon of the butter and cook until the butter has melted. Stir in the sliced onions and cook, stirring occasionally, until soft, about 10 minutes. Reduce the heat to low ("keep warm" setting for electric pressure cookers), add the salt and vinegar, and cook, stirring frequently, until the onions have turned a uniform brown, 15 to 20 minutes.

2. Meanwhile, preheat the oven to 450°F. Make the roux: In a small saucepan over medium heat, mix the remaining 2 tablespoons butter and the flour until the butter has melted and the mixture begins to foam. Continue to cook, stirring occasionally and watching carefully, until this roux turns a nice tan color. Remove the pan from the heat and set aside.

French Onion Soup

3. To deglaze the caramelized onions in the pressure cooker base, pour in the white wine and cook until it evaporates completely. Add the meat stock.

4. Close and lock the lid of the pressure cooker. Cook at high pressure (see "Get *Hip* About the Pressure," page 13) for 5 minutes/all cooker types. When the time is up, open the cooker with the Normal Release method (see page 15).

5. Meanwhile, arrange the bread slices on a baking sheet. Brush the top of each slice with olive oil. Toast in the oven until lightly browned, about 5 minutes. Set the toasts aside and turn the oven to broil.

6. Season the soup with pepper and more salt if you wish. Ladle about ½ cup of the soup into the saucepan with the roux, and whisk until combined. Then whisk the roux mixture into the soup in the pressure cooker base. If you wish, add a few grater swipes of the reserved onion wedge to the soup. Return the uncovered cooker base to medium heat and simmer the soup for a few minutes. Turn off the heat and, if using, stir the Cognac into the soup.

7. To serve, ladle the soup into individual bowls or an ovenproof soup tureen. Sprinkle the cheese shavings over the soup, arrange a layer of toasts on top, and cover the toast with generous amounts of shredded cheese. Place under the broiler until the cheese has melted and turned golden, 3 to 5 minutes.

Chicken Noodle Soup

Serves 4 to 6

Classic comfort food for Americans, this soup is even more delicious when made with homemade stock. Why add fresh carrots and celery if the stock was made with them? Because the veggies from the stock, though curiously intact and perfect, have become absolutely tasteless!

Note: This recipe can be either halved or doubled provided the total volume of the ingredients does not exceed two-thirds of the pressure cooker's capacity.

> 1 tablespoon vegetable oil
> 1 tablespoon unsalted butter
> 1 small yellow onion, chopped
> 2 medium carrots, sliced into ¼-inch-thick rounds
> 2 celery stalks, diced
> 4 chicken thighs, bone in, skin removed
> 4 cups salt-free Chicken Stock (page 48)
> 8 ounces egg noodles or tagliatelle, broken into small pieces
> 1 teaspoon salt
> 1 small bunch flat-leaf parsley, finely chopped

1. Heat the pressure cooker base on medium heat, add the oil and butter, and cook until the butter has melted. Add the onion and sauté until it is translucent, about 5 minutes. Add the carrots, celery, chicken thighs, and stock.

2. Close and lock the lid of the pressure cooker. Cook at high pressure (see "Get *Hip* About the Pressure," page 13) for 15 minutes/stovetop or 18 to 20 minutes/electric (or nonstandard stovetop). When the time is up, open the cooker with the Normal Release method (see page 15).

3. Using tongs, remove the thighs from the pressure cooker and tug out and discard their bones (or freeze for use later in a stock recipe). Delicately break up the meat and return it to the cooker. Return the uncovered cooker base to medium heat. Add the noodles and simmer for the time recommended on the package. Ladle the soup into bowls and sprinkle each serving with chopped parsley.

Chinese Egg-Flower Soup

Serves 4 to 6

If you've just made chicken stock, use some of it piping hot and fresh out of the pressure cooker to make this quick soup! Of course, you can reheat stock you've frozen instead; this is a perfect way to use some of the stock you've frozen. The beaten eggs when stirred into the cooking soup, turn first into shaggy threads and then come to resemble floating bits of torn paper.

6 cups salt-free Chicken Stock (page 48)
2 teaspoons soy sauce
1 teaspoon peeled and grated
   fresh ginger
1 teaspoon sesame oil
1 tablespoon cornstarch or potato starch
2 tablespoons water
2 large eggs, beaten
1 tomato, cut into thin wedges
1 green onion, thinly sliced crosswise

1. Add the stock to a medium conventional saucepan. Stir in the soy sauce, ginger, and sesame oil and bring to a boil over medium-high heat. Whisk together the cornstarch and water in a cup. Pour the slurry mixture into the stock, stirring well, and boil for about 3 minutes. Lower the heat to bring the soup to a gentle simmer.

2. Using a fork or whisk, beat the eggs in a spouted measuring cup. Lightly blocking the spout of the measuring cup to slow the flow of eggs, slowly pour the eggs into the soup in a spiral pattern. Gently stir to break the eggs apart as they cook. Ladle the soup into bowls and top each serving with a few tomato wedges and a sprinkling of sliced green onions.

Foundation Stocks

A delicious, complex stock is the foundation of many recipes. The pressure cooker can quickly make big or small batches of meat, poultry, seafood, and vegetable stock.

While you can include bits of not very pretty vegetables that might be lingering in your refrigerator, the key to making a good meat or poultry stock is starting with quality scrap meat products left over from butchering. In Italy, and I know this is not the rule everywhere, the meat department features little Styrofoam trays with a mix of bones to use for stock. Ask the person behind the meat counter if there are scraps, bones, or the skinny ends of shanks available and, if not, where (and when) to find them. For chicken, ask for a carcass (what's left after they remove the breasts, legs, and wings). You might want to do some advance sleuthing for these butcher's scraps, since a store may break down meats at specific times (even days) or in other locations (find out where!). Cheap cuts can be used as well. For poultry that's usually the wings and backs; for beef and pork it would be the leg and shoulder muscles that are full of nerves and chewy things. These cuts are often very fatty, so it will be extra important to defat your finished stock if you use them.

Meat Stock

Yields 8 to 12 cups double-strength stock

Also known as brown stock, this is an all-purpose, full-flavored stock. Onion skins and tomato paste give it a rich, golden brown color. Strained bits and bones can be discarded—or you may serve the bones and invite diners to scoop out the marrow. The stock is concentrated to double-strength; dilute it with an equal amount of water when ready to use (see "Know Your Strength," page 49). To replicate the salinity of commercial stock, add 1 teaspoon of salt to every 2 cups of diluted stock—or add salt as you find pleasing.

Note: This recipe can be either halved or doubled provided the total volume of the ingredients does not exceed two-thirds of the pressure cooker's capacity.

> 1 tablespoon vegetable oil
> 4½ pounds mixed beef, veal, and pork bones, shanks, and inexpensive cuts of meat
> 2 large unpeeled yellow onions
> 18 whole cloves
> 1 tablespoon whole black peppercorns
> 2 bay leaves
> Cold water, as needed
> 2 tablespoons tomato paste

1. Heat the pressure cooker base on high heat, add oil, and heat briefly. Add the bones and cook on all sides until most of the meat remaining on them is brown; work in batches if needed.

2. Meanwhile, slice the onions in half lengthwise and cut off and discard the root ends. Stick cloves randomly in the cut edge of each half.

3. Add the onions, peppercorns, and bay leaves to the pressure cooker. Pour in cold water to just cover the meat scraps. Add the tomato paste.

4. Close and lock the lid of the pressure cooker. Cook at high pressure (see "Get *Hip* About the Pressure," page 13) for 55 minutes/stovetop or 60 to 65 minutes/electric (or nonstandard stovetop). When the time is up, open the pressure cooker with the Natural Release method (see page 15); this should take 10 to 15 minutes for a stovetop cooker, 20 to 30 minutes for an electric cooker.

5. Carefully strain the contents of the cooker into a stainless steel bowl and let cool to room temperature; discard the solids. To defat the stock, cover the bowl with plastic wrap and refrigerate overnight. The next day, remove the solidified layer of fat. Freeze the stock if not using in the next couple of days.

Variations

Veal Stock

Used to make sauces, like velouté, this stock is meant to lack color, but not flavor! No acids are added to this stock since it might be used with butter and cream and the acid could curdle them.

Follow the Meat Stock recipe, using veal bones only. Replace the yellow onions with peeled white onions, add some fresh herbs such as parsley or thyme, and omit the tomato paste. Do not brown the bones.

Chicken Stock

It's preferable to use a chicken carcass, or two, but if they're not available chicken wings, necks, or backs will also do. Some of the "bones" of younger chickens dissolve; that is because they are not bones at all, but cartilage. After straining the stock, pick any remaining meat out of the strainer to toss in Chicken Noodle Soup (page 45).

Follow the Meat Stock recipe, replacing the meat bones with chicken, or you can use turkey instead. Use carcasses (even from a previously cooked or roasted bird) or parts such as wings, necks, and backs. Replace the tomato paste with ½ cup white wine. Optionally, you can leave out the spices and add a couple of celery stalks snapped in half and a couple of whole carrots. Cut the pressure cooking time to

Plop the Stock

One sign of a good, nutritious stock is that it turns into gelatin when refrigerated. This happens especially with pressure cooker stocks because as they cook, they are more efficient at extracting proteins and minerals from the bones (at least this is so with my double-concentrated recipes). The gel turns quickly into liquid again once heated, so don't be afraid to plop this gelatinous stock into the pressure cooker and then lock the lid. It counts as a liquid—even though it's a gel.

30 minutes/stovetop or 33 to 35 minutes/
electric (or nonstandard stovetop).

Vegetable Stock

Yields 6 to 10 cups
double-strength stock

My Southern Italian mother-in-law, who
does not let anything go to waste, dresses
the strained vegetables from this stock
with balsamic vinegar and serves them as
a side dish (discarding the onion skins and
pointy tips, though). You can include nearly
any seasonal vegetable, just stay away from
cruciferous varieties (broccoli, cauliflower,
or cabbage) because their sulfuric flavor
will dominate the stock.

Note: This recipe can be either halved or
doubled provided the total volume of the
ingredients does not exceed two-thirds of
the pressure cooker's capacity.

> 2 large unpeeled yellow onions,
>   sliced lengthwise in half, root ends
>   removed
> 2 medium carrots, snapped in half
> 2 celery stalks, snapped in half
> 2 medium tomatoes (fresh or canned)
> 1 bunch fresh flat-leaf parsley, tied with
>   string (so it's easy to remove)
> 2 unpeeled garlic
> 1 tablespoon whole black peppercorns
> 2 bay leaves
> Cold water, as needed

1. Add the vegetables, herbs, and spices
to the pressure cooker base. Pour in cold
water to just cover these ingredients.

Know Your Strength

All of the stock recipes instruct you to
just cover the ingredients with water.
Stock pressure cooked this way will
be concentrated to double strength,
meaning you'll dilute it with an equal
amount of water when you are ready to
use it for soup or another recipe—unless
that recipe calls for double-strength
stock. Or you may really enjoy its intense
flavor and if so, use it as you wish.

For example, a 6-quart pressure
cooker that can only be filled to two-
thirds of its capacity (or 4 quarts) can
yield nearly 4 quarts of double-strength
stock, or almost 8 quarts of diluted,
single-strength stock. This is in spite of
the fact that you discard all the solids!
The liquids in those solids have been
squeezed out during pressure cooking,
and until you try it, it's hard to believe
the resulting volume of stock could be so
great. Not only is double-strength stock
more flavorful, it's also easier to store
and takes up less room in the freezer.

If you wish, you can further
concentrate the stock after pressure
cooking—it will take even less space
in your freezer. Strain the stock into
a saucepan or back into the pressure
cooker base and simmer it, uncovered,
over medium-high heat until it has
reduced by half. When ready to use, mix
1 part stock with 2 parts water. Be sure
to label this extra-concentrated stock
"triple-strength" so when you are ready
to use it you can dilute it correctly!

2. Close and lock the lid of the pressure cooker. Cook at high pressure (see "Get *Hip* About the Pressure," page 13) for 10 minutes/all cooker types. When the time is up, open the pressure cooker with the Natural Release method (see page 15); this should take 10 to 15 minutes for a stovetop cooker, 20 to 30 minutes for an electric cooker.

3. Carefully strain the contents of the cooker into a stainless steel bowl and let cool to room temperature. Reserve the solids as my mother-in-law does (see headnote), or discard them. Freeze the stock if not using in the next couple of days.

Seafood Stock

Yields 6 to 10 cups double-strength stock

Use seafood stock as a flavorful base for seafood risotto and fish and shellfish chowders and stews.

Note: This recipe can be either halved or doubled provided the total volume of the ingredients does not exceed two-thirds of the pressure cooker's capacity.

½ cup dry white wine
3 pounds fish bones, fish heads with scales, and shrimp, crab, or lobster shells
1 medium carrot, snapped in half
1 celery stalk (including leaves and stems), snapped in half
1 leek, white and green parts, cut to fit in the cooker and washed well
1 teaspoon fresh thyme leaves
1 bunch fresh flat-leaf parsley, tied with string (so it's easy to remove)
Cold water, as needed

1. Add the wine, bones and shells, vegetables, and herbs to the pressure cooker base. Pour in cold water to cover these ingredients by 1 inch.

2. Close and lock the lid of the pressure cooker. Cook at high pressure (see "Get *Hip* About the Pressure," page 13) for 5 minutes/stovetop or 7 to 8 minutes/electric (or nonstandard stovetop). When the time is up, open the pressure cooker with the Natural Release method (see page 15); this should take 10 to 15 minutes for a stovetop cooker, 20 to 30 minutes for an electric cooker.

3. Carefully strain the contents of the cooker into a stainless steel bowl and let cool to room temperature; discard the solids. Freeze the stock if not using in the next couple of days.

Eggs

"Boiling" or "baking" eggs in the pressure cooker uses a minimum of energy. Though hard-boiling eggs under pressure does not provide any actual time-saving, being able to use fresh eggs and making them easy to peel makes the whole procedure worthwhile.

I first introduced the technique of hard-boiling under pressure on the website in 2011—which started a bit of a mania. I had not been the first person to ever pressure cook an egg, but I was the first to suggest steaming them, work out the timing, figure out that it worked just as well on a fresh egg, and make the jaw-dropping discovery of how easy these eggs were to peel.

Once you try it, you won't make eggs any other way.

Stay Low. Cook eggs using low pressure; it will keep the eggshells from cracking and the yolks from overcooking and turning from bright yellow to an unappetizing gray.

Go Fresh. Forget the convention that eggs must be 10-days-old in order to be easily peeled after boiling. Truly *fresh* eggs—recently out of the chicken—can be hard-boiled in the pressure cooker and they *will* be easy to peel!

Cover up for soft yolks. When you "bake" eggs in the pressure cooker, cover the ramekins with aluminum foil to keep the yolks soft.

8 Uses for Hard-boiled Eggs

With the pressure cooker making hard-boiling and peeling eggs a snap, you may have more than you know what do to with. Here are some tasty ways to use them:

1. **Snacking.** Pop whole into the lunch box for office or school.

2. **Garnishing.** Slice into wedges or rounds to garnish salads or vegetable dishes.

3. **Crumbling.** Chop into small pieces and scatter on just about anything.

4. **Sandwiching.** Add slices to a sandwich instead of, or in addition to, sandwich meat.

5. **Egg Salading.** Chop and use in your favorite egg salad recipe (you can of course put this egg salad in a sandwich).

6. **Stuffing.** Stuff a meatloaf by flattening the ground meat mixture, topping with whole eggs, and rolling them up together. Bake (or pressure cook) as usual.

7. **Layering.** Slice and arrange in a layer in a lasagna or vegetable casserole.

8. **De-glutenifying.** Crumble and use in place of bread crumbs in many recipes, such as meat balls!

Hard-boiled Eggs

Ever noticed that those already hard-boiled eggs at a salad bar are exceptionally easy to peel? They were steamed in a big industrial pressure cooker. You can achieve the same results at home with your pressure cooker. There's not much point in making just one hard-boiled egg in the pressure cooker (you can pressure cook as many eggs as will fit in the steamer basket), so I've included a number of recipes that use a half-dozen, along with a sidebar (page 54) with ideas you can run with on your own.

Basic Hard-boiled Eggs

As many eggs as will fit in your steamer basket

When you first hard-boil eggs in a pressure cooker, it's a good idea to do a test with just one to confirm the cooking time for the size of the egg you are using (you may want to cook just a bit less or more for smaller or larger eggs). After that, you may boil as many at one time as will fit in a single layer in the steamer basket. Always begin with cold eggs, right out of the refrigerator.

Extra-large eggs, cold

1. Add 1 cup of water (or the minimum amount required by your cooker to reach pressure) to the pressure cooker base. Place the eggs in the steamer basket and lower the basket into the cooker.

2. Close and lock the lid of the pressure cooker. Cook at low pressure (see "Get *Hip* About the Pressure," page 13) for 4 minutes/stovetop or 5 minutes/electric (or nonstandard stovetop). When the time is up, open the cooker with the 10-Minute Natural Release method, BUT count only 5 minutes before releasing the valve (see page 15).

3. To stop the cooking, lower the steamer basket with the eggs into a large bowl filled with cold water. When the eggs are cool enough to handle, tap both ends of each on the kitchen counter and then remove the shell. Or store in the refrigerator in a small bowl, to distinguish them from any uncooked eggs that may still linger in your refrigerator.

Hard-boiled Egg Platter

Serves 4 to 6, depending on appetite!

This loose European egg salad is served on a shallow platter instead of in a bowl. It's quite pretty, with red onions, tomatoes, olives, and green herbs—and yummy, too.

6 hard-boiled extra-large eggs
   (page 55)
3 to 4 ripe tomatoes, cut into wedges
½ red onion, very thinly sliced
½ cup black or green olives
Finely chopped fresh flat-leaf parsley or
   fresh basil
Olive oil
White wine vinegar
Salt
Freshly ground black pepper

Using a nonserrated knife, slice each egg lengthwise into 4 wedges. Arrange them on a platter with the tomato wedges. Top them with the onion and olives, scattering them over loosely. Sprinkle the parsley over the top. Drizzle the salad with some oil, vinegar, and a few pinches (or grinds) of salt and pepper.

Hard-boiled Eggs Au Gratin

Serves 6

This combination of hard-boiled eggs and Bolognese sauce (pasta sauce made with meat) is a hearty dish that comes together in no time. Use whatever variety of cheese you like, as long as it can be grated.

6 hard-boiled extra-large eggs
   (page 55)
2 cups Ragù alla Bolognese, hot
   (page 118)
⅓ cup plain dry bread crumbs
1 cup grated mozzarella cheese, or as
   much as you like
Finely chopped flat-leaf parsley

Preheat the broiler. Using a nonserrated knife, slice each egg lengthwise in half. Arrange the eggs, cut side up, in a baking dish. Spoon the sauce over the eggs, and sprinkle the bread crumbs and then the cheese over the top. Place under the broiler until the cheese has melted and is bubbling and the sauce is heated through, about 5 minutes. Sprinkle with parsley and serve.

Classic Deviled Eggs

Yields 12 deviled egg halves

Deviled eggs are a favorite for parties and picnics. Here is the version I think of as classic—change the seasoning as you wish.

6 hard-boiled extra-large eggs
   (page 55)
4 tablespoons mayonnaise
2 teaspoons Dijon mustard
Pinch salt
Paprika, for garnish
Fresh herbs, such as chives,
   for garnish

Using a nonserrated knife, slice each egg in half lengthwise. Gently scoop all the yolks into a small bowl. Add the mayonnaise, mustard, and salt and use an immersion blender to fully combine. Fill each egg white half with a dollop of the yolk mixture and arrange on a serving platter. Sprinkle with paprika and decorate with fresh herbs.

Variations

Smoked Salmon and Dill Deviled Eggs

Follow the Classic Deviled Eggs recipe, substituting ½ cup chopped smoked salmon for the mayonnaise. Omit the paprika and decorate with fresh dill sprigs or green fennel fronds.

Egg Salad and Arugula Sandwiches

Follow the Classic Deviled Eggs recipe, but instead of separating the yolks from the whites, dice and crumble them together. Increase the mayonnaise to 6 tablespoons total, and use a fork to blend it into the eggs along with the mustard and salt. Spread the egg salad on whole wheat bread and top with arugula leaves and halved cherry tomatoes.

Classic Deviled Eggs

"Baked" Eggs

Technically, eggs cooked this way are not really baked—they are pressure-steamed. Pressure cooking not only completes an egg dish faster than does baking it in the oven, but also cooks the eggs more evenly. If the preference is toward a softer yolk, just pressure cook for the same time indicated, but cover the container (or vegetable) tightly with aluminum foil. The extra layer will keep the yolk protected from the super-heated steam that would otherwise instantly harden it on contact.

Prosciutto and Spinach "Baked" Eggs

Yields 4 baked eggs

Most pressure cookers have a low setting. If yours does not, you can still make this recipe but you won't have the option of cooking a "softer" egg since the temperature at high pressure will cook the eggs too quickly. Serve these with toast if you like, and especially for dipping into soft eggs.

Note: This recipe can be halved without any alterations. To double, the ramekins can be stacked in a second or even third layer into the cooker "pyramid style," by offsetting the second layer on the edges of the first.

Olive oil
4 slices prosciutto
4 to 8 whole baby spinach leaves, plus
    2 finely sliced for a garnish
4 extra-large eggs, cold
4 teaspoons grated Pecorino Romano
    cheese
Toast, for serving (optional)

1. Add 1 cup of water (or the minimum amount required by your cooker to reach pressure) to the pressure cooker base; set aside.

2. Add a drop of oil to each of 4 ramekins and rub it over the bottom and sides. Lay a slice of prosciutto into each, and add 1 or 2 whole spinach leaves. Break an egg into each ramekin and sprinkle with the grated cheese, dividing it equally.

3. For a soft egg yolk, cover each ramekin tightly with aluminum foil; for a firm, fully cooked yolk, leave the ramekins uncovered. Place the ramekins in the steamer basket and lower the basket into the pressure cooker.

4. Close and lock the lid of the pressure cooker. Cook at low pressure (see "Get *Hip* About the Pressure," page 13) for 3 minutes/stovetop or 4 minutes/electric (or nonstandard stovetop). When the time is up, open the cooker with the Normal Release method (see page 15). Carefully remove the ramekins, sprinkle the eggs with sliced spinach leaves, and serve immediately.

Prosciutto and Spinach
"Baked" Eggs

Smoked Gouda and Caramelized Onion Cocotte

Follow the recipe for Prosciutto and Spinach "Baked" Eggs, substituting 1 thinly sliced yellow onion for the spinach and finely chopped smoked Gouda cheese for the Pecorino Romano. To begin, caramelize the onions by sautéing over low heat in a little olive oil, adding a splash of balsamic vinegar when they are soft. Divide the onions evenly among the ramekins, pushing them to the sides so that the bottom is partially clear. Break an egg into each ramekin and complete the recipe.

Crème Cocotte

The classic French Cocotte: Follow the recipe for Prosciutto and Spinach "Baked" Eggs, omitting the spinach and prosciutto and placing a dollop of crème fraîche in each ramekin before adding the egg. Sprinkle the eggs with salt and pepper after removing from the cooker.

Tomato Caprese Cocotte

This is my family's favorite cocotte. Follow the recipe for Prosciutto and Spinach "Baked" Eggs, omitting the prosciutto and substituting a few halved cherry tomatoes and some fresh basil leaves for the spinach. Replace the Pecorino Romano with 4 small slices of mozzarella, using 1 slice for each cocotte. For a heartier version, make the cocottes in hollowed-out bell peppers instead of ramekins.

More Eggs

The ease with which you can pressure cook hard-boiled eggs may make it difficult to stop making them! Here are a couple more suggestions for what to do with them.

Chinese Tea Eggs

Yields 4 eggs

Chinese Tea Eggs, also known as Chinese Marbled Eggs, are a common Asian street food. When made at home in the conventional way, the eggs need to be simmered in the seasoning mixture for 2 hours! But the pressure cooker will accelerate the whole process to just 20 minutes cooking time. However, the longer the eggs sit in the simmering liquid, the darker the marbled pattern will be, so I recommend preparing them a day before serving, and refrigerating them in the cooking liquid in the interim. Use a dark Chinese oolong or black tea, such as English Breakfast.

Note: This recipe can be either halved or doubled, provided there is 1 cup of water in the pressure cooker and enough liquid in the heat-proof bowl to cover the eggs.

2 tablespoons dark Chinese oolong or black tea leaves (or 2 tea bags)
4 hard-boiled medium eggs (page 55)
6 tablespoons soy sauce
1 teaspoon salt
2 pieces star anise
1 small stick cinnamon
1 teaspoon cracked black peppercorns

2 strips of citrus zest (lemon, orange, or mandarin orange) (optional)
Water, as needed

1. Add 1 cup of water (or the minimum amount required by your cooker to reach pressure) to the pressure cooker base; set aside.

2. If using tea bags, open them; add the tea leaves to a deep, heat-proof bowl large enough to hold all 4 eggs (such as a ceramic breakfast cereal bowl). Using the back of a soupspoon, lightly tap the eggs all around, cracking, but not breaking, the shells. Put the eggs in the bowl. Add the soy sauce, salt, star anise, cinnamon, peppercorns, and citrus zest. Then pour in water to just cover the eggs. Cover tightly with foil. Place the bowl in the steamer basket and, using a foil sling, (see page 11) and lower the basket into the pressure cooker.

3. Close and lock the lid of the pressure cooker. Cook at low pressure (see "Get *Hip* About the Pressure," page 13) for 20 minutes/stovetop or 23 to 25 minutes/ electric (or nonstandard stovetop). When the time is up, open the pressure cooker with the 10-Minute Natural Release method, BUT count only 5 minutes before releasing the valve (see page 15).

4. Leave the eggs in the soaking liquid until serving. Once they have cooled, transfer the eggs, in the bowl with the tea mixture, to the refrigerator.

Balsamic Pickled Eggs

Yields 6 pickled eggs

Here is a simple way to give a classy zing to hard-boiled eggs. To get the full effect, you need to give the pickling mixture time to penetrate all the way to the yolk. Smaller eggs will pickle faster, about 1½ weeks; extra-large eggs may need 2 weeks. Make a lot and start tasting them during the pickling process. This recipe is adapted from the Washington State University Extension Publication: Pickled Eggs (EB1104). Another easy way to pickle eggs is to drop them in the liquid leftover when you've finished a jar of pickles!

6 hard-boiled medium eggs
   (page 55)
1½ cups balsamic vinegar
1 cup water
3 garlic cloves, halved
3 teaspoons salt
1 teaspoon mixed whole peppercorns
¾ teaspoon dill seeds
¼ teaspoon mustard seeds

Place the eggs in a large glass jar. Add the vinegar, water, garlic, salt, and spices to a small conventional saucepan and heat to almost a boil. Pour over the eggs, cover tightly, and let cool for about 30 minutes. Refrigerate until seasoned, at least 1½ weeks. The eggs will keep, refrigerated, for up to 4 weeks total.

Vegetables

Pressure cooking vegetables preserves more vitamins and minerals than most cooking methods—over 90 percent compared to 60 to 70 percent vitamin retention for vegetables that have been boiled or steamed in the conventional way. Although with pressure cooking the temperature is very high, the cooking time is short, basically flash-cooking vegetables to preserve their color, flavor, and vitamins. Because most vegetables are not very dense, their cooking time is often the same for both stovetop and electric pressure cookers, and you'll see fewer timing adjustments indicated in the recipes in this chapter than in some of the others.

Go digital. Vegetables can be fully cooked in just a few minutes—and overcooked in a few seconds more. Use a digital timer to keep track of cooking time. Before running out to buy a dedicated timer, check the cook top, range hood, and microwave for an integrated timer you can use for pressure cooking. In a pinch, most cell phones also have a timer.

Get out! Remove vegetables from the pressure cooker quickly so that they do not continue cooking. If crunchiness is important, plunge the veggies in a bowl of ice water to stop the cooking.

Keep it. Don't toss the steaming or cooking liquid from the base of the pressure cooker. It is full of nutritious vegetable juice and can be added to stock or used in place of water in another recipe.

Size matters. Just as in conventional cooking, the size of a vegetable will dictate its cooking time. Make sure that all vegetables to be cooked together are similarly sized so that they will cook evenly.

Washing Artichokes

The easiest way to get artichokes squeaky clean—and evict any insects that may have traveled with them from the farm—is to submerge them in cold water with a couple of tablespoons of white vinegar. Swish them around and let them sit for about 15 minutes. Then, rinse well and begin with the recipe.

Steamed Veggies

Steaming vegetables in the pressure cooker means keeping them lifted up and out of the cooking liquid. Place them in a steamer basket so the super-heated steam gently caresses and cooks them. Following are some of my favorite steamed-veggie-and-sauce combos. The Pressure Cooking Timetables (see Appendix pages 269–281) has the basic cooking times for most vegetables. Add your favorite seasoning or mix things up using one of mine.

I'm often asked by readers of the *hip* pressure cooking website if spicing up the steaming liquid will add extra zing to the steamed vegetables. It sounds like a good idea, but in reality the flavor of the steam is 1/1600th the flavor of the liquid producing it, so very little actual flavor will be imparted to the steamed food. So don't throw your spices down the drain, spice up the steaming liquid only if you plan to use it as a sauce or reserve it for another recipe.

Artichokes with Parsley Sauce

Serves 4

Be sure to follow the cooking times given for different size artichokes to avoid overcooking. If you're lucky enough to get fresh artichokes with the stems still attached, *don't* throw the stems away! Prepared properly, they taste as delicious as the tender heart. I have included instructions in the recipe—just in case. Make the parsley sauce while the artichokes are steaming, or ahead of time; it will keep, tightly covered in the refrigerator, for 1 day.

Note: This recipe can be either halved or doubled provided there is at least 1 cup of liquid in the pressure cooker (or your cooker's minimum liquid requirement) and the total volume of the artichokes does not exceed two-thirds of the cooker's capacity.

Parsley Sauce
¼ cup white wine vinegar
¼ cup plain dry bread crumbs (or two crumbled hard-boiled eggs)
½ cup olive oil, plus more as needed
1 bunch fresh flat-leaf parsley (about 4.5 ounces)
2 garlic cloves
1 oil-packed anchovy (optional)
1 teaspoon capers, rinsed and drained
½ teaspoon salt
Freshly ground black pepper

4 medium artichokes

1. To make the parsley sauce, pour the vinegar onto the bread crumbs and set aside. Add the ½ cup oil, the parsley, garlic, anchovy if using, capers, and salt to a mini chopper or blender and finely mince them. Add the bread crumbs and pulse two to three times to combine and season with pepper. Add more oil as needed to obtain your preferred sauce consistency.

2. Add 1 cup of water (or the minimum amount required by your cooker to reach pressure) to the pressure cooker base; set aside.

3. If the artichokes come with stems, cut them off. Peel them with a vegetable peeler and cut into 1-inch sticks. Place the pieces in the water in the pressure cooker (this way they will boil while the artichokes steam above them).

4. If the leaves have sharp spines at the tips, cut off the top of each lower leaf with scissors, then place each artichoke on its side and cut off the entire top with a chef's knife. Insert the steamer basket in the cooker and place the artichokes upright in it.

5. Close and lock the lid of the pressure cooker. Cook at high pressure (see "Get *Hip* About the Pressure," page 13), with all cooker types cooking small artichokes for 4 minutes, medium artichokes for 6 minutes, or large artichokes for 9 minutes. When the time is up, open the cooker with the Normal Release method (see page 15).

6. Using tongs, place an artichoke on a serving plate, and add a few stem pieces on the side. Gently tease the artichokes open, and drizzle the sauce into the crevices and over the stems, dividing it equally among the plates. As you eat the artichokes, dip the upper portion of each leaf into any sauce that's run onto the plate, and when you get to the center, spoon out and discard the fuzzy choke. Slice the heart and dip in the sauce.

Asparagus with Dijonnaise Dipping Sauce

Serves 4 to 6

While the asparagus steam, their stems boil in the cooking liquid below, making an asparagus stock for later use—think risotto! Asparagus cooks quickly, so if you want to serve it hot, be sure to make the sauce before turning on the cooker. Get the thickest asparagus you can find in the store, as very thin asparagus may disintegrate under pressure. This is nice as an hors d'oeuvre or side dish—either way, just let everyone grab a spear or two and dip in!

Note: This recipe can be either halved or doubled provided there is at least 1 cup of liquid in the pressure cooker (or your cooker's minimum liquid requirement) and the total volume of the asparagus does not exceed two-thirds of the cooker's capacity.

1 pound thick asparagus

Dijonnaise Sauce
3 tablespoons mayonnaise
1 teaspoon Dijon mustard
Pinch paprika

1. Add 1 cup of water (or the minimum amount required by your cooker to reach pressure) to the pressure cooker base. Snap off the end of each asparagus spear and add the ends to the cooker. Place the asparagus in the steamer basket and lower it into the cooker.

2. Close and lock the lid of the pressure cooker. Cook at high pressure (see "Get *Hip* About the Pressure," page 13) for 2 minutes/all cooker types. When the time is up, open the cooker with the Normal Release method (see page 15).

3. Quickly lift the steamer basket out of the cooker and, using tongs, immediately transfer the asparagus to a serving dish to keep it from overcooking. Strain the cooking liquid into a food-storage container to use as a stock later; discard the stem ends.

4. To make the Dijonnaise Sauce, mix together the mayonnaise and mustard in a small ramekin. Dust with a pinch of paprika. Serve for dipping the asparagus.

Buttered Brussels Sprouts

Serves 4 to 6

Sprouts are delicious paired with tangy fruit. Here I season them with grated orange zest, but you might like mandarin orange slices, pomegranate seeds, or cranberries—as well or instead!

Note: This recipe can be either halved or doubled provided there is at least 1 cup of liquid in the pressure cooker (or your cooker's minimum liquid requirement) and the total volume of the Brussels sprouts does not exceed two-thirds of the cooker's capacity.

1 pound Brussels sprouts
½ teaspoon salt, plus more if desired
1 tablespoon unsalted butter, diced, at room temperature

1 tablespoon grated orange zest
Freshly ground black pepper

1. Add 1 cup of water (or the minimum amount required by your cooker to reach pressure) to the pressure cooker base. To ensure even cooking, cut any large sprouts in half from top to bottom. Place the sprouts in the steamer basket in an even layer and lower it into the cooker; sprinkle with ½ teaspoon salt.

2. Close and lock the lid of the pressure cooker. Cook at high pressure (see "Get *Hip* About the Pressure," page 13) for 3 minutes/all cooker types. When the time is up, open the cooker with the Normal Release method (see page 15).

3. Lift the steamer basket out of the cooker and immediately tumble the sprouts into a serving dish to keep them from overcooking. Toss with the butter and orange zest and season with pepper and more salt if you wish.

Cauliflower and Gorgonzola Gratin

Serves 4 to 6

Steaming vegetables before you add a gratin topping and then placing the assembled dish under the broiler to melt the cheese guarantees fork-tender vegetables with a perfect bubbling topping! Variations that follow this recipe include a version with broccoli and one with fennel, each seasoned differently; try all three.

Cauliflower and Gorgonzola Gratin

Note: This recipe can be either halved or doubled provided there is at least 1 cup of liquid in the pressure cooker (or your cooker's minimum liquid requirement) and the total volume of the cauliflower does not exceed two-thirds of the cooker's capacity.

1 medium cauliflower
¼ teaspoon salt
¼ cup plain dry bread crumbs
5 ounces Gorgonzola cheese (or other blue cheese), diced
½ cup pine nuts (3 ounces)

1. Add 1 cup of water (or the minimum amount required by your cooker to reach pressure) to the pressure cooker base. Cut the florets from the cauliflower and cut them into 1-inch pieces; reserve the stems for another use. Place the florets in the steamer basket and lower it into the cooker. Sprinkle with the salt.

2. Close and lock the lid of the pressure cooker. Cook at high pressure (see "Get *Hip* About the Pressure," page 13) for 3 minutes/all cooker types. When the time is up, open the cooker with the Normal Release method (see page 15).

3. Turn on the broiler. Lift the steamer basket out of the cooker, tumble the florets into a heat-proof serving dish or individual ramekins, and sprinkle with the bread crumbs, cheese, and pine nuts. Place under the broiler until the cheese is bubbling and just starting to turn golden (about 5 minutes).

Variations

Broccoli, Cheddar, and Crumbled Egg Gratin

Follow the recipe for Cauliflower and Gorgonzola Gratin, substituting broccoli for the cauliflower, 2 crumbled hard-boiled eggs (page 55) for the bread crumbs, and sharp cheddar cheese for the Gorgonzola.

Fennel and Parmesan Cream Sauce Gratin

Follow the recipe for Cauliflower and Gorgonzola Gratin, substituting 2 thickly sliced medium fennel bulbs for the cauliflower, ½ cup heavy cream for the bread crumbs (poured over, not sprinkled!), and grated Parmigiano-Reggiano cheese for the Gorgonzola; omit the pine nuts.

Bread Crumb–Crusted Romano Beans

Serves 4 to 6

Romano beans are flat, wide bean pods that can be eaten whole. They are delicious this way, steamed and then tossed with garlicky bread crumbs and olive oil. Any recipe featuring these tender beans can be made instead with thinner snow peas by halving the pressure cooking time (to 2 minutes), or the rounder and thicker green bean by almost doubling it (to 8 minutes).

Note: This recipe can be either halved or doubled provided there is at least 1 cup of liquid in the pressure cooker (or your cooker's minimum liquid requirement) and the total volume of the beans does not exceed two-thirds of the cooker's capacity.

1 pound fresh romano beans
¼ teaspoon salt
1 tablespoon olive oil
1 garlic clove, minced
½ cup plain dry bread crumbs
1 flat-leaf parsley sprig, chopped

1. Add 1 cup of water (or the minimum amount required by your cooker to reach pressure) to the pressure cooker base. Place the beans in the steamer basket and lower it into the cooker. Sprinkle with the salt.

2. Close and lock the lid of the pressure cooker. Cook at high pressure (see "Get *Hip* About the Pressure," page 13) for 5 minutes/all cooker types. When the time is up, open the cooker with the Normal Release method (see page 15).

3. Meanwhile, heat a large sauté pan over medium heat; add the oil and garlic. As soon as the garlic begins to turn golden, about 1 minute, add the bread crumbs. Mix well and continue to sauté until the crumbs are lightly toasted and crispy. Turn off the heat and mix in the parsley.

4. Lift the steamer basket out of the cooker and immediately tumble the beans into the sauté pan. Using tongs, mix them gently into the crumb mixture to coat well. Transfer to a small serving dish and serve immediately.

Romano Beans in Tomato Sauce

Serves 4 to 6

For an easy but complex side dish, you can steam vegetables above a sauce and then tumble them into it. For example, here a simple tomato sauce cooks in the bottom of the cooker, below Romano beans in a steamer basket.

Note: This recipe can be either halved or doubled provided there is at least 1 cup of liquid in the pressure cooker (or your cooker's minimum liquid requirement) and the total volume of the ingredients does not exceed two-thirds of the cooker's capacity.

1 tablespoon olive oil
2 garlic cloves, smashed
2 cups tomato puree
½ cup water
1 pound fresh romano beans
¼ teaspoon salt
Fresh basil leaves, chopped, for
  sprinkling

1. Heat the pressure cooker base on medium heat, add the oil, and heat briefly. Add the garlic and sauté until golden. Add the tomato puree and water to the pressure cooker base. Place the beans in the steamer basket and lower it into the cooker. Sprinkle with the salt.

2. Close and lock the lid of the pressure cooker. Cook at high pressure (see "Get *Hip* About the Pressure," page 13) for 5 minutes/all cooker types. When the time is up, open the cooker with the Normal Release method (see page 15).

3. Lift the steamer basket out of the cooker and tumble the beans into the sauce in the cooker; mix well to coat. Sprinkle each serving with the fresh basil.

Corn on the Cob

Serves 4 to 6

The fresher the corn, the sweeter it is. That's because as soon as the cob is plucked off the stalk those sweet sugars begin turning into starch. This means that the cooking time could be affected by the age of the cob. So check for doneness before serving—the corn may need a couple more minutes under pressure if it is not very fresh.

Note: This recipe can be either halved or doubled provided there is at least 1 cup of liquid in the pressure cooker (or your cooker's minimum liquid requirement) and the total volume of the corn does not exceed two-thirds of the cooker's capacity.

**4 medium ears corn, husked and
 snapped in half
Salted butter, for serving**

1. Add 1 cup of water (or the minimum amount required by your cooker to reach pressure) to the pressure cooker base. Place corn in the steamer basket and lower it into the cooker.

2. Close and lock the lid of the pressure cooker. Cook at high pressure (see "Get *Hip* About the Pressure," page 13) for 2 minutes/all cooker types. When the time

is up, open the cooker with the Normal Release method (see page 15). Serve the corn immediately, slathered with butter.

Lemon and Anise Carrot Wedges

Serves 4 to 6

Steamed carrots are pretty amazing all by themselves. But dressing them up with a little lemon and the unexpected licorice-y flavor and crunch of anise brings a bit of excitement to them.

Note: This recipe can be either halved or doubled provided there is at least 1 cup of liquid in the pressure cooker (or your cooker's minimum liquid requirement) and the total volume of the carrots does not exceed two-thirds of the cooker's capacity.

**1 lemon
1 pound thick carrots
½ teaspoon anise seeds, lightly crushed
1 teaspoon extra-virgin olive oil**

1. Grate the zest from the lemon and squeeze the juice into a small bowl; mix the zest into the juice and set aside. Cut the carrots in half lengthwise, then cut each piece in half crosswise. Slice the thicker wedges in half lengthwise to make each piece similar in size.

2. Add 1 cup of water (or the minimum amount required by your cooker to reach pressure) to the pressure cooker base. Place the carrots in the steamer basket and lower it into the pressure cooker.

3. Close and lock the lid of the pressure cooker. Cook at high pressure (see "Get *Hip* About the Pressure," page 13) for 4 minutes/all cooker types. When the time is up, open the cooker with the Normal Release method (see page 15).

4. Lift the steamer basket out of the cooker and tumble the carrots into a small serving bowl. Drizzle with the reserved lemon zest and juice, the anise, and oil. Mix delicately and serve.

Eggplant Parmigiana

Serves 4 to 6

The pressure cooker is a great help in prepping vegetables. My collaborator on the Italian version of hippressurecooking. com (www.cucinarehip.it), Martire Pasqualina (or Lina, for short) makes a Parmigiana in the pressure cooker. Eggplant Parmigiana is a casserole that is traditionally made with fried eggplant but Lina steams the slices instead. Here is my slightly more elaborate version—and Lina's original recipe follows as a variation. You can use a ready-made tomato sauce, but either the Fresh Tomato and Basil Sauce or the Super-Easy Tomato Sauce (pages 118 and 119) will be much nicer. Here's a *hip* tip: to quickly slice the eggplants, just put a mandoline over the steamer basket in the cooker, and slice away. Then arrange the slices as directed.

Note: This recipe can be either halved or doubled provided there is at least 1 cup of liquid in the pressure cooker (or your cooker's minimum liquid requirement)

Steam-Purge Eggplant

Eggplant has a bitter liquid that is generally purged before the vegetable is cooked. Instead of salting, pressing, and waiting a couple of hours to do this, you can steam them in the pressure cooker, which does the *exact* same thing in minutes. Follow the procedure described in the Eggplant Parmigiana recipe, and then discard the brown, bitter, steaming liquid.

and the total volume of the eggplant slices does not exceed two-thirds of the cooker's capacity.

> 2 pounds eggplant (not peeled), sliced
>   ¼ inch thick
> 1 large egg
> 2 teaspoons salt
> 1 teaspoon water, or as needed
> Olive oil, as needed
> 2 cups tomato sauce or puree
> 1½ cups plain dry bread crumbs
> 7 ounces mozzarella cheese, grated
> ½ cup grated Pecorino Romano cheese,
>   or other hard grating cheese
> Finely sliced fresh basil leaves, for
>   sprinkling

1. Add 1 cup of water (or the minimum amount required by your cooker to reach pressure) to the pressure cooker base. Insert the steamer basket. Arrange the eggplant slices in the basket so they are standing vertically.

2. Close and lock the lid of the pressure cooker. Cook at high pressure (see "Get *Hip* About the Pressure," page 13) for 5 minutes/all cooker types. When the time is up, open the cooker with the Normal Release method (see page 15). Remove the eggplant from the cooker and divide into four approximately equal portions on a work surface.

3. Preheat the oven to 350°F. In a small bowl lightly whip the egg with the salt and 1 teaspoon water, or just enough to break up

Eggplant Parmigiana

the egg. Rub the inside of an 8 by 13-inch casserole with olive oil and spoon in a bit of the tomato sauce.

4. Transfer one-quarter of the eggplant slices to the casserole, arranging them so they overlap and cover the bottom. Brush this layer with some of the egg mixture and sprinkle one-quarter of the bread crumbs on top. Pour over about one-third of the remaining tomato sauce and sprinkle with one-quarter of the mozzarella. Repeat this layering sequence twice. Then add a final layer of eggplant slices and brush with the egg mixture, pouring any remaining mixture over the top. Sprinkle the remaining bread crumbs and then the remaining mozzarella and the Pecorino Romano over all. Drizzle a little oil on top.

5. Bake the casserole for 20 minutes. Transfer to a wire rack and let it rest and set for 5 to 10 minutes. Sprinkle the sliced basil over the top just before cutting and serving.

Variation

Lina's Parmigiana Light

Follow the recipe for Eggplant Parmigiana, omitting the egg and bread crumbs. Bake for only 10 minutes, or until the cheese has melted (there are no raw eggs in this version so the cooking time is shorter).

Eggplant Stacks

Serves 4 to 6

These little towers of eggplant, ricotta, and tomato, topped with mozzarella, offer another easy way to turn eggplant into a vegetarian main dish.

Note: This recipe can be either halved or doubled provided there is at least 1 cup of liquid in the pressure cooker (or your cooker's minimum liquid requirement) and the total volume of the eggplant slices does not exceed two-thirds of the cooker's capacity.

> 2 pounds unpeeled eggplant, sliced
>   ¼ inch thick
> Olive oil
> 2 cups ricotta cheese (1 pound)
> 1 bunch fresh basil, leaves only, chopped
> 3 garlic cloves, squeezed through a
>   garlic press
> 1 teaspoon salt
> 1 pound fresh ripe tomatoes, sliced
> 8 ounces mozzarella cheese, sliced

1. Add 1 cup of water (or the minimum amount required by your cooker to reach pressure) to the pressure cooker base. Insert the steamer basket. Arrange the eggplant slices in the basket so they are standing vertically.

2. Close and lock the lid of the pressure cooker. Cook at high pressure (see "Get *Hip* About the Pressure," page 13) for 5 minutes/all cooker types. When the time is up, open the cooker with the Normal Release method (see page 15). Remove the eggplant from the cooker and divide into three equal portions on a work surface.

3. Preheat the oven to 350°F. Mix the ricotta, basil, garlic, and salt in a medium bowl until combined. Line a baking sheet with parchment paper. Arrange one-third of the eggplant slices on the baking sheet, spacing them evenly. Top each of the eggplant slices with a swirl of olive oil, a dollop of the ricotta mixture, and 1 tomato slice. Repeat this layering sequence twice, and then top each stack with another eggplant slice. Lay a mozzarella slice on top of each stack. Bake the stacks until the mozzarella has melted, about 10 minutes.

"Roasted" and Caramelized Garlic

Serves 4 to 6 as a appetizer

Roasted garlic is already sweet all by itself, but since we're making this in a third of the usual time, a little sprinkle of sugar and a pass under the broiler enhance the process and give the results a brulée-like crunchy caramelized top. Squeeze the roasted garlic clove onto bread or toast or eat them solo. Be sure to roast several bulbs at once to use in other recipes such as mashed potatoes or a pasta sauce; they keep about a week in the refrigerator.

Note: Provided there is at least 1 cup of water in the base (or your cooker's minimum liquid requirement), you can pressure cook as many garlic bulbs as will fit in the steamer basket of your cooker; increase the sugar and oil accordingly.

1 large garlic bulb
¼ teaspoon turbinado (raw) sugar
1 teaspoon olive oil
Bread slices or toasts, for serving (optional)

1. Add 1 cup of water (or the minimum amount required by your cooker to reach pressure) to the pressure cooker base; insert the steamer basket. Slice off the top of the garlic head (cutting through all the cloves) and place the bulb in the steamer

basket. Save the clove tops to use in another recipe.

2. Close and lock the lid of the pressure cooker. Cook at high pressure (see "Get *Hip* About the Pressure," page 13) for 5 minutes/all cooker types. When the time is up, open the cooker with the 10-Minute Natural Release method (see page 15).

3. Turn on the broiler. Lift the steamer basket out of the cooker. Delicately slide a large serving spoon under the garlic and transfer it to a small heat-proof plate. Dust the sugar on top and drizzle with the oil. Place under the broiler until the top and edges begin to caramelize, about 5 minutes.

4. Serve immediately on hot plates with a butter knife or small spoon. To eat, delicately tease a clove out of its wrapper with the butter knife, or gently squeeze using your fingers, and serve with bread, if desired, or eat on its own.

Orange-Seared Pumpkin

Serves 4 to 6 as a side dish

Steamed pumpkin sautéed and seasoned with fresh orange juice makes a tasty fall or winter side dish. Pumpkin steamed in the pressure cooker is easy to peel and dice and the steaming liquid can be used as a flavorful liquid in another recipe. You can pressure cook spaghetti squash this way too: use the same timing, but tease out the "spaghetti" flesh with a fork instead of dicing it.

Note: This recipe can be either halved or doubled provided there is at least 1 cup of liquid in the pressure cooker (or your cooker's minimum liquid requirement) and the total volume of the pumpkin does not exceed two-thirds of the cooker's capacity.

1 medium pumpkin
2 tablespoons unsalted butter or olive oil
1 orange
1 teaspoon salt, plus more if desired
½ teaspoon freshly ground black pepper

1. Wash the pumpkin well; cut in half and scoop out the seeds. (Discard the seeds or rinse and reserve for other uses.) Cut the pumpkin into wedges that are large, but fit horizontally in the pressure cooker. Add 1 cup of water (or the minimum amount required by your cooker to reach pressure) to the pressure cooker base and stack the wedges, skin side down, in it.

2. Close and lock the lid of the pressure cooker. Cook at high pressure (see "Get *Hip* About the Pressure," page 13) for 5 minutes/all cooker types. When the time is up, open the cooker with the Normal Release method (see page 15).

3. Using tongs, carefully lift out the pumpkin. Remove and discard the peel. Cut the flesh into ½-inch cubes and set aside. Grate the zest from the orange and, in a separate bowl, squeeze the juice; set aside.

4. Heat a sauté pan over medium-high heat, add the butter and orange zest, and cook until the butter has melted. Add the pumpkin and toss to coat well. Cook, stirring infrequently, until heated through and the edges begin to scorch on a few cubes, about 5 minutes. Stir in the salt and pepper; taste and adjust the seasoning if you wish. Drizzle with the reserved orange juice and serve.

Variation

Pumpkin Pulp

For a soft, mashable pumpkin, which is the right consistency for pie or similar recipes, cut and steam the pumpkin as instructed in the recipe for Orange-Seared Pumpkin, but open the pressure cooker using the Natural Release method (see page 14).

Zucchini alla Pizzaiola

Serves 4 to 6

Alla pizzaiola is what Italians call anything that is baked like a pizza—topped with tomato sauce and mozzarella. These steamed zucchini are stuffed and then broiled briefly to be nice and bubbly. In place of the tomato puree, fresh chopped tomatoes or halved cherry tomatoes can be used, as shown in the photo (page 79). If fresh basil is not available (or if you prefer), a generous sprinkling of dried oregano will be equally tasty. You can make similar "pizzas" with eggplant slices, mushroom caps, and even halved artichokes! (See the Appendix, Pressure Cooking Timetables, pages 280–281, for the right steaming times for these alternatives.)

Note: This recipe can be either halved or doubled provided there is at least 1 cup of liquid in the pressure cooker (or your cooker's minimum liquid requirement) and the total volume of the zucchini does not exceed two-thirds of the cooker's capacity.

6 medium zucchini (about 2 pounds)
1 teaspoon salt
½ teaspoon freshly ground
    black pepper
1 tablespoon extra-virgin olive oil
1 cup good-quality tomato puree (or
    sliced cherry tomatoes)
1 small bunch fresh basil (leaves only),
    finely chopped
1 cup shredded or thinly sliced
    mozzarella cheese

1. Add 1 cup of water (or the minimum amount required by your cooker to reach pressure) to the pressure cooker base; insert the steamer basket. Slice the zucchini in half lengthwise. Cut off and discard their ends. Then, depending on the length of each, cut them crosswise into 2 or 3 pieces. Arrange the zucchini in the steamer basket vertically.

2. Close and lock the lid of the pressure cooker. Cook at high pressure (see "Get *Hip* About the Pressure," page 13) for 5 minutes/all cooker types. When the time is up, open the cooker with the Normal Release method (see page 15).

3. Using tongs, delicately lift out the zucchini and arrange it on a heat-proof serving platter. Using a sharp knife, slice along the center of each, cutting about three-quarters of the way through; then gently pull the sides apart to create a crevice.

4. Turn on the broiler. Season the zucchini with the salt, pepper, and oil, dividing them equally. Spoon the tomato puree into the crevices, dividing it equally. Sprinkle the tops first with the basil and then with the mozzarella. Place under the broiler until the cheese is bubbly and has just starting to turn golden, about 5 minutes.

Zucchini alla Pizzaiola

All-Seasons
Potato Salad

Serves 4 to 6

Delicious warm or chilled, this is a great pantry recipe; the only fresh items needed are the potatoes! It is quite a hardy salad and could very well stand on its own as a one-pot vegetarian meal. Pressure cooking whole potatoes makes them too tender to be sliced and then tossed in a salad. The best way to ensure that the potatoes can withstand the mixing and dishing of a salad is to cut them up while raw, and then pressure-steam the pieces.

Note: This recipe can be either halved or doubled provided there is at least 1 cup of liquid in the pressure cooker (or your cooker's minimum liquid requirement) and the total volume of the potatoes does not exceed two-thirds of the cooker's capacity.

> 2 pounds red potatoes, cut into 1-inch chunks
> 1 cup drained marinated artichokes, quartered, with their liquid reserved
> 2 tablespoons extra-virgin olive oil
> 1 cup pitted black salt-cured olives
> Salt
> Freshly ground black pepper
> 2 hard-boiled eggs (page 55), cut into wedges

1. Add 1 cup of water (or the minimum amount required by your cooker to reach pressure) to the pressure cooker base; insert the steamer basket. Distribute the potatoes evenly in the basket.

2. Close and lock the lid of the pressure cooker. Cook at high pressure (see "Get *Hip* About the Pressure," page 13) for 5 minutes/stovetop or 7 minutes/electric (or nonstandard stovetop). When the time is up, open the cooker with the 10-Minute Natural Release method (see page 15).

3. Immediately lift the steamer basket out of the cooker and tumble the potatoes into a salad bowl. Pour in the reserved marinade from the artichokes and tumble to coat. Add the oil, artichokes, and olives and mix well to distribute. Season with salt and pepper. Decorate with the egg wedges just before serving.

Variation

Summer Potato and Bell Pepper Salad

Follow the recipe for All-Seasons Potato Salad, omitting the artichokes, olives, and eggs and adding 1 red and 1 yellow bell pepper, the juice of 1 lemon, and 1 pressed garlic clove. Stem and seed the peppers and cut into strips. Place the strips on top of the potatoes in the steamer basket. After pressure cooking, dress the hot peppers and potatoes with the oil, lemon juice, garlic, salt, and black pepper.

Red, White, and Blue Potato Salad

Serves 4 to 6

A true American classic—made just a little more colorful!

Note: This recipe can be either halved or doubled provided there is at least 1 cup of liquid in the pressure cooker (or your cooker's minimum liquid requirement) and the total volume of the potatoes does not exceed two-thirds of the cooker's capacity.

> 2 pounds assorted red, white, and blue
>   new potatoes, cut into 1-inch chunks
> 2 tablespoons mayonnaise
> 1 teaspoon Dijon mustard
> 2 hard-boiled eggs (page 55), finely
>   chopped
> 1 green onion, finely chopped
> Salt
> Freshly ground black pepper
> Pinch sugar

1. Add 1 cup of water (or the minimum amount required by your cooker to reach pressure) to the pressure cooker base; insert the steamer basket. Distribute the potatoes evenly in the basket.

2. Close and lock the lid of the pressure cooker. Cook at high pressure (see "Get *Hip* About the Pressure," page 13) for 5 minutes/stovetop or 7 minutes/electric (or nonstandard stovetop). When the time is up, open the cooker with the 10-Minute Natural Release method (see page 15).

3. Meanwhile, mix together the mayonnaise and mustard in a salad bowl. As soon as the cooker is opened, lift out the steamer basket and tumble the potatoes into the bowl. Add the eggs and green onions and tumble together until combined and coated with the dressing. Season with salt, pepper, and sugar.

Stewed Veggies

Vegetables that are stewed in the pressure cooker have a distinct advantage over those boiled in a saucepan on the stovetop—their own juice forms a large and flavorful portion of the boiling liquid. Instead of submerging the vegetables in water as you do to boil them in a saucepan, you add just enough water to the cooker for it to reach pressure. Once under pressure, just as with soups, the vegetables, which are 80 to 95 percent water anyway, will release their juice into the boiling water.

Wine-Stewed Broccoli

Serves 4 to 6

A specialty of Southern Italy, *Broccoli affogati,* which literally translates to "drowned broccoli," is served from Sicily to Puglia during the Christmas holidays as a side dish to meat. You may use broccoli crowns only, or include the stems, as you prefer. Cauliflower can be used instead—or for festive color, use both!

Note: This recipe can be either halved or doubled provided there is at least 1 cup of liquid in the pressure cooker (or your cooker's minimum liquid requirement) and the total volume of the vegetables does not exceed two-thirds of the cooker's capacity.

> 2 pounds broccoli (with or without main stems)
> 1 tablespoon olive oil
> 2 garlic cloves, coarsely chopped
> 3 oil-packed anchovies (optional)
> ½ cup of red wine (something tart, such as Chianti)
> 1 teaspoon salt
> 1 cup water, more as needed

½ cup shaved Caciocavallo or Pecorino Romano cheese (shaved using a vegetable peeler)

1. If using broccoli stems, cut them from the crowns and chop them. Separate the crowns into florets. Set the broccoli aside.

2. Heat the pressure cooker base on medium heat, add the oil, and heat briefly. Stir in the garlic and the anchovies if using. Sauté for 2 minutes until the garlic is golden and the anchovies have dissolved. To deglaze the cooker, pour in the wine and continue to cook until it has almost completely evaporated, about 3 minutes. Stir in the broccoli stems if using. Arrange the florets on top and sprinkle with the salt and pour 1 cup water (or the minimum amount required by your cooker to reach pressure).

3. Close and lock the lid of the pressure cooker. Cook at high pressure (see "Get *Hip* About the Pressure," page 13) for 5 minutes/all cooker types. When the time is up, open the cooker using the Normal Release method (see page 15).

4. Delicately tumble the broccoli into a serving dish, pouring the cooking liquid over the top. Decorate with the cheese just before serving.

Bavarian Sweet and Sour Cabbage

3. Give the kraut a final stir, transfer to a serving dish, and serve immediately.

Serves 4 to 6

A traditional German dish that is both sweet and sour, this is a perfect accompaniment to boiled meats or roasted root vegetables. You'll see there isn't much liquid in the recipe, that's because the cabbage has a high water content, which will be released as the pressure cooker heats.

Note: This recipe can be either halved or doubled provided the total volume of the vegetables does not exceed two-thirds of the cooker's capacity.

> 1 tablespoon vegetable oil
> 1 medium onion, sliced
> 1 teaspoon cumin seeds
> 1 small head cabbage (about 1½ pounds), sliced
> 2 teaspoons raw sugar
> 1 teaspoon salt
> ½ cup apple cider vinegar
> ½ cup water

1. Heat the pressure cooker base on medium heat, add the oil, and heat briefly. Stir in the onion and cumin and sauté until the onion has softened. Add the cabbage and stir to distribute evenly. Sprinkle with the sugar and salt and then pour the vinegar and water over the top.

2. Close and lock the lid of the pressure cooker. Cook at high pressure (see "Get *Hip* About the Pressure," page 13) for 3 minutes/all cooker types. When the time is up, open the cooker using the Normal Release method (see page 15).

Mashed Potatoes

Serves 4 to 6

Use this same recipe for mashing *any* root vegetable! I prefer leaving on the skin, for a little extra fiber and protein. If this is not your preference, then simply remove the skin as soon after pressure cooking as you can handle the hot potatoes. The hotter the potatoes, the easier it will be to remove their skin. For mashing, you may use the potato's cooking liquid, steaming liquid from another dish, milk, cream, yogurt, half-and-half, or similar, whatever gives you the taste you like.

Note: This recipe can be either halved or doubled provided there is at least 1 cup of liquid in the pressure cooker (or your cooker's minimum liquid requirement) and the total volume of the potatoes does not exceed two-thirds of the cooker's capacity.

> 2 to 3 pounds medium baking potatoes
> 1 cup water, or more as needed
> Salt
> Cooking liquid, reserved from the potatoes
> ¼ cup whole milk or cream
> Freshly ground black pepper

1. If the potatoes are not similar in size, cut the larger ones into pieces so that they are. Add the potatoes and 1 cup of water (or the minimum amount required by your cooker to reach pressure) to the pressure cooker base; sprinkle with 1 teaspoon salt.

2. Close and lock the lid of the pressure cooker. Cook at high pressure (see "Get *Hip* About the Pressure," page 13) for 10 minutes/stovetop or 13 to 15 minutes/electric (or nonstandard stovetop). When the time is up, open the pressure cooker with the 10-Minute Natural Release method (see page 15).

3. Strain the cooking liquid into a bowl. Then, with a potato masher, begin mashing the potatoes in the cooker base, gradually adding the milk and strained cooking liquid to them as you do so and continuing until they reach your preferred consistency; figure about 2 minutes for rustic texture, 5 minutes for smooth. Season to taste with salt and pepper and transfer to a serving dish.

Stuffed Veggies

The best way to turn a vegetable into a spectacular one-pot meal is to stuff it. The vegetables and fillings in this section of the chapter can be mixed-and-matched; if you do this, use the pressure cooking time in the recipe for the filling, which you can put in whatever vegetable shell you like. Stuffed vegetables are almost always really delicate, so take care when removing them from the cooker.

Ricotta and Basil–Stuffed Peppers

Serves 4 to 6

For stuffing, choose relatively small "square" bell peppers that have a nice base that will allow them to stand up in the pressure cooker.

Note: This recipe can be either halved or doubled provided there is at least 1 cup of liquid in the pressure cooker (or your cooker's minimum liquid requirement) and the total volume of the ingredients does not exceed two-thirds of the cooker's capacity.

> 4 to 6 small boxy bell peppers (any color)
> 1 large egg
> 2 cups ricotta cheese (1 pound)
> 1 cup plain dry bread crumbs
> ½ cup grated Parmigiano-Reggiano or Pecorino Romano cheese
> 1 small bunch fresh basil (leaves only), finely chopped
> 3 garlic cloves, finely minced
> 1½ teaspoons salt
> ¼ teaspoon freshly ground black pepper
> 1 tablespoon olive oil

> 1 medium onion, coarsely chopped
> 1 cup chopped fresh or canned tomatoes, drained with juices reserved
> Water, as needed

1. Slice the top off each bell pepper and set aside. Hollow out the peppers, discarding the ribs and seeds; set the peppers aside.

2. Using a fork, lightly beat the egg in a medium bowl. Add the ricotta and mix well. Add the bread crumbs, Parmigiano-Reggiano cheese, basil, garlic, salt, and black pepper and stir until combined. Spoon the filling evenly into the hollowed peppers; set aside.

3. Heat the pressure cooker base on medium heat, add the oil and heat briefly. Stir in the onion and sauté until soft. Add enough water to the reserved tomato juice to equal 1 cup (or the minimum amount required by your cooker to reach pressure). Add this liquid and the tomatoes to the cooker base. Gently lower the stuffed peppers into the pressure cooker, making sure they stand upright. Then tuck the tops, on their sides, into the spaces between the peppers.

4. Close and lock the lid of the pressure cooker. Cook at high pressure (see "Get *Hip* About the Pressure," page 13) for 5 minutes/all cooker types. When the time

is up, open the cooker using the Normal Release method (see page 15).

5. Using tongs or two spoons, gently transfer the peppers to a serving platter, and place a top on each one. Pour or ladle the tomato sauce over them and serve.

Stagger Veggies in Layers To Make Them Fit

Vegetables can differ quite a bit in size, and so can the shape of the pressure cooker. If all the stuffed vegetables don't fit in the steamer basket or base of the cooker in one layer, arrange the largest ones on the bottom and then make a second layer with the smaller ones, offsetting them on the ones below. This will ensure even distribution of steam so that everything cooks at the same time, no matter the size of the pressure cooker.

Veal-Stuffed Artichoke Halves

Serves 4 to 6

Artichokes cook almost instantly in the pressure cooker, so for this recipe, we will use the steamer basket to slow them down a bit, instead of cooking them in

the sauce as in the previous recipe. The veal is especially tasty but you can use any favorite ground meat mixture without changing the pressure cooking time.

Note: This recipe can be either halved or doubled provided there is at least 1 cup of liquid in the pressure cooker (or your cooker's minimum liquid requirement) and the total volume of the ingredients does not exceed two-thirds of the cooker's capacity.

1 large egg
¼ cup plain dry bread crumbs
2 tablespoons whole milk
¼ cup finely chopped flat-leaf parsley
½ pound ground veal
½ cup grated Parmigiano-Reggiano cheese
½ teaspoon salt
¼ teaspoon freshly grated nutmeg
Pinch freshly ground black pepper
2 to 3 medium artichokes
1 lemon, cut in half crosswise
Baby arugula leaves, for serving (optional)

1. Add 1 cup of water (or the minimum amount required by your cooker to reach pressure) to the pressure cooker base; insert the steamer basket and set aside.

2. Using a fork, lightly beat the egg in a medium bowl. Add the bread crumbs and milk and mix well with the fork. Reserve 1 tablespoon of the chopped parsley and add the remainder to the bowl along with the veal, cheese, salt, nutmeg, and pepper; mix well with your hands until all ingredients are evenly distributed.

3. Remove the tough lower leaves from each artichoke; then place each artichoke on its side and cut off the entire top with a chef's knife, removing the spiny tips of the upper leaves. Then slice each artichoke in half lengthwise, from top to stem, and scoop out the fuzzy choke with a melon baller. Wipe the cut surfaces with a lemon half to keep them from turning brown. Mound the filling into each cavity, dividing it equally. Gently lower the artichokes, stuffed side up, into the steamer basket in the cooker.

4. Close and lock the lid of the pressure cooker. Cook at high pressure (see "Get *Hip* About the Pressure," page 13) for 8 minutes/stovetop or 10 minutes/electric (or nonstandard stovetop). When the time is up, open the cooker using the Normal Release method (see page 15).

5. Lift the steamer basket out of the cooker. One at a time, gently slide a large serving spoon under each artichoke and then, using tongs, to transfer it to a serving platter. Sprinkle with the reserved parsley, dot with arugula leaves if you wish, and serve.

Veal-Stuffed Artichoke Halves

Stuffed Acorn Squash

Serves 4 to 6

This is a fantastic vegetarian main dish for fall, and if you use olive oil instead of butter, it is vegan. So instead of serving a stuffed turkey, serve stuffed squashes! Begin with several small acorn squashes or choose one large one and cut it in half so it fits in your pressure cooker. Be sure to wrap it in a foil sling, (see page 11), so that it's easier to lift out when finished.

Note: This recipe may be halved provided there is at least 1 cup of liquid in the pressure cooker (or your cooker's minimum liquid requirement). It cannot be doubled; to make more, make two batches.

    Acorn squash (see headnote)
    1½ cups fresh bread cubes
    2 celery stalks, chopped
    1 yellow onion, finely chopped
    1 fresh rosemary sprig (leaves only),
        finely chopped
    1 fresh sage sprig (leaves only), finely
        chopped
    1½ teaspoons salt
    Unsalted butter or olive oil
    ¼ cup crumbled amaretti or gingersnap
        cookies

1. Add 1 cup of water (or the minimum amount required by your cooker to reach pressure) to the pressure cooker base; set aside. Slice the top off each acorn squash and scoop out the seeds. (Reserve the tops for another use and the seeds for roasting later.)

2. Mix the bread, celery, onion, rosemary, sage, and 1 teaspoon of the salt in a medium bowl until combined. Sprinkle the remaining ½ teaspoon salt over the inside of the squash and then spoon in the filling, packing well. Lower the squash into the pressure cooker base; if using more than one squash, fit them snugly together. If the squash won't sit upright, crumple aluminum foil into "snakes" and shape them into rings to support the squash. Top the squash with small pats of butter or a swirl of olive oil.

3. Close and lock the lid of the pressure cooker. Cook at high pressure (see "Get *Hip* About the Pressure," page 13) for 10 minutes/stovetop or 13 to 15 minutes/ electric (or nonstandard stovetop). When the time is up, open the cooker using the Normal Release method (see page 15).

4. Using tongs, or the sling, lift the squash out of the cooker and transfer to a serving plate. Cut into individual portions if appropriate. Sprinkle with the cookie crumbs and serve.

Seafood-Stuffed Tomatoes

Serves 4 to 6

A perfect summer dish, this recipe can be served warm, chilled, or room temperature! With the exception of octopus or squid, any seafood available may be used without changing the pressure cooking time.

Note: This recipe can be either halved or doubled provided there is at least 1 cup of liquid in the pressure cooker (or your cooker's minimum liquid requirement) and the total volume of the ingredients does not exceed two-thirds of the cooker's capacity.

> 4 to 6 medium ripe tomatoes
> 1 white fish fillet, cubed
> 1 cup shelled and deveined small shrimp
> 2 hard-boiled eggs (page 55), chopped
> ½ cup plain dry bread crumbs
> Salt
> Freshly ground black pepper
> 2 garlic cloves, finely chopped
> 2 tablespoons olive oil
> 2 tablespoons capers, rinsed and drained
> 1 lemon, cut into wedges, for serving

1. Add 1 cup of water (or the minimum amount required by your cooker to reach pressure) to the pressure cooker base; insert the steamer basket and set aside.

2. Slice the tomatoes in half lengthwise (from stem to base). Use a paring knife to delicately disconnect the ribs from the shell, then use a small spoon to scoop the ribs, seeds, and pulp into a medium bowl. Set the shells aside. Add the fish, shrimp, eggs, bread crumbs, 1 teaspoon salt, ½ teaspoon pepper, and the garlic to the bowl and mix until well combined.

3. Sprinkle the open tomato halves with a little salt and pepper and pour the oil into the tomato halves, dividing it equally. Spoon the filling evenly into the tomatoes and gently lower them into the steamer basket.

4. Close and lock the lid of the pressure cooker. Cook at high pressure (see "Get *Hip* About the Pressure," page 13) for 5 minutes/all cooker types. When the time is up, open the cooker using the Normal Release method (see page 15).

5. Lift the steamer basket out of the cooker, then using tongs or two spoons, transfer to a serving platter. Sprinkle over with the capers, and serve with the lemon wedges on the side.

Potato-Stuffed Onions

Serves 4 to 6

This is a great recipe for turning one portion of leftover mashed potatoes into a meal for four or more. Choose the onions carefully—small round ones will give the best results.

Note: This recipe can be either halved or doubled provided there is at least 1 cup of liquid in the pressure cooker (or your cooker's minimum liquid requirement) and the total volume of the ingredients does not exceed two-thirds of the cooker's capacity.

> 1 cup salt-free Vegetable Stock, more as needed (page 49)
> 3 small round onions (any color)
> 1 cup mashed potatoes (see page 83)
> ½ cup grated Pecorino Romano cheese
> 6 small pats (about ½ tablespoon each) unsalted butter

1. Add the stock to the pressure cooker base; insert the steamer basket and set aside.

2. Cut the onions in half lengthwise, from stem to base, and then remove the root end and tip from each piece. Remove and discard the outer layer of skin. Then scoop out the inside and transfer to a chopping board, leaving a shell about ¼ inch thick (about 3 layers) to stuff: To do this, just delicately insert the edge of a teaspoon between the layers you want to keep and the ones you want to remove.

3. Finely chop the inner layers of the onions and then combine in a medium bowl with the potatoes and cheese. Stuff the onion shells with the mixture and lower them into the steamer basket. Top each stuffed onion with a butter pat.

4. Close and lock the lid of the pressure cooker. Cook at high pressure (see "Get *Hip* About the Pressure," page 13) for 7 minutes/all cooker types. When the time is up, open the cooker using the Normal Release method (see page 14).

5. Lift the steamer basket out of the cooker. One at a time, delicately slide a large serving spoon under each stuffed onion and then, using tongs, transfer it to a serving platter. Drizzle with the steaming liquid and serve immediately.

Stuffed Cabbage Rolls

Serves 4 to 6

Just about every culture has a version of stuffed cabbage rolls; this recipe is a faster version of the classic Northern Italian *Verzolini alla Piacentina*. It's a fantastic way to fancy up leftover cooked meat such as pork from carnitas (see Mexican Pulled Pork page 189), or Mexican Shredded Chicken (page 190).

Note: This recipe can be either halved or doubled provided there is at least 1 cup of liquid in the pressure cooker (or your cooker's minimum liquid requirement) and

the total volume of the ingredients does not exceed two-thirds of the cooker's capacity.

1 cup chopped tomatoes, with their juice
6 Savoy cabbage leaves
2 cups cubed or shredded cooked meat
1 cup plain dry bread crumbs
½ cup grated cheese (your favorite type)
1 large egg
1 teaspoon salt
¼ teaspoon freshly ground black pepper
¾ cup water

1. Add the tomatoes and their juice to the pressure cooker base and set aside. Bring a medium saucepan of water to a boil and dip each cabbage leaf into it to soften; transfer to a strainer in the sink to cool, Discard the boiling water.

2. Add the meat, bread crumbs, and cheese to the bowl of a food processor. Pulse a few times, and then add the egg, salt, and pepper and pulse again until well mixed. Divide the filling into 6 equal portions.

3. Lay the cabbage leaves on a work surface. Place 1 portion of the filling in the middle of the bottom part of each leaf. Fold up the sides over the filling and roll up the leaf. Arrange the rolls in the base of the pressure cooker with their open edges facing down. Pour in the ¾ cup water.

4. Close and lock the lid of the pressure cooker. Cook at high pressure (see "Get *Hip* About the Pressure," page 13) for 5 minutes/all cooker types. When the time is up, open the cooker using the Normal Release method (see page 15).

5. Lift the steamer basket out of the cooker. One at a time, gently slide a large serving spoon under each cabbage roll and transfer it to a serving platter. Drizzle the hot tomatoes over the top and serve immediately.

Faux-Sautéed Veggies

A pressure cooker can hasten the "sauté" of any vegetable. After a quick turn in oil in the uncovered cooker base, a dash of liquid and a few minutes under pressure ensure that the veggies get the benefits of browning first and then retain most of their vitamins and flavor as they fully cook.

Wild Mushroom Sauté

Serves 4 to 6

Use whatever variety of fresh wild culinary mushrooms is available in your region. I especially like chanterelles (*finferli* in Italian) or whatever my family has foraged in the nearby woods. My husband was taught by his father what varieties are edible and he, in turn, is teaching our son and daughter. You can also "sauté" white or any farm-raised mushrooms under pressure, but they need a shorter cooking time than their tougher, wild cousins. Pressure cook white button mushrooms for just 3 minutes. Fresh mushrooms have such a high water content that you don't need to add the usual minimum liquid to the cooker—the mushrooms will quickly give off enough on their own so do not be alarmed by the low quantity of liquid. Adding more liquid would result in a soup, not a sauté!

Note: This recipe cannot be halved. It can be doubled provided the total volume of the ingredients does not exceed two-thirds of the pressure cooker's capacity.

2 tablespoons olive oil
2 garlic cloves, halved
1 pound mushrooms, sliced
¼ cup dry white wine
½ cup water
1 teaspoon salt
¼ teaspoon freshly ground black pepper
1 bunch flat-leaf parsley, finely chopped

1. Heat the pressure cooker base on medium heat. Add the oil and garlic and cook briefly. Then add just enough mushrooms to cover the bottom of the cooker in one layer—about a handful. Let them cook until well-browned on one side, stirring infrequently, for about 4 minutes. To deglaze the cooker, pour in the wine and cook until it has almost completely evaporated. Add the remaining mushrooms, the water, salt, and pepper and mix well.

2. Close and lock the lid of the pressure cooker. Cook at high pressure (see "Get *Hip* About the Pressure," page 13) for 7 minutes/ all cooker types. When the time is up, open the cooker using the Normal Release method (see page 15).

3. Return the uncovered cooker to medium heat and bring the contents to a simmer. Simmer until the liquid has reduced and just coats the mushrooms, about 5 minutes. Taste and adjust the seasoning if you wish. Sprinkle the mushrooms with the parsley and serve immediately.

Variations

Fennel Butter Sauté

Follow the Wild Mushroom Sauté recipe, substituting unsalted butter for the oil, 1 pound sliced fennel (2 small bulbs) for the mushrooms, and Vegetable Stock (page 49) for the water. After pressure cooking, transfer the fennel to a serving dish. Whisk 1 tablespoon all-purpose flour into the liquid in the cooker and simmer as directed until the liquid reaches sauce consistency, about 4 minutes. Drizzle the sauce on the fennel, and sprinkle with a little freshly grated nutmeg just before serving.

Bell Pepper Sauté

Follow the Wild Mushroom Sauté recipe, substituting 1 pound sliced bell peppers (about 3) for the mushrooms. Omit the wine and water and instead, after browning some of the peppers, add 2 chopped tomatoes with their juices and then pressure cook for only 4 minutes. Just before serving, mix in 2 finely minced garlic cloves and 1 tablespoon oil.

Hot and Sour Cabbage, Beijing Style

Serves 4 to 6

This is a tangy, salty side dish and a favorite of mine to serve to anyone who thinks they don't like cabbage. It's truly versatile, pairing particularly well with any meat dish.

Note: This recipe can be either halved or doubled provided there is at least 1 cup of liquid in the pressure cooker (or your cooker's minimum liquid requirement) and the total volume of the ingredients does not exceed two-thirds of the cooker's capacity.

1 tablespoon vegetable oil
5 garlic cloves, halved
One ¼-inch slice fresh ginger, peeled and chopped (or 1 teaspoon ground ginger)
1 teaspoon crushed red pepper flakes
1 small head cabbage (about 1 pound), cut into 4 wedges
¼ cup white vinegar
¼ cup soy sauce
½ cup water
¼ teaspoon cornstarch
1 teaspoon sugar

1. Heat the pressure cooker base on medium heat, add the oil, and heat briefly. Stir in the garlic, ginger, and red pepper flakes. Position the cabbage wedges in the pressure cooker with the thicker, root end down and the tips pointing up. Pour in the vinegar, soy sauce, and water.

2. Close and lock the lid of the pressure cooker. Cook at high pressure (see "Get *Hip* About the Pressure," page 13) for 7 minutes/all cooker types. When the time is up, open the cooker using the Normal Release method (see page 15).

3. Using tongs or two spoons, gently transfer the cabbage wedges to a serving platter; cut each in half crosswise. Return the uncovered cooker base to medium heat and sprinkle the cornstarch and sugar into the cooking liquid. Bring the contents to a boil, stirring often, until thickened. Pour the thickened cooking liquid over the cabbage wedges and serve.

Hot and Sour Cabbage, Beijing Style

Dried Beans and Legumes

The pressure cooker is famous for cutting cooking times, and it does this more with dried beans and legumes than with any other food. I still remember my husband putting on a pot of chickpeas when we first got married. It boiled, simmered, and bubbled for *hours*. We must have had particularly old chickpeas because even after four hours they *still* weren't tender—never again.

Now I measure pressure cooker speed with chickpeas. My first-generation pressure cooker (which huffed and puffed at 9psi or the equivalent of low pressure) could cook soaked chickpeas in twenty minutes—which seemed pretty miraculous to me compared to 4 hours. New-generation pressure cookers that reach 15psi only need 13 minutes. What a difference!

The density of legumes makes it especially necessary for those using electric and nonstandard stovetop pressure cookers (see page 7) to use a longer cooking time, as indicated in the recipes, whereas you will see in the grains chapter, where the key ingredient is less dense, no timing differentiations need to be made for the different types of pressure cookers.

No valves for foamy foods. When pressure cooking legumes and other foods that produce foam, the release method is very important. Normal Release is not safe because foam in the cooker may spray out of the valve during the process. Always release pressure using the Natural or Cold Water Quick Release (see page 15) for a stovetop pressure cooker, and Natural Release for an electric pressure cooker. In the rare instance where it is not practical to wait for the cooker to open, I call for a Slow Normal Release (see page 15)—that's where you turn the release valve very, very slowly or in short spurts and stop for 10 seconds if foam begins to spray out.

Fatten it up. Add about a tablespoon of oil or fat to reduce the foam produced by legumes under pressure. The foam could obstruct the safety mechanisms and spray out of the secondary pressure valve instead of steam. This is especially problematic with venting pressure cookers (with weight-modified or jiggler valves that make lots of noise and release vapor while cooking under pressure), but not a concern for nonventing pressure cookers (with a spring valve that releases very little to no steam during cooking, with very quiet operation). If you don't know what type of valve your pressure cooker has, just add the fat to be on the safe side.

Go only halfway. When pressure cooking legumes, and other foods that expand, never fill the pressure cooker more than half full with beans, cooking liquid, and other ingredients. Some pressure cookers have a little mark with "½" written next to it. If not, eyeball it.

Reduce gas by soaking. Always soak or quick-soak beans before pressure cooking. Soaking removes the indigestible sugars that can cause digestive gas. Also it reduces the cooking time significantly, saving you time and energy—for example dried black beans need to be pressure cooked for 25 minutes and soaked black beans need to be pressure cooked for only 5!

Salt and acid come last. Unless specified by a recipe or technique, do not add salt or acidic ingredients like tomatoes, lemons, or wine during the cooking of dried beans without increasing the cooking time. For example, soaked cannellini beans only need 5 to 7 minutes at high pressure to be cooked, but when tomatoes or salt are added, the cooking time is increased to 20 to 25 minutes!! This time increase is not always a bad thing. It can even be used to your advantage when constructing one-pot meals or dishes with other ingredients that need a longer time to cook (such as BBQ Pork Ribs with Spinach-Bean Salad, page 165).

Stock the stock. Save the cooking water from pressure cooked beans to use in place of a stock or as a soup base. Don't be alarmed if chickpea cooking liquid "gels" just like a meat stock. This is a good sign and example of how nutritious this liquid is!

Boiled Beans

The process of boiling beans in the pressure cooker is not much different from boiling beans in conventional cooking—the big difference here is how little time it takes to get the final result. This is one place where the recipes call for what may be more than the minimum liquid required by your cooker to reach pressure: Don't second guess, use the amount indicated.

Basic Boiled Beans

Yields almost 5 cups cooked beans

Beans prepared this way will give any recipe calling for cooked or canned beans a good start—basic shouldn't mean boring. You can add half an onion or an herb sprig to the cooking liquid. My favorite addition is a bay leaf (lightly crumpled if fresh) and a smashed garlic clove. You can use this method for any type of dried bean; the Appendix: Pressure Cooking Timetable (see pages 270–271) gives the cooking times for each. Read "Get *Hip* About Soaking," pages 100–101. Enjoy these beans in the four salads that follow, or in any of your favorite recipes.

Note: This recipe can be halved provided there are at least 2 cups of water in the cooker base; it can be doubled provided the total volume of the ingredients does not exceed half the pressure cooker's capacity.

2 cups dried beans, soaked, rinsed, and drained
4 cups water
1 herb, choose one:
    bay leaf, fresh thyme sprig, fresh sage sprig

1 to 3 aromatics, choose one from each:
    garlic, onion, shallots
    carrot, bell pepper
    celery, fennel, green bell pepper, parsley stems
1 tablespoon fat, choose one:
    vegetable oil, butter, margarine, rendered fat, 1 thick slice of bacon

1. Place the beans in the pressure cooker base and add the water. Then add your chosen herb, aromatics, and fat.

2. Close and lock the lid of the pressure cooker. Cook at high pressure (see "Get *Hip* About the Pressure," page 13) for the time appropriate for the type of bean and cooker, 5 to 15 minutes. When the time is up, open the pressure cooker with the Natural Release method (see page 15); this should take 10 to 15 minutes for a stovetop cooker, 20 to 30 minutes for an electric cooker.

3. Drain the beans in a colander set over a bowl. Remove the herb and aromatics and reserve the cooking liquid to use in place of stock at a later time. Use the beans in any recipe calling for cooked beans.

Chickpea Caprese Salad

Serves 4 to 6

This classic Italian salad mixes the meaty texture of chickpeas with rich mozzarella and the clean bright flavor of fresh tomatoes. The salad can be made and mixed up to a day ahead, but do not add the basil until just before serving since the acidity of the tomatoes can turn it black.

Note: The pressure cooking time for soaked dried chickpeas is 13 minutes/stovetop cooker or 15 to 20 minutes/electric (or nonstandard stovetop) cooker.

> 2 cups dried chickpeas, cooked (see Basic Boiled Beans page 97) and cooled
> Two 5-ounce balls fresh mozzarella cheese (or one 16-ounce ball dried), chopped
> 2 ripe tomatoes, chopped
> Extra-virgin olive oil
> Salt
> Freshly ground black pepper
> 1 small bunch basil (leaves only), chopped

Stir together the chickpeas, mozzarella, and tomatoes in a medium bowl. Drizzle with oil, sprinkle with salt and pepper, and stir once more. Taste and adjust the seasoning if you wish. Sprinkle with basil just before serving.

Borlotti Bean and Tuna Salad

Serves 4 to 6

This is an Italian summer bean salad that is served chilled. It's usually made with white vinegar, but I like the small hit of sweet you get when using balsamic. If you are able to find it, use imported tuna packed in olive oil for this salad. If you can't find it, use drained water-packed tuna and add 2 tablespoons olive oil. Leave out the fresh oregano until just before serving; if substituting with dry, mix it in with the salad before refrigerating.

Note: The pressure cooking time for soaked dried borlotti beans is 7 minutes/stovetop cooker or 8 to 10 minutes/electric (or nonstandard stovetop) cooker.

> One-quarter red onion, finely chopped
> 1 tablespoon balsamic vinegar
> ½ teaspoon salt
> ½ teaspoon freshly ground black pepper
> One 5- to 7-ounce can imported oil-packed tuna
> 2 cups dried borlotti beans, cooked (see Basic Boiled Beans page 97) and cooled
> ½ teaspoon chopped fresh oregano leaves

Mix the onion, vinegar, salt, and pepper in a small bowl and let macerate for at least 15 minutes. Drain the tuna, reserving the oil. Stir together the tuna and beans in a medium bowl; add about half the reserved tuna oil and the onion mixture and mix well. Sprinkle with the oregano and serve. (Reserve the remaining tuna oil for another use or discard.)

Cannellini, Fennel, and Black Olive Bean Salad

Serves 4 to 6

This salad is especially tasty when mandarin oranges are included, so if they are in season, be sure to mix them in. Make the salad up to a day in advance, but mix in the oranges at the last minute so they don't look tired and soggy.

Note: The pressure cooking time for soaked dried cannellini beans is 4 minutes/ stovetop cooker or 5 to 6 minutes/electric (or nonstandard stovetop) cooker.

2 cups dried cannellini beans, cooked (see Basic Boiled Beans page 97) and cooled
1 fennel bulb, finely chopped
1 cup pitted salt-cured black olives (such as Taggiesche)
2 tablespoons extra-virgin olive oil, plus more if needed
2 tablespoons white vinegar, plus more if needed
Salt
Freshly ground black pepper
2 mandarin oranges, separated into segments (optional)

Stir together the cannellini beans, fennel, and olives in a medium bowl. Drizzle with the oil and vinegar and mix well; season with salt and pepper and add more oil or vinegar if you wish. Stir in the oranges if using.

Black Bean and Corn Salsa Salad

Serves 4 to 6

Make this salad as zesty as you like by adding as much cilantro as appeals to your palate. Serve as a salad, or use as a filling for quesadillas or Tamales (page 156).

Note: The pressure cooking time for soaked dried black beans is 4 minutes/ stovetop cooker or 5 to 6 minutes/electric (or nonstandard stovetop) cooker.

2 cups dried black beans, cooked (see Basic Boiled Beans page 97) and cooled
1 ripe tomato, chopped
One-quarter yellow onion, finely chopped
1 green bell pepper, stemmed, seeded, and finely chopped
1 cup fresh corn kernels (about 2 medium ears)
1 teaspoon salt
Chopped fresh cilantro leaves

Stir together the beans, tomato, onion, bell pepper, corn, and salt in a large bowl. Sprinkle with cilantro and stir once more. Serve.

Get *Hip* About Soaking

The world of legumes has a unique consideration: should those dried beans be soaked before pressure cooking, or not? And if so, what's the way to do it, and when?

To Soak or Not To Soak

Pressure cooking beans from their dried state takes more time and energy than if they have been soaked first, and the end result is, in my opinion, unpleasant. The beans are often split and broken (from the quick rehydration), and none of the indigestible sugars that can cause digestive gas are removed.

Soaking beans ensures even cooking and the removal of those indigestible sugars; it also allows for more interesting pressure cooking techniques such as steaming the beans above a liquid, or boiling them directly in a tomato puree, which would ordinarily be taboo in conventional cooking because it would take too long.

I recommend soaking most dried legumes before pressure cooking, either for 8 to 12 hours or using the quick-soak alternative; see "The Soaks" (page 101) for an explanation of both methods. You can refer to the Pressure Cooking Timetable

(see Appendix pages 270–271) for the basic cooking times for soaked beans. Not all dried beans require soaking, and this chart also shows the cooking times for those that don't, along with the unsoaked cooking times for those that I feel should be, just in case you want to try them that way.

Ooops! I Forgot to Soak

Quick-soaking beans is an alternative to soaking them overnight. It is a process of partially cooking the beans and then rinsing them before fully cooking them in a recipe. A bit of salt is added to keep the skins from breaking. Quick-soaking removes a majority of the indigestible sugars, just like a classic long soak, but only takes 10 minutes in the pressure cooker. Quick-soaked beans can be used in any recipe calling for soaked beans.

Freezing Soaked Beans

To get a head start so I can pressure cook a recipe with beans on a whim, I freeze *soaked* beans so they are always ready to use and quickly infuse with the flavors of a particular recipe. Using frozen soaked beans does not change a recipe's pressure cooking time (which is already so quick)—though the cooker will take a few extra minutes to reach pressure. Here's the method:

Follow the Classic Soak method (see next page), but first measure the beans in 1-cup quantities and soak each cupful individually. This way, even though they will close to double in size during soaking, you'll

know later what quantity of dried beans you started with—important for following most recipes. After soaking, draining, and rinsing, package each cupful separately in a food storage bag and flatten it. Next, put each bag in the freezer horizontally—when the contents are frozen the bags can be stored vertically to save space.

When it's time to make any recipe calling for soaked beans, simply grab a bag of frozen soaked beans, whack it on the countertop to break it up a little bit, and use as the recipe indicates.

The Soaks

Split peas and lentils do not need to be soaked before pressure cooking. Generally, every other kind of dried legume will benefit from being soaked prior to pressure cooking. Of course, fresh beans that you shell yourself don't need to be soaked—and since not everyone has access to these fresh beans, or the desire to shell them, I have not included their cooking times in the Pressure Cooking Timetable (see Appendix page 270), but it's the same as their soaked dried counterpart. For soaking, always work with measured 1- or 2-cup quantities of beans, and note the quantity so you'll know what you started with when ready to add to a recipe.

Classic Soak: 8 to 12 hours or overnight

1. Rinse and drain the dried beans.
2. Put the beans in a large mixing bowl and fill with plenty of cold water—4 cups of water to each cup of beans or more (more water will do a better job of removing indigestible sugars). Set aside at room temperature for at least 8 hours or overnight. Halfway (approximately!) through the soaking, drain and rinse the beans and then continue the soaking with fresh water.
3. Drain and rinse the beans again before using in any recipe calling for soaked beans (or freeze for later use).

Quick-soak: 10 minutes

1. Rinse and drain the dried beans.
2. Put the beans in the pressure cooker. For each cup of beans add 4 cups of water and 1 teaspoon of salt.
3. Pressure cook at high pressure for 2 minutes for all cooker types (see "Get *Hip* About the Pressure," page 13).
4. Open the pressure cooker using the Natural Release method (10 to 15 minutes, see page 15).
5. Drain and rinse the beans before using; their skins may appear a little wrinkled and this is normal. Use in any recipe calling for soaked beans. Discard the quick-soaking liquid. Also rinse out the pressure cooker.

Cannellini in Tomato-Sage Sauce

Serves 4 to 6

This classic Tuscan dish, *cannellini all'uccelletto*—cooked in the same fashion as a small bird—can be used as an accompaniment to meat. Cannellini beans don't usually need 15 to 20 minutes to be pressure cooked, but adding tomatoes to the cooking liquid nearly triples their cooking time. However, cooking the beans separately first and then adding tomatoes and pressure cooking again does not bring significant time-saving in this case. By the way, the tomatoes will contribute about 1½ cups of cooking liquid to the ingredients mix.

Note: This recipe can be halved provided there are at least 1½ cups of liquid in the cooker base; it can be doubled provided the total volume of the ingredients does not exceed half the pressure cooker's capacity.

3 garlic cloves; 2 smashed, 1 minced
  and reserved
1 tablespoon olive oil (everyday quality)
2 fresh sage sprigs (reserve 2 leaves for
  a garnish)
1 cup water
1 pound ripe tomatoes, coarsely chopped
  (or whole cherry tomatoes or one
  14.5-ounce can chopped tomatoes with
  their juices)
1 cup dried cannellini beans, soaked,
  rinsed, and drained
1½ teaspoons salt
½ teaspoon freshly ground black pepper
Extra-virgin olive oil

1. Add the 2 smashed garlic cloves to the cooker base with the everyday olive oil and sage sprigs and heat on low heat (keep warm setting for electric cookers) to slowly infuse the oil with the garlic and sage. Swish the contents around occasionally. When the garlic starts to turn golden, after about 4 minutes, add the water, tomatoes, and cannellini beans.

2. Close and lock the lid of the pressure cooker. Cook at high pressure (see "Get *Hip* About the Pressure," page 13) for 15 minutes/stovetop or 18 to 20 minutes/electric (or nonstandard stovetop). When the time is up, open the pressure cooker with the Natural Release method (see page 15); this should take 10 to 15 minutes for a stovetop cooker, 20 to 30 minutes for an electric cooker.

3. When the cooker is open, remove and discard the sage stems and stir in the minced garlic, salt, and pepper; taste and adjust the seasoning if you wish. Using a slotted spoon, transfer the beans to a serving dish, swirl in a little extra-virgin olive oil and decorate with the reserved sage leaves.

Variation

Tomato Cannellini with Sausage

Follow the Cannellini in Tomato-Sage Sauce recipe, adding about ½ pound sausage (your favorite kind) cut into 1-inch pieces: Before adding the smashed garlic and sage sprigs, heat the pressure cooker base on medium heat, add the everyday olive oil, heat briefly, and then add the sausage and cook until browned. Reduce the heat to low, add the garlic and sage, and continue as directed in the recipe.

Cannellini in
Tomato-Sage Sauce

Cuban Refried Beans

Serves 4 to 6

Most Latin cultures have their own version of refried beans. Although the type of bean and the condiments change, the technique is similar in all: Cook the beans with aromatics and then either drain and fry them with more spices OR sauté these spices separately and mix in before serving. *Frijoles negros* is quintessentially Cuban—the little shot of vinegar at the end makes their flavor both satisfying and crisp. This recipe is a terrific side dish for *ropa vieja, or* Cuban Pulled Beef (page 191).

Note: This recipe can be halved provided there are at least 1½ cups of liquid in the cooker base; it can be doubled provided the total volume of the ingredients does not exceed half the pressure cooker's capacity.

2 cups dried black beans, soaked and
    drained
2 cups water
1 bay leaf
2 tablespoons olive oil
1 large onion
1 green bell pepper
2 garlic cloves
1 teaspoon dried oregano, crumbled
1 teaspoon ground cumin
1 teaspoon salt
¼ teaspoon freshly ground black pepper
2 tablespoons white wine vinegar
Chopped fresh cilantro leaves, for
    serving

1. Place the beans, water, bay leaf, and 1 tablespoon of the oil in the pressure cooker base.

2. Close and lock the lid of the pressure cooker. Cook at high pressure (see "Get *Hip* About the Pressure," page 13) for 5 minutes/stovetop or 6 minutes/electric (or nonstandard stovetop). When the time is up, open the pressure cooker with the Natural Release method (see page 15); this should take 10 to 15 minutes for a stovetop cooker, 20 to 30 minutes for an electric cooker.

3. Meanwhile, chop the onion and bell pepper and mince the garlic. Heat a medium sauté pan on high heat; add the remaining 1 tablespoon oil and heat briefly. Stir in the onion and bell pepper. Cook until the onion has softened and starting to turn golden around the edges; then stir in the garlic, oregano, and cumin and sauté for another 30 seconds. Remove the vegetables from the heat and set aside.

4. As soon as the cooker is open, check that the beans are the desired consistency; they should be a bit like a stew. If not, puree just a small portion of them (while still in the cooker) with an immersion blender to make them creamier.

5. Return the pressure cooker base to medium-high heat and bring the beans mixture to a boil. Stir in the salt, black pepper, and vinegar. Lower the heat to medium-low and simmer, mixing infrequently, for about 5 minutes. Then tumble the sautéed vegetables into the beans, mix well, and heat through. Serve the beans with a generous sprinkling of cilantro.

Variation

Mexican Refried Beans

Frijoles is the Mexican version of refried beans. Follow the Cuban Black Beans recipe, replacing the black beans with kidney (or borlotti) beans, omitting the bell pepper and vinegar, and adding 1 teaspoon crushed red pepper flakes to the sautéing onion. Pressure cook the beans for 7 minutes/stovetop cooker or 8 to 10 minutes/electric (or nonstandard stovetop) cooker.

Drunken Cowboy Chili

Serves 6 to 8

When serving this chili con carne to sensitive eaters, I only add a pinch of crushed red pepper flakes. If you like it spicy, believe it or not, 1 teaspoon goes a long way in the pressure cooker, infusing plenty of spicy heat through the whole chili, and making it quite spicy indeed! Two variations follow, one vegetarian and one even hotter.

Note: This recipe can be halved provided there are at least 1½ cups of liquid in the cooker base; it can be doubled provided the total volume of the ingredients does not exceed half the pressure cooker's capacity.

1 tablespoon vegetable oil
3.5 ounces smoked pancetta or bacon, chopped

1 medium yellow onion, chopped
1 celery stalk, chopped
1 bunch fresh cilantro or parsley, stems and leaves chopped separately
8 ounces ground beef (or mixed meats such as pork, veal, or lamb)
1 tablespoon ground cumin
1 tablespoon ground coriander
1 tablespoon unsweetened cocoa powder
1 teaspoon crushed red pepper flakes
1½ cups beer
1½ cups chopped ripe tomatoes (or one 14.5-ounce can chopped tomatoes with their juices)
1 cup dried cranberry or pinto beans, soaked, rinsed, and drained
1 bay leaf
2 teaspoons salt
Sour cream, for serving

Careful with the Red Pepper Flakes!

The hotness of crushed red pepper flakes appears to magnify in the pressure cooker tenfold. What seems like magic is really just the even distribution and infusion of the hot pepper's oils into every part of the dish that occurs in pressure cooking. In conventional cooking, the eater gets a hit of heat only when he actually bites on a hot pepper flake that is floating around in the dish. Generally a pinch is mild, and a teaspoon is spicy! After making a few recipes that include red pepper flakes, you'll have an idea of how to adjust for more or less heat as suits your taste.

1. Heat the pressure cooker base on medium heat; add the oil and heat briefly. Add the pancetta and sauté until it is almost crispy, about 5 minutes. Then add the onion, celery, and cilantro stems (reserving the leaves for garnish) and sauté until the onion has softened, about 4 minutes. Move the contents to the side in the pressure cooker. Add the beef and stir to break it up. Sauté, stirring infrequently, until browned on at least one side and the juices have evaporated, 5 minutes, or longer if it is very wet.

2. Sprinkle the cumin, coriander, cocoa powder, and red pepper flakes over the meat and stir to combine. Sauté for 1 minute more to toast the spices lightly. To deglaze the cooker, stir in the beer. Add the tomatoes, beans, and bay leaf and mix well.

3. Close and lock the lid of the pressure cooker. Cook at high pressure (see "Get *Hip* About the Pressure," page 13) for 25 minutes/stovetop or 28 to 30 minutes/electric (or nonstandard stovetop). When the time is up, open the pressure cooker with the Natural Release method (see page 15); this should take 10 to 15 minutes for a stovetop cooker, 20 to 30 minutes for an electric cooker.

4. Fish out and discard the bay leaf. Add the salt; taste and adjust the amount if you wish. Return the uncovered cooker to medium heat and simmer for about 5 minutes or until the chili has reduced to the desired thickness.

5. Ladle the chili into individual bowls and top each with a dollop of sour cream and sprinkling of the cilantro leaves.

Variations

Veggie Chili

Follow the Drunken Cowboy Chili recipe, replacing the meat with 1 pound sliced mushrooms and using only ¾ cup beer.

5-Alarm Chili

Make the Drunken Cowboy Chili super spicy by doubling the crushed red pepper flakes to 2 teaspoons, and adding 1 teaspoon freshly ground black pepper and 1 teaspoon cayenne pepper. HOT!

Dal

Dal is Indian comfort food. It is served over rice, or eaten with roti, an especially delicious Indian flatbread. Indian cuisine encompasses *hundreds* of dals. For a Westerner's introduction, any Madhur Jaffrey cookbook will include a fine example of dal recipes that can be easily translated to the pressure cooker.

Dal is traditionally made of lentils or other whole or split beans that have had their hulls removed (and the word for these special beans is *dal* as well). Find these legumes at your local Indian market or online. Although it's not traditional, some specialty split beans many be replaced with regular lentils or common beans. In the following recipes substitutions are noted where appropriate.

The consistency of cooked dal can range anywhere from creamy to soupy. The recipes here lean toward creamy; should you want yours to be more soupy, after pressure cooking, mix in a cup or two of boiling water (as much as gives you the desired consistency), then adjust the amount of salt to reflect the greater yield.

Toor Dal

Serves 4 to 6

The technique for toor dal and its variations is the same: pressure cook the legumes with a few spices and on the side make another aromatic blend to mix in just before serving. If your neighborhood grocery doesn't carry the Indian seasonings, they are often available at natural foods stores and other specialty markets. Rinse the toor dal before soaking them.

Note: This recipe can be either halved or doubled provided the total volume of the ingredients does not exceed half the pressure cooker's capacity.

Toor Dal
2 cups dried toor dal (pigeon peas) or
  lentils

4 cups water
2 tablespoons vegetable oil
1 tablespoon peeled and finely chopped
  fresh ginger
1 tablespoon pressed garlic
2 teaspoons garam masala
1 teaspoon ground turmeric
1 teaspoon amchoor (mango powder)
2 teaspoons salt

Aromatic Blend
3 tablespoons ghee or vegetable oil
1 teaspoon cumin seeds
1 teaspoon mustard seeds
2 bay leaves
Pinch asafetida or a strip of lemon zest
4 whole red chili peppers or 1 teaspoon
  crushed red pepper flakes
1 teaspoon paprika

Boiling water, as needed

1. Rinse and drain the toor dal. Pour toor dal into a medium bowl, cover with water and let soak for about 30 minutes. Rinse and drain the toor dal and then transfer to the base of the pressure cooker. Add the water, oil, ginger, garlic, garam masala, turmeric, and mango powder.

2. Close and lock the lid of the pressure cooker. Cook at high pressure (see "Get *Hip* About the Pressure," page 13) for 7 minutes/stovetop or 8 to 10 minutes/electric (or nonstandard stovetop). When the time is up, open the pressure cooker with the Natural Release method (see page 15); this should take 10 to 15 minutes for a stovetop cooker, 20 to 30 minutes for an electric cooker.

3. Meanwhile, prepare the aromatic blend: Heat the ghee in the a small saucepan over medium heat and when it is hot add the cumin and mustard seeds. When the seeds begin to crackle, stir in the bay leaves, chilis, and paprika. Remove from the heat, add the asafetida, and stir well.

4. When the cooker is open, mix the dal well and add the 2 teaspoons salt. If it is thick add some boiling water to achieve the consistency as you desire. Pour the aromatic blend over the dal just before serving.

Variations

Moong Dal

Follow the Toor Dal recipe, replacing the toor with dried moong (mung beans). There is no need to presoak them, so just add them to the cooker with the 4 cups water and the other ingredients in the first step.

Masoor Dal with Spinach

Follow the Toor Dal recipe, replacing the toor with dried masoor (red split lentils), and adding 2 cups chopped spinach in the first step. Cook at high pressure for 1 minute/all cooker types. Alternatively, you may use common lentils, in which case do not presoak them but just rinse, drain, and add them to the cooker with the 4 cups water and other ingredients in the first step, then cook at high pressure for 10 minutes/stovetop cooker or 13 to 15 minutes/electric (or nonstandard) cooker.

Lobiya Dal with Squash

Follow the Toor Dal recipe, replacing the toor with lobiya (black-eyed peas), and adding 2 cups of chopped and peeled pumpkin, or winter squash, such as acorn or butternut, in the first step. There is no need to presoak these beans, so just rinse, drain, and add them to the cooker with the 4 cups water and the other ingredients in the first step. Cook at high pressure for 6 minutes/stovetop cooker or 8 to 9 minutes/electric (or nonstandard) cooker.

Urad Dal

Serves 4 to 6

Urad is easy to spot at your Indian grocer. They look exactly like black beans, but are so much smaller and cuter. Don't let their cuteness fool you—urad are as hard as little rocks and so definitely benefit from an overnight soak. Should you not find urad, black beans are a good substitute. This recipe is adapted from Madhur Jaffrey's *At Home with Madhur Jaffrey.*

The pressure cooking time for soaked dried urad is 8 minutes/stovetop cooker or 9 to 10 minutes electric (or nonstandard stovetop) cooker; for soaked dried black beans it is 4 minutes/stovetop cooker or 5 to 6 minutes/electric (or nonstandard stovetop) cooker.

Note: This recipe can be either halved or doubled provided the total volume of the ingredients does not exceed half the pressure cooker's capacity.

> 2 cups dried urad dal or black beans, cooked, plus 2 cups of their cooking liquid reserved (page 97)
> 6 tablespoons tomato paste
> ¼ cup chopped fresh cilantro
> 2 teaspoons salt
> 2 teaspoons peeled and very finely grated fresh ginger
> 2 garlic cloves, minced
> ¾ cup heavy cream
> 2 tablespoons unsalted butter

1. Add the urad dal with their reserved cooking liquid, the tomato paste, cilantro, salt, ginger, and garlic to the pressure cooker base.

2. Close and lock the lid of the pressure cooker. Cook at high pressure (see "Get *Hip* About the Pressure," page 13) for 5 minutes/all types of cookers. When the time is up, open the pressure cooker with the Natural Release method (see page 15); this should take 10 to 15 minutes for a stovetop cooker, 20 to 30 minutes for an electric cooker.

3. Quickly stir in the cream and butter, melting it with the residual heat of the pressure cooker. Taste and add more salt if you wish and serve.

Aloo Chana

Serves 4 to 6

A hearty one-pot-meal dal that includes protein from the beans and starch from the potatoes, this is usually served over hot rice or with roti, a grilled Indian flatbread.

The pressure cooking time for soaked dried chickpeas is 13 minutes/stovetop cooker or 18 to 20 minutes electric (or nonstandard stovetop) cooker.

Note: This recipe can be either halved or doubled provided the total volume of the ingredients does not exceed half the pressure cooker's capacity.

> 1 tablespoon vegetable oil
> 1 teaspoon cumin seeds
> 1 teaspoon crushed red pepper flakes
> 1 teaspoon garam masala
> 1 teaspoon ground coriander
> 1 teaspoon mango powder (amchoor)
> 1 teaspoon ground turmeric
> 3 tomatoes, cut into chunks
> 1 cup dried chickpeas, cooked (see Basic Boiled Beans page 97), plus 1 cup of their cooking liquid
> 2 large potatoes, cut into chunks
> 1 teaspoon salt
> Thinly sliced white onion, for serving (optional)
> Chopped fresh cilantro, for serving (optional)
> Steamed hot rice or roti, for serving (optional)

1. Heat the pressure cooker base on medium heat, add the oil, and heat briefly. Add the cumin seeds and cook for a few seconds, until they crackle. Add the red pepper flakes, garam masala, coriander, mango powder, and turmeric and stir well. Add the tomatoes and sauté for about 1 minute. Stir in the chickpeas, their reserved cooking liquid, and the potatoes.

2. Close and lock the lid of the pressure cooker. Cook at high pressure (see "Get *Hip* About the Pressure," page 13) for 7 minutes/stovetop or 8 to 9 minutes/electric (or nonstandard). When the time is up, open

the pressure cooker with the Natural Release method (see page 15); this should take 10 to 15 minutes for a stovetop cooker, 20 to 30 minutes for an electric cooker.

3. Stir in the salt; adjust the amount if you wish. Serve, sprinkled with sliced onions and chopped cilantro if you like.

Aloo Chana

Bean Dips

The word "dips" no doubt suggests chips and crudités, but these bean dips are also excellent spread in sandwiches or wraps and they make terrific soup bases as well.

Arugula and Toasted Pine Nut Hummus

Yields about 2 cups

It's green! In this version of hummus, toasted pine nuts take the place of the usual tahini—which is a toasted sesame seed paste. The arugula gives the dip color and pep. Although chickpeas only need 13 minutes to pressure cook, we're adding a couple of extra minutes to make sure they are super-tender for a creamy puree.

Note: This recipe can be either halved or doubled provided the total volume of the ingredients does not exceed half the pressure cooker's capacity.

> 3 cups water
> 1 cup dried chickpeas, soaked, rinsed, and drained (see "Get *Hip* About Soaking," pages 100–101)
> 1 tablespoon vegetable oil
> 3 garlic cloves, divided
> ½ cup pine nuts (3 ounces)
> 1 lemon
> 2 cups arugula
> 1½ teaspoons salt
> 2 tablespoons extra-virgin olive oil

1. Add the water, chickpeas, vegetable oil, and 2 of the garlic cloves to the pressure cooker base.

2. Close and lock the lid of the pressure cooker. Cook at high pressure (see "Get *Hip* About the Pressure," page 13) for 15 minutes/stovetop or 18 to 20 minutes/electric (or nonstandard stovetop). When the time is up, open the pressure cooker with the Natural Release method (see page 15); this should take 10 to 15 minutes for a stovetop cooker, 20 to 30 minutes for an electric cooker.

3. Meanwhile, toast the pine nuts in a dry skillet over low heat until golden. Grate the zest from the lemon and squeeze its juice in a small bowl. Set aside a few arugula leaves to use as a garnish.

4. Drain the chickpeas, reserving all of the cooking liquid, and let them cool. Pour the chickpeas into the bowl of a food processor; add ½ cup of the reserved cooking liquid, the arugula, pine nuts, lemon juice and zest, and the remaining garlic clove. Pulse to mix and keep adding cooking liquid until the desired consistency is reached (you may need to incorporate an additional 1 cup). Add the salt, adjusting the amount as desired. Scoop the hummus into a dipping bowl. Make a deep groove on top and drizzle with the extra-virgin olive oil; garnish with the reserved arugula leaves.

Classic Chickpea Hummus

Follow the Arugula and Toasted Pine Nut Hummus recipe, replacing the arugula, pine nuts, and lemon zest with 2 heaping tablespoons tahini and 2 teaspoons ground cumin. Dust with paprika if you wish.

Smoky Black Bean Dip

This bean dip is flavored with smoked chipotle peppers. Follow the Arugula and Toasted Pine Nut Hummus recipe, but replace the chickpeas with black beans, cooking them for 6 minutes/stovetop cooker or 8 to 10 minutes electric (or nonstandard stovetop) cooker. Omit the arugula and pine nuts and replace the lemon with 2 limes. Add 3 teaspoons ground chipotle pepper or smoked paprika to the food processor before pulsing the cooked beans. Decorate with a few fresh mint sprigs if you wish.

Red Bean and Sun-dried Tomato Spread

Follow the Arugula and Toasted Pine Nut Hummus recipe, but replace the chickpeas with cranberry or borlotti beans, cooking them for 8 minutes/stovetop cooker or 9 to 10 minutes/electric (or nonstandard stovetop) cooker. Replace the arugula and pine nuts with ¾ cup drained oil-packed, sun-dried tomatoes. Garnish the spread with 1 tablespoon rinsed and drained capers or a thinly sliced sun-dried tomato.

Top to bottom: Smoky Black Bean Dip, Red Bean and Sun-dried Tomato Spread, Classic Chickpea Hummus

Rice and Beans

Rice and beans are a natural one-pot meal. Although the cooking times of the rice and beans differ, we make up for this difference by cooking them sequentially— this allows the rice to cook in the beans' flavorful and nutritious cooking liquid.

Congri— Black Beans and Rice

Serves 4 to 6

Many Latin cultures from Spain to Peru have their own versions of beans and rice. We're going to make *congri,* which is Cuba's version. This recipe can also be prepared by cooking the rice and beans separately, but I prefer to use the cooking liquid from the black beans to cook the rice—changing its color to an unexpected gray, but adding a rainbow of flavor. Make this recipe vegetarian by leaving out the bacon and replacing it with 1 tablespoon of vegetable oil.

Note: This recipe can be either halved or doubled provided the total volume of the ingredients does not exceed half the pressure cooker's capacity.

4 ounces bacon (or the traditional whole smoked pork trotter), diced
1 cup dried black beans, soaked, rinsed, and drained
2 cups water, or more as needed
1 bay leaf
2 tablespoons vegetable oil
1 medium yellow onion, diced

1 medium green bell pepper, stemmed, seeded, and diced
1 teaspoon ground cumin
1 teaspoon dried oregano
½ teaspoon ground white pepper
1½ cups medium or long-grain white rice (such as basmati)
1 tablespoon white vinegar
2 teaspoons salt
2 garlic cloves, minced

1. Add the bacon to the pressure cooker base, heat on low heat ("keep warm" setting for electric cookers), and let the bacon slowly render its fat. Turn up the heat to medium and continue to cook until the bacon begins to crisp, about 7 minutes. Add the black beans, 2 cups of water, and bay leaf.

2. Close and lock the lid of the pressure cooker. Cook at high pressure (see "Get *Hip* About the Pressure," page 13) for 4 minutes/stovetop or 5 to 6 minutes/ electric (or nonstandard stovetop). When the time is up, use the Slow Normal Release method (see page 15) to very carefully release the pressure and open the cooker.

3. Drain the beans, reserving all their cooking liquid in a 4-cup heat-proof measuring cup. Add water to bring the liquid to the 3-cup mark. The beans are not finished cooking yet so don't worry if they're very al dente now, they will continue cooking with the rice. Set the beans aside.

4. Return the pressure cooker base to medium heat (don't wash it first). Add 1 tablespoon of the oil and heat briefly. Add the onion, bell pepper, cumin, oregano, and white pepper and sauté until the onion has begun to soften. Stir in the rice, beans, and reserved cooking liquid, vinegar, and salt; mix well.

5. Close and lock the lid of the pressure cooker. Cook at high pressure for 3 minutes/all cooker types. When the time is up, this time open the pressure cooker with the 10-Minute Natural Release method (see page 15).

6. Meanwhile, heat the remaining 1 tablespoon oil in a small skillet over medium-low heat. Add the garlic and cook, watching carefully, until it begins to turn golden.

7. When the cooker is open, mix the garlic-infused oil into the rice and bean mixture. Taste and add more salt if you wish and serve.

Variations

Red Bean Congri

Follow the Congri—Black Beans and Rice recipe, but use borlotti beans instead of black beans. Cook them at high pressure for 7 minutes/stovetop cooker or 8 to 10 minutes/electric (or nonstandard stovetop) cooker, and then use the Normal Release method (see page 14) to open the cooker.

New Orleans Red Beans and Rice

Follow the Congri—Black Beans and Rice recipe, but use cranberry beans instead of black beans. Cook them at high pressure for 7 minutes/stovetop cooker or 8 to 10 minutes/electric (or nonstandard stovetop) cooker, then use the Slow Normal Release method (see page 15) to open the cooker. Cut 8 ounces andouille sausage into rounds, and brown the sausage in the heated oil in the cooker base before sautéing the onion and bell pepper. Sprinkle chopped green onions over the finished dish before serving.

Pasta and Sauces

The pasta recipes are in their own category because, really... a whole book can be written *just* about pasta in the pressure cooker! There are many variations and techniques from each and every region of Italy. Where onions and butter rule in the North, garlic, oil, and a pinch of crushed red pepper flakes are kings of the South. Plus each city has its own classic sauce and each household puts its own twist on it.

The minestrone recipes, however, are in the soups chapter, page 37. Because minestrone, as Italians know it, is not exclusively enriched by pasta: rice, farro, and barley are equal accomplices.

Dice and chop! Always use chopped or diced whole tomatoes either fresh or from a can and not just tomato puree. These tomato products release their liquid quickly so the there is no chance the tomatoes can scorch before the cooker reaches pressure.

Sauté aromatics. Before pressure cooking, onions, shallots, garlic, and leeks should be carefully sautéed to remove their harsh raw flavor. Onions should be sautéed until softened, which may take about 5 minutes; garlic until golden, which could take anywhere from 30 seconds to a minute depending on how thinly it's sliced; leeks and shallots anywhere in between.

Brown and caramelize. The main ingredient in the sauce, be it meat or vegetable, benefits from a sear in the hot pressure cooker base, followed by a little browning. Doing so improves the flavor of each ingredient. Skipping this step will mean all ingredients just boil together and give the sauce a boring one-dimensional flavor.

Deglaze and evaporate wine fully. Unless instructed otherwise, always evaporate the wine completely when making pasta sauce to avoid any unpleasant acidic or dominating flavors.

Quick-open to reduce excess liquid. There is almost no evaporation during pressure cooking so opening the pressure cooker quickly after cooking helps the contents evaporate—often needed to keep a sauce from being runny. Use the Normal Release method (see page 14) and then remove the pressure cooker lid and let the cooker sit, uncovered and off the heat. After about 5 minutes the contents in the cooker will

have reduced considerably, just from evaporation—and the sauce will still be hot!

Finish the sauce first, and *then* throw pasta in its cooking water. Here's the trick to making sure pasta does not get cold, sticky, and limp when you are pressure cooking a sauce, but boiling the pasta in the conventional way: Start boiling water for the pasta as soon as you have all of the ingredients for the sauce in the pressure cooker, but don't toss the dry pasta into the water until the sauce is finished pressure cooking—pasta waits for no man, woman, child, or sauce!

Time it. When pressure cooking pasta in the sauce, adjust the timing in the recipe to the specific pasta shape and type being used; see "Pressure Cook Pasta to al Dente" (see page 127) for specific pasta timing information.

Salt correctly. Add the salt when you add the pasta. If using dried beans that were quick-soaked with a teaspoon of salt (see The Soaks, page 101) adjust the salt quantity accordingly. In Italy, we say that the pasta cooking water should be as salty as the Mediterranean Sea—that's about 30 grams per liter, by the way (or a tablespoon of salt for every 4 cups of water). Salty!

Fresh herbs, please. Dried herbs absorb liquid from the sauce to rehydrate and don't have any juice to donate the way fresh herbs do. Added bonus of fresh herbs: the stems are flavorful, too! But pick those out before serving. In a pinch, if fresh herbs are not available, replace each sprig with ½ teaspoon of the dried herb and crumble the leaves between your fingers to release what little oil remains before tossing them in the cooker.

Pasta Sauces

A pressure cooker can make a sauce in as much time as it takes to boil a big pot of water. Sauces are perfect candidates for cooking in the smaller pressure pan that often comes with a set, though the classic stockpot-type cooker will also work. The recipes here all begin with sauté, browning, and evaporation steps because pressure cooking a mix of raw ingredients, as is often recommended by other cooks, results in a highly unbalanced, acidic, and flat sauce.

Basic Meat Ragù

Yields enough sauce for one 1-pound package of pasta

When visiting a pressure cooker manufacturer in Germany I made this recipe to show them how good an easy Italian ragù (basic meat sauce) can be. I got into a heated argument with the company's cooking demo manager. "Ground beef is fully cooked in 5 minutes, why pressure cook it for 15?!?" she asked in her most incredulous-sounding German. The answer lies in the Italian tradition of simmering meat sauces beyond just-cooked meat, but to continue instead until every last bit of the meat and its juices have melted into the sauce—doing this in the pressure cooker means 15 minutes, not 5.

I prefer to use ground chuck for my sauce; its fat adds flavor that won't be obtained from lean ground beef. Serve this sauce over reginette, pappardelle, fettuccine, or a short tube pasta that can capture the sauce, such as rigatoni or penne. Alternatively, use the sauce for filling one lasagna casserole.

Note: This recipe cannot be halved. It may be doubled provided the total volume of the ingredients does not exceed two-thirds of the pressure cooker's capacity.

2 tablespoons unsalted butter
1 tablespoon olive oil
1 medium yellow onion, chopped
1 fresh thyme sprig
1 fresh oregano sprig
½ teaspoon salt
¼ teaspoon freshly ground black pepper
1 medium carrot, chopped
1 celery stalk, chopped
10½ to 16 ounces ground beef chuck
2 garlic cloves, crushed
⅓ cup red wine (whatever you're having with dinner)
1 cup chopped or crushed tomatoes
½ cup tomato puree
½ cup water (for electric pressure cooker only)

1. Heat the pressure cooker base on medium heat, add 1 tablespoon of the butter and the olive oil, and heat until the butter has melted. Add the onion, thyme, oregano, salt, and pepper and sauté, stirring infrequently, until the onion has softened. Stir in the carrot and celery.

2. Move the contents to the side in the pressure cooker. Add the beef and garlic and stir to break up. Sauté, stirring infrequently, until the beef is brown on at least one side and the juices have evaporated, for 5 minutes, or longer if there are a lot of juices. To deglaze the cooker, stir in the red wine and cook until it evaporates completely. Pour in the chopped tomatoes and the tomato puree; add the water if using.

3. Close and lock the lid of the pressure cooker. Cook at high pressure (see "Get *Hip* About the Pressure," page 13) for 15 minutes/stovetop or 18 to 20 minutes/ electric (or nonstandard stovetop). When the time is up, open the pressure cooker with the Normal Release method (see page 15).

4. Fish out and discard the herb stems. Add the remaining 1 tablespoon butter to the sauce and stir until melted. Serve the sauce over pasta or incorporate in lasagna or a similar recipe.

Variation

Ragù alla Bolognese

Follow the Basic Meat Ragù recipe, adding 4 ounces chopped bacon (or guanciale or smoked pancetta) before sautéing the onion, and replacing the chopped tomatoes with 1 cup meat stock (see page 47) and 4 tablespoons tomato paste. After pressure cooking, stir in 1 tablespoon cream instead of butter.

Ragù alla Napoletana

This ragù is common throughout the south of Italy. Thrifty Italian cooks can squeeze two courses (or even two meals) from one recipe by cooking chops or another cut of meat in the tomato sauce, removing the meat, serving the sauce over pasta for a first course, and then serving the meat separately for the second, or main course, along with a green salad.

Follow the Basic Meat Ragù recipe, omitting all of the herbs and replacing the ground beef with any cut of pork, veal, or beef you have on hand—particularly chops—browning it as you would the ground beef. When you have finished pressure cooking, lift out the meat and transfer it to a serving plate. Cover, and keep warm to serve as a second course.

Fresh Tomato and Basil Sauce

Yields enough sauce for one 1-pound package of pasta

When tomatoes are plentiful, red, ripe, and well . . . cheap, make a lot of batches of this sauce to store in the freezer and brighten up a winter meal. Serve this sauce over spaghetti or fresh homemade pasta of your choice.

Note: This recipe cannot be halved. It may be doubled provided the total volume of the ingredients does not exceed two-thirds of the pressure cooker's capacity.

1½ pounds ripe tomatoes (4 to 5 tomatoes)
½ teaspoon salt
1 bunch fresh basil
2 tablespoons olive oil (everyday quality)
3 garlic cloves, coarsely chopped

¼ cup water (for electric pressure cooker only)

1 tablespoon extra-virgin olive oil

1. Halve as many of the tomatoes as will cover the base of your pressure cooker (3 to 4). Chop the rest in large pieces and transfer them to a bowl, scraping in their liquid, too. Sprinkle the salt over the chopped tomatoes. Reserve 1 sprig of the basil and snip the leaves off the remaining basil, chop them, and set them aside.

2. Heat the pressure cooker base on medium heat, add the 2 tablespoons of everyday olive oil, and heat briefly. Arrange the tomato halves, cut side down, in the cooker base and let them fry, without stirring, until caramelized, about 4 minutes. Flip the tomatoes over, sprinkle with the garlic, and pour the chopped tomatoes and their juices into the cooker. Add the water if using. Lay the reserved basil sprig on top.

3. Close and lock the lid of the pressure cooker. Cook at high pressure (see "Get *Hip* About the Pressure," page 13) for 5 minutes/all cooker types. When the time is up, open the pressure cooker with the Normal Release method (see page 15).

4. Fish out and discard the basil stem. Using a fork, break up the tomato halves and their skins. Return the uncovered cooker base to medium-high heat and cook until the contents have reduced to a sauce consistency, about 5 minutes more.

5. Pour the sauce over pasta, sprinkle with the chopped basil, and swirl on the extra-virgin olive oil. Serve immediately.

Super-Easy Tomato Sauce

Yields enough sauce for one 1-pound package of pasta

When I'm pressed for time and even chopping an onion seems like it will take too long, I make this super-fast and easy tomato sauce. Adding a carrot is a trick I learned from my Southern Italian mother-in-law to tame down the acidity of any tomato (be it fresh or tinned) without resorting to using sugar or baking soda. This sauce complements any shape fresh or dried pasta.

Note: This recipe cannot be halved. It may be doubled provided the total volume of the ingredients does not exceed two-thirds of the pressure cooker's capacity.

2 tablespoons olive oil (everyday quality)

1 medium carrot, grated

3 garlic cloves, smashed

1 teaspoon dried oregano

1 cup tomato puree

1 cup chopped fresh or canned tomatoes, with their juices

½ cup water or stock (for electric pressure cookers only)

½ teaspoon salt

1 tablespoon extra-virgin olive oil

1. Heat the pressure cooker base on medium heat. Add the everyday oil and heat briefly; then stir in the carrot and garlic and sauté until the garlic just starts to turn golden. Crumble the oregano between your fingers to release the oils and then sprinkle into the pressure

cooker. Stir in the tomato puree, chopped tomatoes, water if using, and salt.

2. Close and lock the lid of the pressure cooker. Cook at high pressure (see "Get *Hip* About the Pressure," page 13) for 5 minutes/all cooker types. When the time is up, open the pressure cooker with the Normal Release method (see page 15).

3. Pour the sauce over pasta and serve immediately.

Variations

Spicy Arrabbiata Sauce

Follow the Super-Easy Tomato Sauce recipe, adding ½ teaspoon crushed red pepper flakes with the garlic.

Spicy Puttanesca Sauce

A Roman pasta dish of dubious and colorful origins—said to be used by prostitutes to attract customers for a meal, and maybe more!

Follow the Super-Easy Tomato Sauce recipe, adding 8 anchovies and 2 chopped fresh hot chili peppers (or 1 teaspoon crushed red pepper flakes) when sautéing the carrot and garlic. After releasing pressure, sprinkle the sauce with ½ cup chopped pitted black olives, 1 tablespoon rinsed and drained capers, and a little chopped fresh parsley. Serve with a swirl of olive oil on any pasta shape.

Eggplant Sauce

Yields enough sauce for one 1-pound package of pasta

A traditional Sicilian dish, *Pasta alla Norma* is named after the opera by Vincenzo Bellini: *La Norma*. It can be served with any kind of pasta, but the most popular combinations in Italy are on spaghetti or rigatoni. The Cacioricotta cheese I recommend for serving is an aged and salted ricotta cheese.

Note: This recipe cannot be halved. It may be doubled provided the total volume of the ingredients does not exceed two-thirds of the pressure cooker's capacity.

3 tablespoons olive oil, plus more for serving
2 medium eggplants, cubed or sliced into thin strips
3 garlic cloves, smashed
1½ cups high-quality canned whole tomatoes
1 fresh basil sprig (leaves only), chopped
½ cup water or stock (for electric pressure cookers only)
½ teaspoon salt
Freshly grated Cacioricotta or Pecorino Romano cheese, for serving

1. Heat the pressure cooker base on medium heat, add the 3 tablespoons oil, and heat briefly. Stir in the eggplant, spreading it over the bottom of the cooker, and sauté until it starts to turn golden, about 7 minutes. Stir in the garlic, tomatoes, half the basil, water if using, and salt.

2. Close and lock the lid of the pressure cooker. Cook at high pressure (see "Get *Hip* About the Pressure," page 13) for 5 minutes/all cooker types. When the time is up, open the pressure cooker with the Normal Release method (see page 15).

3. Pour the sauce over pasta and serve with a swirl of oil, a sprinkling of the remaining basil, and some grated cheese.

Artichoke and Black Olive Ragù

Yields enough sauce for one
1-pound package of pasta

This is *not* a classic Italian recipe—but it should be! It's a luscious combination of vegetables that steals the show from any pasta that may accompany it. This sauce is the perfect filling for vegetarian lasagna (see Sloppy Lasagna page 127), or for saucing a filled pasta like ravioli or a substantial wide egg pasta for a hearty one-dish meal.

Baby artichokes don't have a choke—the unpleasant fuzzy area buried at the center that must be removed from mature artichokes. All the prep they require is to pull off their outer leaves and then cut them in half or quarters as indicated in your recipe. If baby artichokes are not available, cut large artichokes into wedges after removing their choke (see instructions page 66).

Note: This recipe cannot be halved. It may be doubled provided the total volume of the ingredients does not exceed two-thirds of the pressure cooker's capacity.

3 tablespoons olive oil
1 pound baby artichokes, sliced lengthwise into quarters
1 medium yellow onion, chopped
1 teaspoon salt
¼ teaspoon freshly ground black pepper
Generous pinch crushed red pepper flakes
1 medium carrot, chopped
1 celery stalk, chopped
3 garlic cloves, lightly mashed
2 cups chopped fresh or canned tomatoes, with their juices
2 tablespoons tomato paste
½ cup water (for electric pressure cookers only)
½ cup pitted black olives, coarsely chopped

1. Heat the pressure cooker base on medium heat, add 2 tablespoons of the oil, and heat briefly. Add the artichokes and sauté, stirring infrequently, until they are golden on one side. Using a slotted spatula, transfer them to a plate and set aside.

2. Add the remaining 1 tablespoon oil to the cooker along with the onion, salt, black pepper, and red pepper flakes and sauté until the onion has softened. Add the carrot, celery, and garlic and mix well. Then add the chopped tomatoes, tomato paste, water if using, and the artichokes and stir well to incorporate.

3. Close and lock the lid of the pressure cooker. Cook at high pressure (see "Get *Hip* About the Pressure," page 13) for 5 minutes/all cooker types. When the time is up, open the pressure cooker with the Normal Release method (see page 15).

4. Mix in the olives. Serve over pasta or incorporate in lasagna or a similar recipe.

Variation

Primavera and Saffron Sauce

Follow the Artichoke and Black Olive Ragù recipe, replacing the artichokes with 1 diced waxy potato (such as a red potato) and 2 diced medium zucchini. Add several saffron threads when sautéing the onions. Swirl with your best olive oil before serving.

Artichoke and Black Olive Ragù

Speck and Porcini Mushroom Sauce

Yields enough sauce for one 1-pound package of pasta

Sugo alla Tirolese is an autumn dish from Trentino-Alto Adige, in northern Italy bordering Austria. It's made with fresh porcini mushrooms—which are not easy to find outside of Italy. So this version uses common grocery-store mushrooms and reconstituted dry porcini. Speck is a pepper-crusted smoked prosciutto; if you are not able to find it, bacon will do nicely. Beer is not an original part of the recipe, but Trento is dotted with Germanic rough-hewn, wood-paneled drinking taverns and, in my mind, beer is a better fit for this dish than wine. This sauce complements wide pasta such as pappardelle, fettuccine, or any long, rich, egg pasta.

Note: This recipe cannot be halved. It may be doubled provided the total volume of the ingredients does not exceed two-thirds of the pressure cooker's capacity.

½ cup dry porcini mushrooms
Boiling water (about 1 cup)
1 tablespoon unsalted butter
6 ounces speck (or bacon), finely diced
1 shallot, finely diced
1 pound fresh portobello, cremini, or
    white button mushrooms, sliced
¼ cup beer
3 tablespoons heavy cream
Salt
Freshly ground black pepper

1. Measure the porcini into a 1-cup heat-proof measuring cup. Add boiling water up to the 1-cup mark. Cover with plastic wrap and let steep for 10 minutes.

2. Meanwhile, heat the pressure cooker base on low heat ("keep warm" setting for electric cookers), add the butter, and melt. Add the speck and sauté until crispy. Strain soaked mushrooms through a fine-mesh strainer to remove particles and dust. Add the shallot and fresh mushrooms to the cooker and brown on one side, stirring infrequently. To deglaze the cooker, pour in the beer and let it evaporate almost completely. Pour in the porcini mushrooms and their soaking liquid.

3. Close and lock the lid of the pressure cooker. Cook at high pressure (see "Get *Hip* About the Pressure," page 13) for 5 minutes/stovetop or 6 to 7 minutes/electric (or nonstandard stovetop). When the time is up, open the pressure cooker with the Normal Release method (see page 15).

4. Mix the cream into the sauce and simmer everything together for about 1 minute (no need to heat the cooker for this, the residual heat in the sauce is sufficient). Season with salt and pepper and serve over pasta.

Pasta and Sauce Cooked Together

Pressure cooking pasta in the sauce results in an incredibly rich flavor that can *only* be achieved in the pressure cooker. Instead of being boiled in water and covered with sauce, the pasta *absorbs* the sauce and becomes more intensely flavored. This is exactly what Italian chefs are aiming for when they stop boiling pasta before it's done and then finish it in the sauce. Cooking the pasta directly in the sauce from the start is something that is just not possible *without* a pressure cooker.

Note: Regardless of the extra water specified for electric pressure cookers in the following recipes, some electric cookers may not be able to cook pasta and sauce together at all. Pasta and sauce flirt precariously with the minimum liquid requirements of a cooker and not all cookers pass with flying colors. Do a test run with your family to make sure yours can, before inviting guests to be disappointed by an unanticipated failure in this area.

The pasta sauces in the previous section can also be used with this technique, but because many of them contain meat or ingredients that would not be cooked at the same time as the pasta, make the sauce first, then open the pressure cooker and stir in the raw pasta. Add enough water to submerge the pasta and calculate the cooking time using the technique in "Pressure Cook Pasta to al Dente," page 127.

Any short to medium-length hard semolina pasta can be pressure cooked in sauce or in water. Nests of dried egg fettuccine can also be pressure cooked, but only in water, and they should be strained when done since they require more water to cook than they will absorb. Frozen or dried stuffed pasta, like ravioli or tortellini, may work—follow a specific recipe to be sure you don't get a watery sauce—because they absorb much less water than dry pasta.

Pasta al Pomodoro

Serves 4 to 6

A classic that can now be just as fast as just making a sauce! In fact, that's exactly what you do here: Put together the tomato sauce, but before pressure cooking it, add the pasta and then cook all at once. Use really good-quality pasta and olive oil, you will taste the difference!

Note: This recipe cannot be halved. It may be doubled provided the total volume of the ingredients does not exceed half the pressure cooker's capacity.

3 tablespoons extra-virgin olive oil
1 medium carrot, grated
3 garlic cloves, smashed
1 teaspoon dried oregano
1 cup tomato puree
1 cup chopped fresh or canned tomatoes, with their juices
2 teaspoons salt
One 16-ounce package any short pasta
Water, as needed

1. Heat the pressure cooker base on medium heat. Add 2 tablespoons of the oil and heat briefly. Stir in the carrot and garlic and sauté until the garlic just starts to turn golden. Crumble the oregano between your fingers to release the oils and then sprinkle into the pressure cooker. Stir in the tomato puree, chopped tomatoes, and salt. Add the pasta and water to cover. Mix well to submerge the pasta. For electric pressure cookers, add an extra 1 cup water.

2. Close and lock the lid of the pressure cooker. Cook at low pressure (see "Get *Hip* About the Pressure," page 13) for 4 minutes/all cooker types or for half the cooking time indicated on the pasta package. When the time is up, open the pressure cooker with the Normal Release method (see page 15).

3. Swirl the remaining 1 tablespoon oil over the pasta and sauce, stir, and let stand, uncovered, for 2 minutes before serving.

Pasta al Pomodoro

Sloppy Lasagna

Sloppy Lasagna

Serves 4 to 6

This is not your traditional lasagna as there is really no way to stack and layer rectangular pasta in a round pressure cooker and get even close to the result you would normally get from the oven. However, the flavor is all there and so are the satisfyingly long mozzarella strands that stretch from the pressure cooker—or serving dish—to the plate. Use any "wavy" pasta: lasagna strips, campanelle, or reginette are all fine choices

Note: This recipe cannot be halved. It may be doubled provided the total volume of the ingredients does not exceed half the pressure cooker's capacity.

Basic Meat Ragù or Artichoke and Black Olive Ragù (pages 117 and 121), prepared and hot in the cooker
1 teaspoon salt

One 8- or 9-ounce package wavy lasagna strips (not precooked), broken into 2-inch pieces
Water, as needed
8 ounces mozzarella cheese, diced

1. Add the salt and lasagna strips to the cooker, mixing them into the hot sauce. Pour in just enough water to cover the pasta (if using an electric cooker, add an extra ½ cup water). Smooth down the top pieces of pasta so they are submerged as you do this.

2. Close and lock the lid of the pressure cooker. Cook at low pressure (see "Get *Hip* About the Pressure," page 13) for 4 minutes/all cooker types or for half the cooking time indicated on the pasta package. When the time is up, open the pressure cooker with the Normal Release method (see page 15).

3. Sprinkle the mozzarella over the lasagna; stir, and let stand, uncovered, for 2 minutes before serving.

Pressure Cook Pasta to al Dente

To achieve al dente results for pressure cooked pasta, it is important to cook at low pressure and use only half the recommended cooking time for each shape. For example, if the pasta package says the shape needs 9 to10 minutes of conventional boiling, it should be pressure cooked for 5 minutes at low pressure; 12 to 13 minutes would be 6 minutes at low pressure, and so on. The cooking time is the same for all types of pressure cookers.

Pasta e Broccoli alla Romana

Serves 4 to 6

The broccoli can be replaced with trimmed broccolini, or even better, a trimmed romanesco cauliflower; that amazing green cauliflower with the spiky swirled florets.

Note: This recipe can be either halved or doubled provided the total volume of the ingredients does not exceed half the pressure cooker's capacity.

- 1 tablespoon olive oil (everyday quality)
- ¼ teaspoon crushed red pepper flakes
- 3 oil-packed anchovies
- 3 garlic cloves
- One 16-ounce package fusilli, campanelle, or pennette pasta
- 8 ounces broccoli florets, cut into approximately ½-inch pieces
- 2 teaspoons salt
- 3 cups salt-free Vegetable Stock, or as needed (page 49)
- 1 tablespoon extra-virgin olive oil
- ¼ cup Pecorino Romano cheese shavings (cut using a vegetable peeler)

1. Heat the pressure cooker base on medium heat, add the everyday olive oil, and heat briefly. Stir in the red pepper flakes, anchovies, and 2 of the garlic cloves. Sauté until the anchovies have broken up and the garlic is lightly golden. Add the pasta, broccoli, and salt and mix well. Pour in just enough stock to cover the pasta, smoothing down the top pieces so they are submerged as you do this. If using an electric cooker, add an extra ½ cup stock.

2. Close and lock the lid of the pressure cooker. Cook at low pressure (see "Get *Hip* About the Pressure," page 13) for 5 minutes/all cooker types, or for half the cooking time indicated on the pasta package. When the time is up, open the pressure cooker with the Normal Release method (see page 15). Meanwhile, mince the remaining garlic clove.

3. Mix the minced garlic into the pasta and sauce and then swirl the extra-virgin olive oil over the top. Stir and let stand, uncovered, for 2 minutes before serving. Dust each plate with some flakes of Pecorino Romano

Pasta Without Sauce

Serves 4 to 6

While pasta cooked in its sauce is extra flavorful, not every sauce requires cooking (for example a fresh basil pesto). What to do? You can pressure cook pasta in plain water, without sauce, and have it ready quickly. The oil included keeps the pasta from foaming and spraying out of the valve when you release the pressure, so don't skip it. Be sure to use a pasta shape that is suitable for pressure cooking (see "Pasta You Should Not Pressure Cook," page 129).

Note: This recipe can be either halved or doubled provided the total volume of the ingredients does not exceed half the pressure cooker's capacity.

1 tablespoon olive oil
One 16-ounce package pasta
2 teaspoons salt
Water, as needed

1. Heat the pressure cooker base on medium heat; add the oil, pasta, and salt. Pour in just enough water to cover the pasta (if using an electric cooker, add an extra ½ cup water). Smooth down the top pieces of pasta so they are submerged as you do this.

2. Close and lock the lid of the pressure cooker. Cook at low pressure (see "Get *Hip* About the Pressure," page 13) for 4 minutes/all cooker types, or for half the cooking time indicated on the pasta package. When the time is up, open the pressure cooker with the Normal Release method (see page 15).

3. Immediately tumble the pasta into a bowl and toss with your chosen sauce. No need to strain!

Pasta You Should Not Pressure Cook

Not all pasta types are suitable for pressure cooking. Use the conventional pot of boiling water to cook these, following the package directions:

- Any pasta that requires 7 minutes or less cannot be cooked to al dente in the pressure cooker, it will be overcooked.

- Fresh pasta needs less than 5 minutes to be cooked without pressure, so is not appropriate for pressure cooking.

- Spaghetti. You must not break spaghetti in half to fit it in your pressure cooker. Ever. Not only is it bad luck, but more practically, the short strands will splatter sauce all over your shirt as you try to twirl them around your fork.

- Orecchiette. These have a tendency to fall into little stacks and will turn into a solid mass in the pressure cooker.

- Very small pasta intended for soups— like stelline, quadratini, orzetto—could clog the safety mechanisms of your pressure cooker. However, they can be added after pressure cooking to the sauce (or a soup) in the open pressure cooker. Follow a specific recipe (see page 37 for more information).

- Potato gnocchi need to stop cooking when they float; if you cannot see them you cannot stop your pressure cooker. However, there is a pasta "shape" called gnocchetti that is made of semolina flour and it is okay to pressure cook.

Pasta and Beans

It's easy to play with the ratios in these recipes. If you want a lot of legumes, use 2 cups of soaked beans and 1 cup of uncooked pasta. If you want a lot of pasta, use 2 cups of pasta with just 1 cup of beans—the remainder of the recipe, including the liquid, can remain unchanged. The finished consistency of *pasta e fagioli* should be more stew than soup.

Since legumes, even soaked legumes, need so much more time to cook than pasta these recipes are made in two phases. The first flavors and precooks the beans, and then for the second phase (which can also be done without pressure) the pasta is added and cooked in the bean's cooking liquid.

Classic Pasta e Fagioli

Serves 4 to 6

This is the pasta and legume combination most familiar outside Italy, and this version is actually a very slight variation of the classic recipe from the Veneto region. Broken pieces of egg fettuccine or lasagna are a traditional choice for this dish, but any short pasta will also work well (if pressure cooking the pasta, read "Pasta You Should Not Pressure Cook," page 129). Read "Get *Hip* About Soaking," page 100, before beginning.

Note: This recipe can be either halved or doubled provided the total volume of the ingredients does not exceed half the pressure cooker's capacity.

> 1 tablespoon olive oil (everyday quality)
> 1 tablespoon unsalted butter
> 4 ounces smoked pancetta (or bacon), chopped

1 medium carrot, cut into large dice
1 medium yellow onion, cut into large dice
2 celery stalks, cut into small dice
1 fresh rosemary sprig
1 fresh sage sprig
1 cup dried borlotti beans, soaked, rinsed, and drained
4 cups water, plus more to cook the pasta if needed
2 tablespoons tomato paste
2 teaspoons salt
½ teaspoon freshly ground black pepper
2 cups egg fettuccine or similar egg pasta, broken into 1-inch pieces if appropriate
Good quality extra-virgin olive oil, for serving
Grated cheese (your favorite type), for serving

1. Heat the pressure cooker base on medium heat, add the everyday olive oil, and butter, and cook until the butter has melted. Add the pancetta and sauté until it releases its fat. Stir in the carrot, onion, and celery and sauté until softened, about 5 minutes. Add the rosemary and sage and sauté everything together for 1 minute more. Then add the beans and the 4 cups water.

2. Close and lock the lid of the pressure cooker. Cook at high pressure (see "Get *Hip* About the Pressure," page 18) for 7 minutes/stovetop or 8 to 10 minutes/electric (or nonstandard stovetop). When the time is up, use the Slow Normal Release method (see page 14) to very carefully release the pressure. The beans have not finished cooking yet; they will continue to cook with the pasta.

3. Fish out and discard the herb stems. Stir in the tomato paste, salt, and pepper. Use an immersion blender to puree a small portion of the beans—just pulse for 5 seconds right in the cooker. Stir in the pasta. If the pasta is not covered by the cooking liquid, add water until it is, and if using an electric cooker, add an extra ½ cup water.

4. Close and lock the lid of the pressure cooker. Cook at low pressure for 4 minutes/all cooker types or for half the cooking time indicated on the pasta package. When the time is up, open the pressure cooker with the Normal Release method (see page 14).

5. Stir the pasta and beans together well. Taste and season with more salt or pepper if you wish. Add a swirl of extra-virgin olive oil and a dusting of cheese to each serving.

Variations

Limas with Gnocchetti alla Contadina

This is a peasant dish and *alla contadina*— "the way of the farmer's wife"—means that it's usually made with whatever veggies you have on hand. So there is no right or wrong way to make this recipe. Here is my favorite rendition. My kids think that the giant beans are pasta . . . shhh!

Follow the Classic Pasta e Fagioli recipe, omitting the celery and replacing the borlotti beans with 1½ cups dried lima, corona, gigante, or other large white beans (soak them); the tomato paste with about 1 cup chopped tomatoes and their liquid (or enough to submerge the pasta); the egg pasta with an eggless scoop-type such as gnocchetti, nuvolette, or conchiglie (clouds or shells); and the grated cheese with chopped parsley. Pressure cook the beans for 10 minutes/stovetop cooker or 11 to 13 minutes/electric (or nonstandard stovetop) cooker, or check the Pressure Cooking Timetable (see Appendix page 271 for the bean type being used) and do not puree them. Complete the recipe as written.

Pasta e Fagioli alla Toscana

This dish of cannellini, pasta, and herbs is incredibly simple but has a very robust flavor, thanks in part to a pinch of crushed red pepper flakes; it will be truly enhanced if you can finish with a really tangy and tart Tuscan olive oil.

Follow the Classic Pasta e Fagioli recipe, omitting the pancetta, and replacing the onion with 3 lightly crushed garlic cloves, the borlotti with 1½ cups dried cannellini beans (soak them), and the egg pasta with 8 ounces ditalini pasta. Add a pinch crushed red pepper flakes to the oil and butter; add 2 small chopped tomatoes with the tomato paste. Pressure cook the beans for 7 minutes/stovetop cooker or 8 to 9 minutes/electric (or nonstandard stovetop) cooker and puree for a creamy consistency as directed. Cook the pasta for half the time indicated on its package.

Chickpeas and Pasta

Also known as *Pasta e Ceci,* this winter Italian classic is particularly phenomenal with small shells, gnocchetti, or a pipe pasta that will scoop up the chickpeas! The potato dissolves into the stew and makes it creamy. Choose Pecorino Romano for the grating cheese.

Follow the Classic Pasta e Fagioli recipe, adding a small diced potato and 1 bay leaf with the carrot and onion. Replace the borlotti with 1 cup dried chickpeas (soak them). Pressure cook the beans for 15 minutes/stovetop cooker or 18 to 20 minutes/electric (or nonstandard stovetop) cooker and puree about half the bean mixture right in the cooker. Just before serving, stir in 2 tablespoons of the best ricotta you can find (even better if it's from sheep's milk).

Grains

Grains cooked in the pressure cooker require precise liquid ratios, much more so than in conventional cooking; this is to make up for the fact that there is almost no evaporation during cooking. With too little liquid, you risk burning and scorching the grain, but using too much makes it mushy and unpleasant.

Owners of electric and nonstandard stovetop pressure cookers (see page 7) will be pleased to read that *refined* grains (such as white rice, polenta, and pearled farro) cook to *exactly* the same doneness in the specified time, whether at 9, 11, 13 or 15psi—no more adjustments to cooking time for the various cookers! Refined grains rehydrate very quickly under pressure. So quickly, in fact, that a tad more or a tad less pressure *barely* make a difference! However, this isn't true for whole grains such as brown rice, which are denser, like dried beans; these require different cooking times in the different cookers.

Breads recipes are also in this chapter—after all, flour is made from ground grain.

133

Measure it. Liquid to grain ratios are very important in pressure cooking. Use measuring cups or the same vessel (a glass, etc.) to accurately measure both grain and liquid. The Pressure Cooking Timetable (see Appendix pages 270–271) contains liquid ratios for most grain varieties.

Reuse it. Extra cooking and steaming liquid saved from pressure steaming vegetables or boiling legumes and meat is a perfect substitute for the water needed when pressure cooking grains.

No more than half full. When pressure cooking grains (as with legumes and other foods that expand), never fill the pressure cooker more than half full with ingredients, including the liquid. Some pressure cookers have a little mark with "½" written next to it. If not, eyeball it.

Fatten it up. Grains tend to produce copious amounts of foam when cooked; to reduce this foam and preclude it spraying out of the pressure regulating valves, add a teaspoon of fat to the pressure cooker: use oil, butter, or a fat rendered from bacon or another meat.

Perfectly Cooked Grains

Italians treat any rice or grain like pasta. They boil it in tons of water until tender, and then dump out all of the extra water through a strainer. Learning to cook grains in the pressure cooker resulted in a revelation of taste and texture for me, as I hope it will for you.

With the proper liquid amount, pressure cooked grains never get "soggy" or "mushy," but instead retain a little bit of their character in each springy bite. Careful measurement ensures that each grain absorbs just enough water to be al dente when done, with no water left in the cooker to drain. But I make one exception to this rule for Italian rice—it's just better cooked in more water.

1-Minute Quinoa

Serves 6 to 8;
about 5 cups cooked quinoa

The ratio for perfect pressure cooked quinoa is 1½ cups water to 1 cup quinoa. Red, black, or rainbow quinoa can be used instead of the common white variety; they all require the same cooking time.

Note: This recipe can be either halved or doubled provided there is at least 1 cup of liquid in the pressure cooker (or your cooker's minimum liquid requirement) and the total volume of the ingredients does not exceed half the cooker's capacity.

2 cups whole-grain quinoa, rinsed
   and drained
3 cups water
2 teaspoons salt

1. Place the quinoa, water, and salt in the pressure cooker base.

2. Close and lock the lid of the pressure cooker. Cook at high pressure (see "Get *Hip* About the Pressure," page 13) for 1 minute/all cooker types. When the time is up, open the pressure cooker with the 10-Minute Natural Release method (see page 15).

3. Fluff the quinoa with a fork and serve.

Variation

1-Minute Golden Quinoa

My favorite way to make this recipe is by mixing 1½ cups white quinoa and ½ cup of any other color. It makes this dish exciting and colorful. Follow the 1-Minute Quinoa recipe, adding 2 teaspoons ground cumin, 1 teaspoon ground turmeric, and 3 crushed garlic cloves. After cooking, add more salt if you wish.

Quinoa Olive Salad

Serves 6 to 8

A more nutritious alternative to rice or pasta salad, this salad is equally tasty made with any type of quinoa, or a mix. Taggiesche and Niçoise olives are both good choices for this, or you may use whatever black olive is your favorite.

1-Minute Quinoa (page 135), prepared
1 cup pitted black olives, finely chopped
1 bunch fresh thyme (leaves only)
½ cup pine nuts (3 ounces)
2 tablespoons extra-virgin olive oil
Freshly squeezed juice of half a lemon

Tumble the quinoa into a salad bowl and let it cool for a few minutes, then mix in the olives, thyme, pine nuts, oil, and lemon juice.

Cilantro-Lime Quinoa

Serves 6 to 8

This salad is particularly striking when made with black quinoa.

1-Minute Quinoa (page 135), prepared
1 cup fresh cilantro leaves
Freshly squeezed juice of 2 limes
2 garlic cloves, coarsely chopped
2 tablespoons olive oil

Tumble the quinoa into a salad bowl and let it cool for a few minutes. Meanwhile, using the chopper attachment of an immersion blender, puree the cilantro, lime juice, garlic, and oil. Mix the puree into the quinoa.

Perfect Brown Rice

Serves 4; about 3 cups cooked rice

This technique works with both long-grain and short-grain brown rice. It is also the method to use for red, green, and black rice; like brown rice, these still have their bran, which is colored differently in different rice varieties.

Note: This recipe can be either halved or doubled provided there is at least 1 cup of liquid in the pressure cooker (or your cooker's minimum liquid requirement) and the total volume of the ingredients does not exceed half the cooker's capacity.

1½ cups brown rice
2½ cups water
½ teaspoon salt
1 teaspoon olive oil

1. Place the rice, water, salt, and oil in the pressure cooker base.

2. Close and lock the lid of the pressure cooker. Cook at high pressure (see "Get *Hip* About the Pressure," page 13) for 18 minutes/stovetop or 20 to 22 minutes/electric (or nonstandard stovetop). When the time is up, open the pressure cooker with the 10-Minute Natural Release method (see page 15).

3. Fluff the rice with a fork and serve.

Variation

Perfect Wild Rice

This grain, native to the Great Lakes region, is not really rice at all. It is a seed of a grass that is grown in water. Although the wild crop is still harvested, wild rice is now cultivated as well, and so is more widely available than it once was. Wild rice may not absorb all the cooking liquid; if there is liquid left in the cooker when you open it, either scoop out the grain with a slotted spoon or drain it in a strainer. Follow the Perfect Brown Rice recipe, but use 3 cups water for every 1 cup rice. Cook on high pressure for 22 minutes stovetop/24 to 26 minutes electric (or nonstandard stovetop) cooker.

Perfect Long-Grain White Rice

Serves 4

This is the method for pressure cooking any refined or white rice in the market that is labeled as long grain and has not been parboiled. You can cook basmati rice this way, though the Perfect Basmati Rice variation that follows will yield lengthened, individually separate grains that are the more traditional hallmark of this fragrant rice.

Note: This recipe can be either halved or doubled provided there is at least 1 cup of liquid in the pressure cooker (or your cooker's minimum liquid requirement) and

Brown Rice Cooking Time

Brown rice is not a horticultural variety of rice, it is simply rice of any type that has been husked but retains its bran layer, which gives it its color and makes it take longer to cook than white rice. There are endless varieties of white rice and each starts life as brown rice. My local grain store has brown versions of Jasmine, Basmati, even Arborio and Carnaroli rice—and *each* has its own cooking time!

I follow the technique from Jill Nussinow (www.theveggiequeen.com) to determine the pressure cooking time for *any* brown rice variety that I'm not completely sure about. Simply look at the recommended cooking time on the package, halve it, and use that cooking time at high pressure. For example, if the package says 50 to 60 minutes, pressure cook it for 25 minutes in a stovetop cooker or 30 minutes in an electric (or nonstandard stovetop) cooker. This works with any brown, red, green, or black rice (which are just different colors of the rice hull).

If the brown rice package, or bulk bin, does not have the cooking time indicated, you can always try the generic brown rice cooking time which 18 minutes/stovetop or 20 to 22 minutes/electric (or nonstandard stovetop) cooker, at high pressure, using the 10-Minute Natural Release method (see page 15) to open the cooker.

the total volume of the ingredients does not exceed half the cooker's capacity.

1½ cups long-grain white rice
3 cups water
½ teaspoon salt
1 teaspoon vegetable oil or unsalted butter

1. Place the rice, water, salt, and oil in the pressure cooker base.

2. Close and lock the lid of the pressure cooker. Cook at high pressure (see "Get *Hip* About the Pressure," page 13) for 4 minutes/all cooker types. When the time is up, open the pressure cooker with the 10-Minute Natural Release method (see page 15).

3. Fluff the rice with a fork and serve.

Variations

Perfect Basmati Rice

When prepared traditionally, Indian rice needs both a good rinse and a short, 10 to 15 minute soak (and then draining) to help the grains stretch out into amazingly long kernels. Follow the Perfect Long-Grain White Rice recipe, but use 1¼ cups water for every 1 cup rice and omit the oil. Before cooking, rinse the rice in a strainer, set the strainer in a bowl of water to soak and then lift the strainer to drain the rice. Cook on high pressure for 2 minutes/all cooker types.

Perfect Jasmine Rice

Asian rice needs a good rinse and drain before cooking. Follow the Perfect Long-Grain Rice recipe, but use 1¼ cups water for every 1 cup rice and omit the oil. Cook on high pressure for 1 minute/all cooker types.

Perfect Arborio or Carnaroli Rice

Serves 4

Italian rice varieties are often sprayed with vitamins to make them more nutritious, so it is recommended not to rinse them before cooking. When Italians prepare these for use in a salad instead of for risotto, they boil them in a lot of water and drain the excess liquid after cooking. For pressure cooker preparation, instead of steaming as for the other rice types, we're going to boil Italian rice as is done traditionally, but with a little less water and a lot less time! A strainer with legs is the best type to use here—the holes on a colander are too large, but your hands won't be free to hold a strainer that's not self-supporting.

Note: This recipe can be either halved or doubled provided there is at least 1 cup of liquid in the pressure cooker (or your cooker's minimum liquid requirement) and the total volume of the ingredients does not exceed half the cooker's capacity.

1½ cups Arborio or Carnaroli rice
4 cups water
1 teaspoon salt
1 teaspoon vegetable oil or unsalted butter

1. Place a strainer in your sink. Place the rice, water, salt, and oil in the pressure cooker base.

2. Close and lock the lid of the pressure cooker. Cook at high pressure (see "Get *Hip* About the Pressure," page 13) for 3 minutes/all cooker types.

When the time is up, open the pressure cooker with the Slow Normal Release method (see page 15).

3. Drain the rice in the strainer and rinse with cold water to stop further cooking.

The 10-Minute Natural Release Is Key

Opening the pressure cooker with the 10-Minute Natural Release is an essential part of most grain recipes because during this release, the steam in the cooker continues to cook the grains. Even after the pressure has gone down and the cooker is closed, the steam is continuing to cook the grains. If the pressure cooker is opened right after pressure cooking, the grains will be underdone. But letting the steam do its work without any additional heat, which might cause scorching or overcooking, ensures perfectly steamed, piping hot grains. Stovetop cookers: This applies to you, too; leave the cooker closed until the full 10 minutes have elapsed even if the signal shows that all of the pressure has gone down (see page 14.)

Pilafs, Risottos, and Paella

Risotto is actually a type of pilaf—where the grain and sometimes another ingredient are sautéed in butter or oil before boiling or steaming. And in the pressure cooker, paella is treated very similarly to risotto.

While pilafs, like the steamed rice recipes in the first part of this chapter, use the 10-Minute Natural Release method and thus finish cooking as the pressure comes down, opening the pressure cooker for risotto and paella is a race against time. Risottos and paellas are DONE when pressure cooking is done, so open the cooker quickly, using the Normal Release method as called for in the following recipes, or the Cold-Water Quick Release method if you're comfortable using it (see page 15).

Armenian Rice Pilaf

Serves 4 to 6

Those of a certain age will remember the Rice-a-Roni advertisements and might think that the combination of pasta and rice was an invention of Kraft Foods. But in truth, it's a common dish in Armenia!

Note: This recipe can be either halved or doubled provided there is at least 1 cup of liquid in the pressure cooker (or your cooker's minimum liquid requirement) and the total volume of the ingredients does not exceed half the cooker's capacity.

2 tablespoons unsalted butter
1 tablespoon olive oil
½ cup vermicelli or angel hair pasta, broken into 1-inch pieces
2 cups long-grain white or basmati rice
4 cups salt-free Chicken Stock, preferably double-strength (page 48)
2 teaspoons salt

1. Heat the pressure cooker base on medium heat, add the butter and oil, and cook until the butter has melted. Add the vermicelli and stir well to coat. Sauté until the pieces just begin to turn golden. Add the rice; stir well to coat and toast for about 1 minute. Add the chicken stock and salt.

2. Close and lock the lid of the pressure cooker. Cook at high pressure (see "Get *Hip* About the Pressure," page 13) for 3 minutes/ all cooker types. When the time is up, open the pressure cooker with the 10-Minute Natural Release method (see page 15).

3. Mix the pilaf well, pulling up the rice from the bottom of the pressure cooker to the top before serving.

Variation

Turkish Pilaf

Follow the Armenian Rice Pilaf recipe, replacing the vermicelli with orzo pasta and the Chicken Stock with salt-free Meat Stock (page 47), preferably double-strength.

Indian Veggie Pullow

Serves 4 to 6

This commonly cooked rice pilaf is enhanced with peas, carrots, fried onions, and spices; it is also called *pilau* and *pulao*. Since the rice is rinsed and soaked, it needs a very short pressure cooking time—most of the cooking of this rice dish is actually done without any energy, while the pressure is releasing, using only the residual heat after you've removed the pressure cooker from the heat (see "The 10-Minute Natural Release Is Key," page 139) The pullow is traditionally served with raita, which is a cucumber and yogurt sauce.

Note: This recipe can be either halved or doubled provided there is at least 1 cup of liquid in the pressure cooker (or your cooker's minimum liquid requirement) and the total volume of the ingredients does not exceed half the cooker's capacity.

½ cup cashews
2 cups basmati rice
4 tablespoons ghee or vegetable oil
1 large onion, finely chopped
3 cardamom pods, lightly crushed
3 or 4 whole cloves, lightly crushed
1 tablespoon smashed garlic
1 tablespoon peeled and grated fresh
   ginger
½ teaspoon crushed red pepper flakes
1 teaspoon ground coriander
½ teaspoon ground turmeric
½ teaspoon ground cinnamon
1 cup frozen petite green peas

1 cup coarsely chopped cauliflower
   florets (1-inch pieces)
2 carrots, peeled and diced
3 cups water
2 teaspoons salt

1. Toast the cashews in a dry skillet over low heat until golden. Place the rice in a fine-mesh strainer and rinse it. Rest the strainer with the rice in a bowl and cover with water to soak.

2. Meanwhile, heat the pressure cooker base on medium heat, add the ghee, and heat briefly. Stir in the onion and fry until golden, about 7 minutes. Stir in the cardamom and cloves and sauté for about 1 minute. Lift the strainer so the rice can drain. Add the garlic, ginger, red pepper flakes, coriander, turmeric, and cinnamon to the onion mixture and sauté for another 30 seconds. Then add the peas, cauliflower, carrots, and rice; mix well. Sauté for about 3 more minutes. Stir in the water and salt.

3. Close and lock the lid of the pressure cooker. Cook at high pressure (see "Get *Hip* About the Pressure," page 13) for 3 minutes/all cooker types. When the time is up, open the pressure cooker with the 10-Minute Natural Release method (see page 15).

4. Fluff the pullow with a fork; taste and add more salt if you wish. Sprinkle the cashews over the top.

Variation

Chicken Pullow

Follow the Indian Veggie Pullow recipe, adding a cup or two of chopped cooked chicken along with the onion. Or you can begin by sautéing 2 raw diced boneless and skinless chicken breasts, but make sure they are cooked through before adding the other ingredients; the pressure cooking time is not sufficient to cook them. Replace the water with salt-free Chicken Stock (page 48).

Perfect Risotto No Matter the Ingredients

Adding vegetables and seafood to a pressure cooker risotto recipe can throw off the precious liquid ratio. Vegetables and seafood are 70 to 90 percent water, so the addition of a couple of zucchini could contribute almost an extra cup of liquid to the risotto, throwing off the ratio and resulting in mushy, or worse, burst rice grains.

To maintain the ratio, put the "wet" ingredients, be they chopped vegetables or seafood, in the measuring cup where you will measure the stock—a large 4-cup measuring cup or 1-liter pitcher work well. To ensure that the pressure cooker has enough initial liquid to reach pressure, pile the vegetables in the measuring vessel up to the 3-cup (or 750ml) mark. Add the stock, or water, to the measuring vessel, filling it until it registers the amount specified in your recipe, then add just a little dash more. Add the wet ingredients and stock to the pressure cooker at the same time. One thing to remember though—if your recipe calls for sautéing onions, leeks, shallots, or garlic before you add the other ingredients, do so in the usual manner.

With this technique the risotto will always turn out perfectly—no matter the ingredients you choose to add!

Spumante Risotto

Serves 4 to 6

Spumante is Italy's champagne. I make this risotto with leftover wine from birthday parties and New Year's celebrations. You can use any sparkling wine or even sparkling cider. Make this risotto extra-fancy by substituting a drizzle of truffle oil or a teaspoon of truffle spread for the final butter.

Note: This recipe can be either halved or doubled provided there is at least 1 cup of liquid in the pressure cooker (or your cooker's minimum liquid requirement) and the total volume of the ingredients does not exceed half the cooker's capacity.

> 1 tablespoon olive oil
> 2 tablespoons unsalted butter
> 1 large white onion, diced
> 2 cups Arborio or Carnaroli rice
> ½ cup Spumante
> 4 cups salt-free Chicken Stock (page 48)
> 2 teaspoons salt
> ¼ teaspoon ground white pepper
> 3 tablespoons grated Parmigiano-Reggiano cheese, plus more to serve at the table

1. Heat the pressure cooker base on medium heat; add the oil and 1 tablespoon of the butter and heat until the butter has melted. Stir in the onion and sauté until softened. Add the rice, stirring to coat well. While you continue to stir, look carefully at the rice, it will first become wet and look slightly transparent and pearly, then it will slowly begin to look dry and solid white again—this is the signal that the rice is perfectly toasted (do not brown or burn it). At that point pour in the wine. Scrape the bottom of the pressure cooker gently, and keep stirring until all of the wine has evaporated. Stir in the stock, salt, and pepper.

2. Close and lock the lid of the pressure cooker. Cook at high pressure (see "Get *Hip* About the Pressure," page 13) for 7 minutes/all cooker types. When the time is up, open the pressure cooker with the Normal Release method (see page 15).

3. Add the remaining 1 tablespoon butter to the risotto, and sprinkle the Parmigiano-Reggiano over the top; stir until well mixed and the butter has melted. Serve, passing more cheese at the table.

Variations

Risotto with Zucchini Flowers

In Italian we call this *Risotto ai Fiori di Zucchine.* Follow the Spumante Risotto recipe, adding 12 zucchini flowers: Slice each flower crosswise into 3 sections. Reserve the sections that are only petals; chop the bases into small pieces and add them to the pressure cooker while sautéing the onion. When finished pressure cooking, stir the reserved flower petals into the risotto along with the butter and cheese; they will cook instantly in the heat of the rice.

Risotto with Porcini Mushrooms

To make *Risotto ai Funghi Porcini,* follow the Spumante Risotto recipe, replacing the Spumante with a dry red wine such as Sangiovese or Chianti, adding 1 cup dried porcini mushrooms, and using only as much stock as indicated here: Place the mushrooms in a 4-cup measuring cup and add hot water to the 2-cup mark; cover with plastic wrap and let soak for 30 minutes. Then fill the measuring cup with the stock to just over the 4-cup mark (see "Perfect Risotto No Matter the Ingredients," page 142). Complete the recipe, adding the mushrooms and stock after the wine has evaporated. When ready to serve, sprinkle with fresh thyme leaves.

Risotto with Saffron and Peas

To make *Risotto alla Milanese*, as this dish is called in Italian, follow the Spumante Risotto recipe, replacing the Spumante with a dry white wine and adding 1 teaspoon saffron threads (or 2 packets of powdered saffron), and 1 cup shelled fresh peas. Stir in the saffron when the onion has softened. Add the peas with the stock. (Read "Saffron Savvy," page 148.)

Spumante Risotto

Risotto with Mixed Shellfish

Serves 4 to 6

Risotto ai Frutti di Mare is another classic Italian risotto. It's perfectly suited for summer—but with so many great selections of frozen seafood available today, it can easily be made any time of the year. Depending on the seafood mix you're using we separate the seafood from the in-shell shellfish. If you like, instead of water, use liquid leftover from cooking octopus or other seafood (see page 204). Read "Perfect Risotto No Matter the Ingredients," (page 142), before beginning.

Note: This recipe can be either halved or doubled provided there is at least 1 cup of liquid in the pressure cooker (or your cooker's minimum liquid requirement) and the total volume of the ingredients does not exceed half the cooker's capacity.

> 3 cups mixed seafood (shrimp, calamari, clams, etc.)
> Water, as needed
> 2 tablespoons olive oil, plus more to finish
> 3 garlic cloves, chopped
> 3 oil-packed anchovies
> 2 cups Arborio or Carnaroli rice
> Freshly squeezed juice of 1 lemon
> 2 teaspoons salt
> ¼ teaspoon ground white pepper
> 1 bunch flat-leaf parsley, chopped
> Lemon wedges, for serving

1. Separate the shellfish from the other seafood and set the shellfish aside. Add the remaining seafood to a 4-cup measuring cup and add water to just over the 4-cup mark.

2. Heat the pressure cooker base on medium heat, add the oil, and heat briefly. Stir in the garlic and anchovies and sauté until the garlic is golden and the anchovies are broken up. Add the rice, stirring to coat well. While you continue to stir, look carefully at the rice, it will first become wet and look slightly transparent and pearly; then it will slowly begin to look dry and solid white again. At that point pour in the lemon juice. Scrape the bottom of the pressure cooker gently, and keep stirring until all of the juice has evaporated. Stir in the seafood and water and the salt and pepper. Place the shellfish on top without stirring any further.

3. Close and lock the lid of the pressure cooker. Cook at high pressure (see "Get *Hip* About the Pressure," page 13) for 6 minutes/all cooker types. When the time is up, open the pressure cooker with the Normal Release method (see page 15).

4. Stir the risotto. Swirl some oil over the top and sprinkle with parsley. Serve with lemon wedges.

Barley Risotto with Leeks and Speck

Serves 4 to 6

Italians call barley *orzo*, and risotto made with barley is *orzotto*. Trento-Alto Adige is a northern region of Italy that borders Austria and is famous for a smoked, pepper-encrusted prosciutto called speck. Hence the Italian name for this recipe: *Orzotto alla Trentina*. I have seen speck in well-stocked supermarkets and Italian delis in the United States. Should you not be able to find it, you can substitute pancetta or bacon, though you should reduce the oil in this recipe since the substitutions bring plenty of extra fat to the party.

Note: This recipe can be either halved or doubled provided there is at least 1 cup of liquid in the pressure cooker (or your cooker's minimum liquid requirement) and the total volume of the ingredients does not exceed half the cooker's capacity.

1 tablespoon olive oil
4 ounces speck, chopped
2 leeks, halved lengthwise and thinly sliced crosswise
1½ cups pearled barley
½ cup white wine
3 cups Vegetable Stock (page 49)
Freshly ground black pepper
1 tablespoon unsalted butter
1 tablespoon grated Parmigiano-Reggiano cheese, plus more to pass at the table
Salt

1. Heat the pressure cooker base on medium heat, add the oil, and heat briefly. Add the speck and sauté until crispy. Stir in the leeks and sauté for a few more minutes. Stir in the barley, coating it well with the leek mixture. Pour in the wine and cook, stirring, until completely evaporated. Add the stock.

2. Close and lock the lid of the pressure cooker. Cook at high pressure (see "Get *Hip* About the Pressure," page 13) for 20 minutes/all cooker types. When the time is up, open the pressure cooker with the Normal Release method (see page 15).

3. Stir the orzotto; mix in the butter and 1 tablespoon of the Parmigiano-Reggiano, and season with salt and pepper. Serve, passing more cheese at the table.

Farro Risotto with Radicchio and Gorgonzola

Serves 4 to 6

There are two main types of radicchio: Treviso, which has long, skinny, almost rectangular leaves, like Belgian endive, and the common globe shape, which has round leaves like a cabbage. Either type can be used to make this *Farotto al Radicchio*, and whichever you choose, you'll want to pressure cook only the tougher white portions of the leaves. To preserve its magnificent color, just wilt the more tender red part by stirring it into the cooked risotto.

Note: This recipe can be either halved or doubled provided there is at least 1 cup of liquid in the pressure cooker (or your cooker's minimum liquid requirement) and the total volume of the ingredients does not exceed half the cooker's capacity.

1 small round radicchio or
   2 Treviso radicchios
1 tablespoon unsalted butter
1 small yellow onion, diced
2 cups pearled farro
½ cup dry red wine
3 cups salt-free Vegetable Stock
   (page 49)
1 teaspoon salt
4 ounces creamy Gorgonzola cheese, cut
   into cubes

1. Separate the red and white parts of the radicchio; if using the long skinny Treviso radicchio, separate the leaves and slice out the white rib from each. For the common round type, just cut off the bottom, the mostly white part of the globe and then halve the top part and cut out the white center. The separation of white and red does not require surgical precision—just do your best to divide them. Finely chop each color separately and set the red portion aside.

2. Heat the pressure cooker base on medium heat, add the butter, and cook until melted. Stir in the onion and sauté until it begins to soften. Add the white portion of the radicchio and farro and stir to mix well. Sauté for 1 minute more; then pour in the wine and cook, stirring, until it has completely evaporated. Add the stock and salt.

3. Close and lock the lid of the pressure cooker. Cook at high pressure (see "Get *Hip* About the Pressure," page 13) for 9 minutes/all cooker types. When the time is up, open the pressure cooker with the Normal Release method (see page 15).

4. Add the reserved red radicchio and the Gorgonzola to the risotto and mix until the radicchio has wilted and the cheese has melted. Serve.

Gorgonzola Soft or Hard

There are many kinds of Gorgonzola cheese in Italy, but only two main types are exported. A soft (*cremoso),* which has more cream, and hard (*piccante*), which is more crumbly and strongly flavored. If either of these is not available to you—or not within the budget—any blue cheese will do (but it will alter the flavor significantly). If you have a choice, use the creamy Gorgonzola in the Farro Risotto with Radicchio and Gorgonzola; if using the crumbly Gorgonzola add a splash or two of heavy cream after pressure cooking to compensate. For the Polenta Crostini on page 153, use the crumbly Gorgonzola.

Quick Mixed Paella

Serves 4 to 6

Paella Mixta Express is what Spaniards call "paella made in the pressure cooker" to distinguish it from true paella, which is made in a special wide, shallow pan that makes the rice very dry, with a golden bottom crust. This recipe won't replace the true paella, but it's a delicious and quick facsimile. A wide, shallow, pressure braiser would be the ideal pressure cooker to use for this because it will maximize the size of the delicious crust. But a common stockpot pressure cooker will still coax the rice into a respectable little crust.

Note: This recipe can be either halved or doubled provided there is at least 1 cup of liquid in the pressure cooker (or your cooker's minimum liquid requirement) and the total volume of the ingredients does not exceed half the cooker's capacity.

4 tablespoons olive oil
4 skinless chicken thighs
6 ounces pork sausage, cut into 1-inch pieces (about 2 sausages)
1 yellow onion, chopped
1 red bell pepper, stemmed, seeded, and chopped
1 green bell pepper, stemmed, seeded, and chopped
Large pinch saffron threads (or 2 packets saffron powder)
2 cups short-grain rice
3 cups salt-free Vegetable Stock or Seafood Stock (pages 49 and 50)
⅛ teaspoon ground turmeric
2 teaspoons salt
2 cups mixed shellfish (mussels, clams, langoustines, and shrimp)

1. Heat the pressure cooker base on medium heat, add the oil, and heat briefly. Add the chicken and sausage and fry until golden, stirring infrequently. Transfer the meat to a dish and set aside. Add the onion and green and red bell peppers to the cooker and sauté until the onion begins to soften, about 4 minutes. Then stir in the saffron, rice, and meat, and sauté everything together for 2 minutes. Add the stock, turmeric, and salt, mixing well. Arrange the shellfish on top and do not mix further.

2. Close and lock the lid of the pressure cooker. Cook at high pressure (see "Get *Hip* About the Pressure," page 13 for 6 minutes/ all cooker types. When the time is up, open the pressure cooker with the Normal Release method (see page 15).

3. Mix the paella well and then cover and let stand for 1 minute before serving.

Saffron Savvy

Saffron is usually "bloomed" in a bit of water and then added to risotto along with the stock, but in pressure cooking, it tends to disappear when incorporated in this way. To ensure that the saffron threads (or powder) retain their color and flavor during the pressure cooking stage, add them dry to the sautéing onions (or similar ingredients) before adding the stock.

Include a bit of crunchy rice from the base of the cooker with each portion.

"Perfect Risotto No Matter the Ingredients," page 142). Complete the recipe as written.

Paella Valenciana Express

This Valencian version of paella has no seafood and is delicious made with rabbit instead of chicken, but chicken is good, too. Follow the Quick Mixed Paella recipe, omitting the seafood, doubling the chicken to 12 ounces (8 pieces), and adding 1 cup shelled fresh or frozen peas before pressure cooking.

Variations

Paella Marisco Express

This is an all-seafood paella. Follow the Quick Mixed Paella recipe, omitting the chicken and sausage. Add 6 ounces mixed seafood (not shellfish) with the stock as follows: Place the seafood in a 4-cup measure and then fill the measure with stock to just over the 4-cup mark (see

149

Grains

Steamed Grains Bain-Marie

Cooking "bain-marie" in the pressure cooker is like using a double boiler—ingredients are mixed in a dish that is placed in the steamer basket, over water. This is a perfect method for anyone who is consistently getting scorched rice in the pressure cooker, which can happen using a lower-quality pressure cooker, or particularly tricky cooker/cooktop combination. It's also good for creating a one-pot meal by using the steam from a recipe cooking in the bottom of the cooker base to cook rice or another grain in a bowl above it (see the One-Pot Meals chapter, page 209).

Steaming grains bain-marie requires a heat-proof container, foil sling (see page 11), and steamer basket (see page 10). Even if the container is large enough to double these recipes, I do not recommend it, as the cooking of the grain may be uneven. Halving and even quartering a grain recipe cooked bain-marie is not a problem, since the cooker will reach pressure with the steaming liquid and not the grain's cooking liquid.

Bain-Marie South African Yellow Rice

Serves 4 to 6

Although sweet, this rice is often an accompaniment to meats—like South Africa's national dish *Bobotie*, which is a spice-laden ground meat and egg custard casserole—a very fancy moussaka.

- 1½ cups long-grain rice, rinsed
- 1½ cups water for the rice
- ½ cup raisins
- 1 tablespoon butter
- 1 teaspoon sugar
- 1 teaspoon ground turmeric
- ½ teaspoon ground cinnamon
- Small pieces of cinnamon stick, for a garnish (optional)

1. Add 1 cup of water (or the minimum amount required by your cooker to reach pressure) to the pressure cooker base; insert the steamer basket and set aside.

2. Add the rice, the 1½ cups water, raisins, butter, sugar, turmeric, and cinnamon to a 4-cup heat-proof dish. Stir to mix well and lower into the pressure cooker, using a foil sling (see page 11); do not cover the bowl.

3. Close and lock the lid of the pressure cooker. Cook at high pressure (see "Get *Hip* About the Pressure," page 13) for 3 minutes/all cooker types. When the time is up, open the pressure cooker with the 10-Minute Natural Release method (see page 15).

4. Lift the heat-proof bowl out of the cooker. Fluff the rice with a fork, decorate with cinnamon stick pieces if you like, and serve.

Bain-Marie Brown Rice with Salted Peanuts

Follow the method described in the South African Yellow Rice recipe, replacing all the ingredients with 1½ cups brown rice, 2¼ cups water, ½ cup salted roasted peanuts, and 1 teaspoon olive oil, and then pressure cook for 18 minutes/stovetop or 20 minutes/electric (or nonstandard stovetop) cooker.

Bain-Marie Buttered Barley and Herbs

Follow the method described in the South African Yellow Rice recipe, replacing all the ingredients with 1½ cups pearled barley, 2¼ cups water, ¼ cup crushed fresh mixed herbs (your choice), 1 tablespoon butter, 1 teaspoon salt, and 1 finely minced garlic clove. Pressure cook for 20 minutes/all cooker types.

Bain-Marie Pearled Farro with Sun-Dried Tomato Pesto

A bit of pesto seasons this dish while it steams, and then enhances it more afterward. If you like, make it with basil pesto instead of sun-dried tomato; the results are equally good. Follow the method described in the South African Yellow Rice recipe, replacing all the ingredients with 1½ cups pearled farro, 3 tablespoons prepared sun-dried tomato pesto, and ½ teaspoon salt, and then pressure cook for 5 minutes/all cooker types. Mix in 2 more tablespoons pesto before serving.

Bain-Marie South African Yellow Rice

Polenta and Masa

Polenta, a ground cornmeal that is mixed with water and cooked into a tasty, versatile mush, is fairly tricky to prepare in the pressure cooker. You need to know that it *may* scorch and stick to the base of the cooker—though nothing that an overnight soak can't fix!

Masa, a flour ground from specially treated corn, is used in several ways in Mexican and Central American cuisine; it is usually cooked by steaming for several hours. In the pressure cooker these hours are turned to minutes as the masa is plumped and cooked by the pressurized steam.

Basic Polenta Recipe

Serves 2 to 4; about 5 cups

A Northern Italian tradition that is incredibly versatile, polenta forms a mush that is soft when first made but firms up when it cools. It can be baked, grilled, or fried, and is often served with a sauce or topping. It can be sliced or cut into shapes before this second cooking; several recipes using it follow this one.

Coarse-ground polenta is also called *bramata;* coarse cornmeal can be used instead. Do not use instant or fine-ground polenta (also called *fioretto*), because the starch exits and solidifies so quickly that it hardly has any time to cook at all before it begins to burn—not just scorch—in the bottom of the pressure cooker.

Note: This recipe can be either halved or doubled provided there is at least 1 cup of liquid in the pressure cooker (or your cooker's minimum liquid requirement) and the total volume of the ingredients does not exceed half the cooker's capacity.

4 cups water or stock
1 tablespoon olive oil or unsalted butter
1 teaspoon salt
1 cup coarse-ground polenta or cornmeal

1. Add the water and oil or butter to the pressure cooker base and bring to a boil, uncovered, on high heat. Add the salt. Then, stirring clockwise, begin sprinkling in the polenta. As soon as it is all in, give the contents a final stir and quickly close and lock the lid of the cooker.

2. Cook at high pressure (see "Get *Hip* About the Pressure," page 13) for 8 minutes/all cooker types. When the time is up, open the pressure cooker with the Slow Normal Release method (see page 15).

3. Mix the polenta with a long-handled spoon, being careful to avoid any superheated spurts from the hot mass. Pour into individual plates, to serve while soft, or onto a serving platter, where it will firm up before cutting into portions. A rustic presentation, which recalls how farmers would just pour the cauldron of polenta down the length of a long wood country table, is to pour the polenta onto a large wooden cutting board.

Grilled Polenta

Serves 4 to 6

You'll want to plan ahead just a bit for this because the polenta must be poured out of the pressure cooker into a casserole or baking dish and allowed to cool and firm up before you can grill it. You can even do this a day ahead and refrigerate it overnight. Cut the polenta to the desired size right before grilling—or use cookie cutters to make fun shapes for the kids. If grilling isn't an option for you, you can brown the polenta using the oven broiler.

> Basic Polenta (page 152), prepared
>   and hot in the cooker
> Olive oil
> About ½ cup of your favorite marinade

Rub a 10 by 13-inch casserole or baking dish with oil and pour the hot polenta into it as soon as you open the cooker, spreading it quickly to level. Let it cool until it solidifies (for several hours).

Heat a gas or charcoal grill. Slice the polenta into rectangles or squares and brush both sides with the marinade. Place directly on the grill rack and grill for a few minutes on each side—or until there is a lightly golden crunchy outside layer. Serve hot.

Polenta Crostini

Serves 4 to 6

This is my favorite appetizer to bring to potlucks—just be sure to ask ahead if you can use your host's oven. I bring the polenta already cut and laid out on baking sheets, with all of the toppings in separate containers, and then assemble on site so I can serve when the crostini are hot and bubbly, just out of the oven. As with the Grilled Polenta, plan ahead so the hot, soft polenta has time to cool and solidify. Top these polenta cutouts with the Wild Mushroom Sauté (page 191) or Artichoke and Black Olive Ragù (page 121) to serve as a side dish or even a vegetarian entrée. Or sprinkle them with crumbled Gorgonzola cheese just before you bake them, and then enjoy them with the topping all bubbly and melted.

> Basic Polenta (page 152), prepared
>   and hot in the cooker
> Butter
> Olive oil
> Freshly ground black pepper
> Wild Mushroom Sauté (page 91),
>   Artichoke and Black Olive Ragù
>   (page 121), or crumbled Gorgonzola
>   cheese, or another topping of your
>   choice.

Butter a baking sheet and pour the hot polenta onto it, spreading it quickly to level. Let it cool, uncovered, until it solidifies (for several hours).

Preheat the oven to 400°F. Butter or oil a second cookie sheet. Use cookie cutters to cut out shapes (personally, I prefer round). Place the cutouts on the second cookie sheet; brush the tops with oil and sprinkle with pepper; then spoon a bit of your chosen topping onto each. Bake for 20 minutes. Serve hot.

Polenta Lasagna

Serves 6 to 8

This is an alternative for anyone who is trying to cut back or avoid gluten—but delicious in its own right, too. It can even be made with white polenta! Fill this lasagna with just about anything—any of the pressure cooker pasta sauces (pages 117 to 125) is ideal. You'll need to make two batches of Basic Polenta, one at a time, with the first ready to pour out of the cooker when you begin this recipe. Allow about 3 hours from start to finish so the first batch of polenta has time to firm up. Make a filler sauce while it cools.

If you like, do most of the assembly the day ahead and then you'll need just 20 minutes baking time before serving. See "Three Ways to Speed Up Polenta Lasagna" (page 155) for time-saving options.

> 2 batches Basic Polenta (page 152), with the first prepared and hot in the cooker
> Artichoke and Black Olive Ragù (page 121) or another sauce, prepared
> Olive oil
> 8 ounces mozzarella cheese, grated
> ½ cup grated Parmigiano-Reggiano (or your favorite hard cheese)
> 2 tablespoons cold butter, chopped

1. Oil a 10 by 13-inch casserole and pour the first batch of polenta into it, spreading it quickly to an even layer. Let it cool until it begins to solidify, about 2 hours.

2. Pour the sauce over the polenta in the casserole and spread it out evenly. Sprinkle with half the grated mozzarella.

3. Prepare the second batch of polenta and pour it into the middle of the casserole, over the cheese, quickly spreading it out to the edges. If you're not ready to bake the lasagna, once the polenta cools you may cover the casserole and refrigerate it up to 24 hours.

4. Preheat the oven to 375°F. Sprinkle the polenta lasagna first with the remaining mozzarella and then with the Parmigiano-Reggiano over the top layer of polenta. Dot with butter and bake, uncovered, until heated through and the top is bubbly and golden, about 20 minutes.

Three Ways to Speed Up Polenta Lasagna

If you are pressed for time, follow the Polenta Lasagna recipe but assemble it in one of these ways.

1. **The Assembled Polenta:** With this method, there is a high risk of polenta "crackage" but nothing that can't be covered up with plenty of cheese! You need two same-size casseroles. Start off with a double batch of polenta, pouring half into each of the casseroles. Let both cool. Spread the sauce and cheese on one and invert the other over it. Complete the recipe as written.

2. **Individual Polenta Stacks:** This option makes cute individual portions. You need a lot of small ramekins (8 to 10 small, or 6 medium). Pour the polenta into them, filling each about three-quarters full. Allow to firm up, then invert each to release the polenta; slice each piece in half horizontally, return one half to each ramekin. Add sauce and cheese, top with the other portion of polenta, and complete the recipe as written.

3. **Daredevil Polenta Lasagna:** This option is for pressure cooker polenta experts only, as it requires quick movements in assembling the polenta while hot and soft—there is no time to figure things out or troubleshoot! Make the sauce for the filling first and set aside. Then make a double batch of polenta and pour half into the prepared casserole. Moving quickly (before the half in the cooker begins to solidify) pour the sauce onto the hot polenta in the casserole and sprinkle with the cheese (no spreading or stirring!) and then pour the rest of the polenta on top and complete the recipe as written.

Tamales

Yields about 36 tamales

Traditional Mexican corn-husk tamales are filled with cooked *carnitas* or black beans or even the local seafood! Made the conventional way they can take hours to steam, but steaming is just a matter of minutes with the pressure cooker.

If you live near a Mexican grocery store, you may be able to purchase premixed *masa* dough. Otherwise, many grocery stores and natural food markets carry sacks of masa harina, which is flour from a specially treated corn. Each brand will have its own preparation instructions on the package, so follow those to prepare the masa dough for this recipe. You may use the *carnitas* cooking liquid in place of some or all of the water needed to make the dough.

Note: Make as many tamales as you wish; to double this recipe, make two batches.

One 6-ounce package corn husks
   (36 to 40 husks)
Boiling water, for soaking the husks
3 cups masa harina flour, prepared
   according to instructions on package
   (about 6 cups masa harina dough)
Carnitas (see Mexican Pulled Pork,
   page 189) or Boiled Black Beans
   (see Basic Boiled Beans page 97), or
   another filling of your choice
½ cup prepared chili sauce

1. Add 2 cups of water to the pressure cooker base, insert the steamer basket, and set aside.

2. Rinse the corn husks and lay them in a large shallow dish such as a casserole. Pour in enough boiling water to cover the husks and then place a heavy object, like a smaller casserole, in the dish to keep them submerged.

3. Set up a tamale assembly area on a work surface, arranging the soaking corn husks, masa dough, the filling, and chili sauce in a row, with the pressure cooker at the chili sauce end. Before starting to construct the tamales, flip the corn husks in the casserole so the ones that were soaking on the bottom are now on the top.

4. Lay out 1 to 3 corn husks with the inside facing up and wipe dry with a kitchen towel. Spread an even layer of *masa* in the top two-thirds of each husk, leaving a border to fold up along both sides. Spoon a small amount of filling along the center of the masa. Drizzle chili sauce over the filling. Carefully fold the side borders over the filling and then fold up the bottom third of the tamale—*don't squeeze*. Leave the tops open and place the tamales upright in the pressure cooker. If you are making just a few tamales, tie them together in groups of three with kitchen string so that they form a bit of a tripod and can stand up in the steamer basket on their own. Otherwise pack them so they all stand up. If the basket becomes tightly packed, stop and set aside the remaining ingredients for a second batch.

5. Close and lock the lid of the pressure cooker. Cook at high pressure (see "Get *Hip* About the Pressure," page 13) for 15 minutes/all cooker types. When the time is up, open the pressure cooker with the Natural Release method " page 15).

6. Serve the tamales hot, in their wrappers.

Steamed Breads

Bread can be steamed either in a heat-proof bowl or in the classic manner, in a coffee can. Pressure cooking bread in a coffee can results in a lovely cylindrical loaf that is easy to slice into rounds. A heat-proof bowl produces more of a round "pie" that is sliced and served in wedges.

The first recipe in this chapter and its variation feature classic sweet-but-not-for-dessert steamed breads that are best done in a heat-proof bowl. The second recipe and variations are for savory breads that would do well in a can. But really, you can use either container for any of the recipes, just check for doneness; a toothpick inserted in the bread should come out dry. If necessary, return to the cooker and pressure cook a bit longer. The final recipe is for bread that is cooked on small squares of parchment paper set right in a steamer basket.

Chunky Maple Syrup Cornbread

Yields 1 small loaf

Cooking cornbread and other sweet breads in the pressure cooker provides only a marginal time-saving over baking them in an oven. However, it takes 70 percent less energy, so there is no need to preheat and run the oven (especially nice in the summer) and, best of all, this cooking can be piggybacked with any other recipe (see Get *Hip* About Making Meals Under Pressure, page 210). This bread is just as good made with honey as with maple syrup. And if you don't have corn kernels, don't worry—leave them out.

Note: You may halve this recipe as long as you bake it in a smaller container.

However, it cannot be doubled; the bread would be too thick to cook properly with steam and be deeper than it is wide and that's just . . . weird (my son's favorite phrase of the moment).

1 cup all-purpose flour
1 cup yellow cornmeal or coarse-ground polenta
1 tablespoon baking powder
½ teaspoon salt
¾ cup milk (any kind)
¼ cup maple syrup
¼ cup vegetable oil, plus more for oiling the bowl
2 large eggs
¾ cup fresh or frozen and thawed corn kernels, rinsed and drained

1. Add 2 cups of water to the pressure cooker base, insert the steamer basket, and set aside. Oil a 4-cup heat-proof bowl (or 1-pound coffee can); dust it with flour and set aside.

2. Add the flour, cornmeal, baking powder, and salt to a medium bowl and mix with a fork until thoroughly combined. Measure the milk, maple syrup, and oil into a large measuring cup; add the eggs and break up well with a fork.

3. Pour the milk mixture into the flour mixture and stir until just combined. Stir in the corn. Pour the batter into the prepared bowl. Using a foil sling, (see page 11), lower the filled bowl into the pressure cooker; do not cover the bowl.

4. Close and lock the lid of the pressure cooker. Cook at high pressure (see "Get *Hip* About the Pressure," page 13) for 15 minutes/stovetop or 18 to 20 minutes/electric (or nonstandard stovetop). When the time is up, open the pressure cooker with the Normal Release method (see page 15).

5. Lift the bowl out of the pressure cooker. Insert a toothpick in the center to test for doneness; if it comes out dirty, lower the bowl back into the pressure cooker and pressure cook for 5 more minutes. If it comes out clean, turn the bread out of the bowl and then place it, flat side down, on a heat-proof plate. Pat the top of the bread dry and serve, or heat the broiler and slide the bread under it for a few minutes until the top is crunchy and golden.

Variation

Date and Walnut Bread

Follow the Chunky Maple Syrup Cornbread recipe, adding 1 teaspoon cinnamon with the dry ingredients, increasing the milk to 1 cup, and replacing the corn kernels with an equal amount of chopped dates plus ¾ cup coarsely chopped walnuts.

Steamed Savory White Bread

Yields 1 small loaf

Having a difficult time finding savory bread recipes that could be steamed, I adapted a white-flour Irish soda bread recipe. This cooks in less than half the time needed in the oven, and tastes terrific served warm with butter. It won't replace your oven-baked bread, but is a great alternative if you are camping, boating, or RV'ing! Cooking times may vary depending on the width and materials of the container used. By the way, the container doesn't have to be a coffee can—a 1-pound baby formula can or dry milk powder can is just as good; alternatively, you may use a 4-cup heat-proof bowl.

Note: You may halve this recipe as long as you bake it in a smaller container. However, it cannot be doubled; the bread would be too thick to cook properly with steam and be deeper than it is wide.

Vegetable oil
2 cups all-purpose flour
½ teaspoon baking soda
1 teaspoon salt
1¼ cups whole-milk plain yogurt
   (or buttermilk, or milk mixed with
   1¼ tablespoons vinegar)
Butter, for serving

1. Generously oil a 1-pound coffee can and set it aside.

2. Add the flour, baking soda, and salt to a medium bowl and mix with a fork until thoroughly combined. Add the yogurt and stir lightly to incorporate; then knead briefly with your hands in the bowl. The mixture should be a bit chunky and slightly sticky.

3. Gather the dough together and see if it will hold together as a clumsy ball. If it won't, sprinkle a little water over it and knead lightly for a minute longer. Shape the mixture into a cylinder and lower it in the prepared can, brush a little oil onto the top. Cover the top of the can with aluminum foil, tying it securely with kitchen string to keep it tightly closed during steaming.

4. Place the can in the steamer basket and then lower the basket into the pressure cooker base. Add hot water (directly from the tap) to the cooker base to come halfway up the sides of the can.

5. Close and lock the lid of the pressure cooker. Cook at high pressure (see "Get *Hip* About the Pressure," page 13) for 15 minutes/stovetop or 18 to 20 minutes/ electric (or nonstandard stovetop). When the time is up, open the pressure cooker with the 10-Minute Natural Release method (see page 15).

6. Carefully lift the container out of the pressure cooker. Remove the foil and test the bread for doneness by inserting a toothpick or skewer; if it comes out dirty, lower the container back into the pressure cooker and pressure cook for 5 more minutes. If it comes out clean, unmold the loaf and transfer it to a wire rack to rest for 10 minutes before slicing. Serve warm with butter.

Variations

Whole Wheat Sunflower Seed Bread

Follow the Steamed Savory White Bread recipe, replacing half the all-purpose flour with whole wheat flour, and stirring in ½ cup shelled sunflower seeds before kneading.

Smoked Mozzarella and Herb Bread

Follow the Steamed Savory White Bread recipe, adding ¼ cup finely chopped mixed fresh herbs, 1 finely minced garlic clove, and ½ cup shredded smoked mozzarella cheese with the yogurt.

Pimiento Olive Bread

Follow the Steamed Savory White Bread recipe, adding 1 cup drained and chopped pimiento-stuffed olives with the yogurt.

Chinese Steamed Buns

Yields 6 buns

Chinese *mantou* are plain steamed buns. Lightly sweet, they can be served during the main course or dipped in condensed milk for dessert. They are cute little buns and can also be sliced open and stuffed like mini sandwiches, or (as the Chinese sometimes do) deep-fried. (You can do this right after pressure cooking).

Note: This recipe makes about six buns, enough to fill one pressure cooker steamer basket. Should you have more than one steamer basket, this recipe can easily be doubled and the baskets can be stacked in the cooker; there is no need to increase the

Chinese Steamed Buns

amount of water added to the cooker base if you do this.

2¼ cups all-purpose flour
9 tablespoons warm water, for the bread
1 teaspoon instant dried yeast
1 tablespoon sugar
1 teaspoon vegetable oil

1. Add 1 cup of water (or the minimum required by your cooker to reach pressure) to the pressure cooker base. Insert the steamer basket and set aside.

2. Add the flour to the bowl of a stand mixer fitted with a dough hook. Add the 9 tablespoons water, yeast, and sugar to a cup and mix well. Slowly mix the water mixture into the flour, incorporating it to form a dough. Knead with the mixer until the dough forms a ball, then add the oil and continue kneading for about 10 minutes more. Plop the dough onto a lightly floured surface and let it rest for 5 minutes.

3. Roll out the dough to approximately a 10 by 13-inch rectangle. Then roll up from one long side, making a spiral. Cut off the uneven ends and slice into 6 equal pieces. Cut 6 squares of wax paper, each slightly larger than an upright dough slice. Place each slice, seam side down, on a piece of paper and arrange them in the steamer basket.

4. Close and lock the lid of the pressure cooker. Let the buns rise in the closed cooker (not heated) for 45 minutes.

5. When the dough has risen, cook at high pressure (see "Get *Hip* About the Pressure," page 13) for 3 minutes/all cooker types. When the time is up, open the pressure cooker with the 10-Minute Natural Release method (see page 15).

6. Serve immediately, or cover tightly and refrigerate. To reheat, pressure cook for 1 minute at high pressure, then open the cooker with the Normal Release method.

Meat and Poultry

Meats prepared in the pressure cooker become incredibly tender and flavorful. They cook in their own juice in addition to any liquid that is called for in the recipe and, much as with similarly prepared vegetables, their flavor is intensified compared to the results in conventional cooking.

One caveat about pressure cooking meat is that it needs to be quickly and tightly covered when pulled out of the cooker—but not for the reason you'd think! Unlike meat that has been roasted and baked in the oven, pressure cooked meat doesn't need to rest to allow its juices to redistribute. To the contrary, the worry with pressure cooked meat is its super-heated juices might quickly evaporate, leaving it tough and dry. Opening the pressure cooker with the Natural Release method, which will allow the juices in the meat to cool down to a non-pressure boiling temperature, helps to keep the meat moist as well. This evaporation phenomenon does not affect boiled meat—but pressure-steamed, braised, and roasted meat will need special care when it's fresh out of the cooker, or it will quickly become tough, dry, and tasteless.

Time-check for success. Although the pressure cooking rule of thumb is to cut cooking time to about one-third of the time required in conventional preparation, the pressure cooking time really depends on the cut of meat. Check the recommended cooking time for your specific cut of meat in your cooker's instruction manual or the Pressure Cooking Timetable (see Appendix, pages 276–278). Too little time will give you a raw dish, and too much time will extract all of the juices out of the meat, turning the cooking liquids into a flavorful stock, but leaving the meat itself tasteless.

Infusion matters. The cooking liquid is the star here and will infuse the meat with boundless flavor. The liquid could be wine, beer, water, stock, coconut milk, or tomato sauce, and pepped up with various herbs and spices.

Regulate liquid. Use the amount of liquid appropriate to the cooking method. To braise use the least amount of liquid required for your pressure cooker to reach pressure (usually 1 to 2 cups). To boil, depending on the dish, you can either just cover the meat or even get away with covering it only halfway, this ensures that the liquid is not too diluted (the meat will release its own juices, too). Steaming is much more forgiving; the liquid must be at least the minimum amount required, but not so much that it can reach the bottom of the steamer basket.

Go Fresh! Whenever possible use fresh herbs. Pressure cooking maximizes the flavor of every ingredient in the cooker, blending and infusing them. You want the flavorful oils and water that fresh herbs give to your recipe. You can toss them in whole, stems

and all, before closing your pressure cooker—the leaves will fall off during cooking—then remove and discard the woody stems after cooking!

Marinate. If time allows, marinate meat before cooking. It's a great way to fully coat the exterior and get the tenderizing process underway. You can make a marinade out of any combination of herbs (rosemary, thyme, or as you like); spices (cumin, curry, etc.); aromatics (garlic, onions, etc.); fat (oil, or spread on a bit of butter or lard); and acid (lemon, vinegar, tomato); plus salt and pepper.

Brown or broil. Browning meat prior to pressure cooking, or crisping it under the broiler after, adds both color and flavor. It only takes a few extra minutes, but can really take out the boring boiled blahs.

Wine about it. While it may boil away and reduce during conventional cooking, this is not the case with pressure cooking, which leaves the original uncooked wine taste eerily and unpleasantly intact. Don't skip the recipe instructions to evaporate or reduce the wine!

Reduce to a glaze or gravy it. When the cooking is finished, let the meat rest in its serving dish for a few minutes, tightly covered with aluminum foil. In the meantime you can reduce the cooking liquid still in the pressure cooker base to enhance the dish. Reduce to about half and thicken with potato starch or flour to make a gravy. Or reduce even more, to a syrupy consistency (about one-quarter of the original quantity) to make a glaze, then return the meat to the cooker, turning to coat and reheat.

Steamy Meats

There are two ways to steam meats in the pressure cooker: the first is the conventional manner, in which the meat sits in a steamer basket and its juice and fat dribble into the base of the cooker (where another dish can be cooking). The second is the Asian method, where the meat is placed in a heat-proof bowl that captures the juices, which are then thickened into a sauce with a little cornstarch.

There is no need to brown meats prior to steaming, but they can be broiled afterward.

BBQ Pork Ribs with Spinach-Bean Salad

Serves 4 to 6

Here two components cook at once: The meat sits in the steamer basket, dribbling its juices into the beans boiling below, which gives them an exquisite flavor! Though the BBQ in the title refers to the flavor and not the cooking method, the results should fool all but your most observant guests. The slide-under-the-broiler finish gives this dish a scorch that is both beautiful and delicious—the meat, of course, can also be finished on a *real* barbecue! Read "Get *Hip* About Soaking," pages 100–101.

Note: This recipe cannot be halved or doubled as it contains precise ingredient and liquid amounts to ensure that the beans are not cooked in too much liquid. To make more, prepare two batches.

1½ pounds baby back pork ribs
1 cup prepared barbecue sauce
Salt
Freshly ground black pepper
1 tablespoon olive oil
1 yellow onion, cut into large dice
1½ cups water
1 cup dried cannellini beans, soaked, rinsed, and drained
1 bay leaf
1 garlic clove, finely chopped
6 ounces fresh spinach (about 3 cups; baby spinach is nice)

1. Cut the ribs apart. Coat them on all sides with most of the barbecue sauce and sprinkle with salt and pepper; set the remaining sauce aside. Arrange the ribs in a steamer basket; you can stand them somewhat vertically to get them to fit. Set aside.

2. Heat the pressure cooker base on medium heat, add the oil, and heat briefly. Stir in the onion and sauté until soft, about 4 minutes. Add the water, beans, and bay leaf and stir.

3. Lower the rib-filled steamer basket into the pressure cooker and then close and lock the lid. Cook at high pressure (see

BBQ Pork Ribs with
Spinach-Bean Salad

"Get *Hip* About the Pressure," page 13) for 20 minutes/stovetop or 23 to 25 minutes/electric (or nonstandard stovetop). When the time is up, open the pressure cooker with the 10-Minute Natural Release method (see page 15).

4. Set the upturned lid of the cooker on your countertop. Carefully lift the steamer basket out of the cooker and place it on the lid; cover with aluminum foil. Fish out and discard the bay leaf from the beans, and mix in 1 teaspoon salt, the garlic, and spinach. Using a slotted spoon, scoop the bean mixture into a large casserole (big enough to hold the ribs in one layer) with low sides. Using tongs, arrange the ribs on top of the beans and brush with the remaining barbecue sauce.

5. Turn on the broiler. Broil the casserole until the sauce on the ribs is lightly caramelized, 3 to 5 minutes. Serve immediately.

Variation

Bitter Chocolate Pork Ribs with Black Beans

Here's a totally different take on barbecued ribs: With a different set of ingredients, classic American barbecue goes South of the Border! Follow the BBQ Pork Ribs with Spinach-Bean Salad recipe, replacing the cannellini beans with black beans and the spinach with 1 each chopped green and red bell peppers. Also replace the barbecue sauce with the following mixture: ¼ cup unsweetened dark cocoa powder, 3 tablespoons vegetable oil, 2 tablespoons honey, 1 tablespoon ground cumin, 1 teaspoon salt, 1 teaspoon ground white pepper, and 1 teaspoon smoked paprika.

Nonna Laura's Meatballs

Serves 4 to 6

My Italian grandmother was a professor of geology at the prestigious University of Pavia, and while not a particularly prolific cook, she was making freezer meals before they became "the thing." I fondly remember our weekly visits when she served wholly un-Italian morning tea and later, would slide those convenient, frosted little rectangular aluminum tubs out of her freezer. Those tubs contained out-of-this-world delicious meatballs!

Ground meat mixtures with bread tend to plump a bit in the pressure cooker because the bread absorbs the steam and expands, so you will want to make fairly small meatballs to compensate. I recommend using a melon baller to measure and portion out the ground meat. And yes, you can freeze them too. When cooled, tumble the meatballs into a gallon-size resealable food storage bag for later use.

If you don't have the time, or inclination, to make the béchamel, simply serve the meatballs plain and reserve the steaming liquid to use as meat stock.

Note: This recipe can be halved provided there is at least 1 cup of liquid in the pressure cooker base (or your cooker's minimum liquid requirement). It cannot be doubled; to make more, prepare two batches.

½ cup finely ground plain dry bread
   crumbs
1 cup whole milk
1 pound of mixed ground meats (a little
   over 5 ounces each of veal, pork, and
   beef)
½ medium yellow onion, very finely
   chopped
½ cup grated Parmigiano-Reggiano or
   Grana Padano cheese
1 teaspoon salt
½ teaspoon freshly ground black pepper
¼ teaspoon freshly grated nutmeg
1 large egg

Béchamel Gravy
½ cup whole milk, or as needed
1 tablespoon unsalted butter
2 tablespoons all-purpose flour
Salt
Ground white pepper
Freshly grated nutmeg

1. Place the bread crumbs in a medium bowl and stir in the milk. Mix well and let rest for about 5 minutes. Meanwhile, add 1 cup of water (or the minimum required by your cooker to reach pressure) to the pressure cooker base. Insert the steamer basket and set aside.

2. Add the ground meat, onion, cheese, salt, black pepper, and nutmeg to the bread-crumb mixture. Mix with your hands until well combined. Push the meat to the side of the bowl and add the egg to the resulting empty hollow. Using a fork, break up the egg and then mix it into the meat mixture with your hands.

3. Use a melon baller, or for larger meat balls, a 1-tablespoon measuring spoon, to portion the meat mixture. Delicately roll meatballs between your palms. Arrange the meatballs in the steamer basket in two snug layers, offsetting the balls in the top layer

between the ones below. (If they don't all fit, you'll need to cook a second batch, reusing the steaming liquid.)

4. Close and lock the lid of the pressure cooker. Cook at high pressure (see "Get *Hip* About the Pressure," page 13) for 8 minutes/stovetop or 9 to 10 minutes/ electric (or nonstandard stovetop). When the time is up, open the pressure cooker with the 10-Minute Natural Release method (see page 15).

5. Delicately transfer the meatballs to a casserole, cover tightly, and keep warm. Cook a second batch if necessary. Remove the steamer basket from the cooker.

6. To make the gravy, pour the steaming liquid from the pressure cooker into a heat-proof 2-cup measuring cup. Add milk to equal 1½ cups. Return the pressure cooker base to medium heat; add the butter and cook until melted. Sprinkle in the flour and stir with a whisk or fork until it turns golden and then bubbles and looks foamy. Then slowly whisk in the milk mixture. Continue whisking for a few more minutes until the gravy has thickened. Whisk in salt, white pepper, and a little nutmeg to taste. Pour the gravy over the meatballs in the casserole and serve.

Variation

Meat Loaf Ring

Follow Nonna Laura's Meatball recipe, adding the finely chopped leaves of 1 small bunch parsley with the cheese. Instead of rolling into individual meatballs, shape the mixture into a long loaf and delicately lay it into the steamer basket, connecting the ends to make a ring. Serve with béchamel gravy generously poured on top.

Chinese Steamed Chicken with Green Onions

Serves 2 to 4

My permanent move back to Italy ignited an interest in cooking Chinese cuisine. After living in San Francisco (a city with a sizeable Chinatown and constant flow of new immigrants) for twenty-five years, I really miss the chance to indulge in international cuisine. Things are slowly changing in Italy, but non-Italian restaurants are few and far between here.

I am a proud student of Pei Mei and her vintage cookbooks written for the Taiwanese housewife and dutifully translated into English. This recipe is adapted to the pressure cooker from *Pei Mei's Cookbook Volume 1*.

Note: This recipe can be halved provided there is at least 1 cup of liquid in the pressure cooker base (or your cooker's minimum liquid requirement). It can be doubled, if your pressure cooker is tall enough, by adding a second steamer basket and second heat-proof dish. DO NOT crowd or stack the meat in one dish as it will interfere with the cooking.

3 tablespoons vegetable oil

1 tablespoon rice wine

1 tablespoon peeled and finely grated fresh ginger

1 teaspoon salt

2 whole chicken legs with thighs attached

5 green onions

1. To make a marinade, whisk together the oil, rice wine, ginger, and salt in a cup. Put the chicken in a baking dish or resealable food storage bag, add the marinade, and turn the chicken until well coated. Refrigerate for at least half an hour, but no more than two.

2. Add 1 cup of water (or the minimum required for your cooker to reach pressure) to the pressure cooker base. Insert the steamer basket and place a heat-proof bowl in it, using a foil sling, (see page 11). Place the chicken legs in the bowl. Cut 2 green onions in half crosswise and thinly slice a third; add them to the chicken. Pour any remaining marinade juices over the chicken.

3. Close and lock the lid of the pressure cooker. Cook at high pressure (see "Get *Hip* About the Pressure," page 13) for 10 minutes/stovetop or 12 to 14 minutes/electric (or nonstandard stovetop). When the time is up, open the pressure cooker with the 10-Minute Natural Release method (see page 15).

4. Meanwhile, chop the 2 remaining green onions. When the cooker is open, lift out the heat-proof bowl and separate the chicken thighs from the drumsticks and transfer to a serving dish or individual plates. If you wish, pour the juices in the heat-proof bowl into a small saucepan and place over medium heat, whisk in a pinch of cornstarch, and boil until thickened. Serve the chicken with the juices, thickened or not, poured over each portion. Top with the chopped green onions.

Chinese Lemon Chicken

___

Serves 2 to 4

This version of *Ling Mung Jing Gai,* chicken steamed with fresh lemons, was inspired by Eileen Yin-Fei Lo's book *The Chinese Kitchen.* While the method is similar to that of Chinese Steamed Chicken with Green Onions, the seasoning is completely different.

Note: This recipe can be halved provided there is at least 1 cup of liquid in the pressure cooker base (or your cooker's minimum liquid requirement). It can be doubled, if your pressure cooker is tall enough, by adding a second steamer basket and second heat-proof dish. DO NOT crowd or stack the meat in one dish as it will interfere with the cooking.

2 tablespoons soy sauce

1 tablespoon rice wine

1 tablespoon oyster sauce

2 teaspoons sesame oil

1 tablespoon peanut oil

2 teaspoons peeled and grated fresh ginger

2 teaspoons sugar

2 teaspoons salt

⅛ teaspoon freshly ground black pepper

2 whole chicken legs, thighs and drumsticks attached

Pinch cornstarch (optional)

1 lemon, thinly sliced

2 green onions, thinly sliced

1. To make the marinade, whisk together the soy sauce, rice wine, oyster sauce, sesame oil, and peanut oil in a cup; then whisk in the ginger, sugar, salt, and pepper until blended. Put the chicken in a baking dish or resealable food storage bag, add the marinade, and turn the chicken until well coated. Refrigerate at least half an hour, but no more than two.

2. Add 1 cup of water (or the minimum required for your cooker to reach pressure) to the pressure cooker base. Insert the steamer basket and place a heat-proof bowl in it, using a foil sling (see page 11). Place the chicken legs and their marinade in the bowl.

3. Close and lock the lid of the pressure cooker. Cook at high pressure (see "Get *Hip* About the Pressure," page 13) for 10 minutes/stovetop or 12 to 14 minutes/electric (or nonstandard stovetop). When the time is up, open the pressure cooker with the 10-Minute Natural Release method (see page 15).

4. Lift the heat-proof bowl out of the cooker. Separate the chicken thighs from the drumsticks and transfer to a serving dish or individual plates. If you wish, pour the juices in the heat-proof bowl into a small saucepan and place over medium heat. Whisk in a pinch of cornstarch and boil until thickened. Serve the chicken with the juices, thickened or not, poured over each portion, and top with the lemon slices and green onions.

Steamed Beef with Spicy Rice Powder

Serves 2 to 4

This recipe is my adaptation for the pressure cooker of a recipe from *Pei Mei's Chinese Cookbook* (Volume 1).

Note: This recipe can be halved provided there is at least 1 cup of liquid in the pressure cooker base (or your cooker's minimum liquid requirement). It can be doubled, if your pressure cooker is tall enough, by adding a second steamer basket and second heat-proof dish. DO NOT crowd or stack the meat in one dish as it will interfere with the cooking.

- 2 green onions, thinly sliced crosswise
- Half a star anise
- 1 tablespoon soy sauce
- 1 tablespoon rice wine
- 1 teaspoon peeled and grated fresh ginger
- 1 teaspoon sugar
- ½ teaspoon salt
- 3 tablespoons water
- 8 ounces beef, thinly sliced (flank or sirloin)

Spicy Rice Powder
- 1 cup uncooked long-grain white rice
- 2 star anise
- 1 teaspoon freshly ground black pepper

1. To make the marinade, mix together about three-quarters of the green onions, the half star anise, soy sauce, rice wine, ginger, sugar, salt, and water in a small bowl. Put the beef in a baking dish or resealable food storage bag, add the marinade, and turn the beef until well coated. Let sit at room temperature for about half an hour.

2. Meanwhile, to make the spicy rice powder, heat a medium sauté pan over medium-low heat. Add the rice, star anise, and pepper and stir to mix. Cook until the rice is lightly toasted, about 3 minutes. Transfer the mixture to a food processor and pulse several times until it has the consistency of bread crumbs.

3. Add 1 cup of water (or the minimum required by your cooker to reach pressure) to the pressure cooker base; insert the steamer basket and a heat-proof bowl, using a foil sling (see page 11). Drain the beef and discard the marinade. Put ½ cup of the spicy rice powder on a plate and dip the beef in it, turning to coat all sides of each slice. Arrange the beef in the heat-proof bowl in a single layer. Reserve the remainder of the spicy rice powder for another use; it can be stored tightly covered with your spices.

4. Close and lock the lid of the pressure cooker. Cook at high pressure (see "Get *Hip* About the Pressure," page 13) for 8 minutes/stovetop or 10 to 12 minutes/ electric (or nonstandard stovetop). When the time is up, open the pressure cooker with the 10-Minute Natural Release method (see page 15).

5. Lift the heat-proof bowl out of the cooker. Serve the beef hot, with the remaining green onions sprinkled over the top.

Juicy Braised Meats

Braising is a wet cooking method in which the ingredients are placed in a small amount of liquid. In pressure cooking, this liquid should be no more than the minimum needed for the cooker to reach pressure and maintain it for the required pressure cooking time. Knowing this minimum requirement is crucial because both the meat and vegetables will release flavorful juices during cooking and the cooking liquid will increase instead of evaporating as in conventional cooking; if you start with too much liquid in the cooker, the impact of these juices will be diluted.

A low wide pressure braiser is ideal, but not required, for the recipes in this section. The large surface area allows for browning meat in a single batch and ensures that the meat will be in contact with the hottest part of the cooker—the base—while braising.

Neapolitan Beef Rolls

Serves 4 to 6

Braciole alla Napoletana is a popular dish found in the Campania region of Italy. Like Ragù alla Napoletana (page 118), this dish is often turned into two—the sauce used for a pasta course and the meat served as the main dish, often over mashed potatoes. The tomatoes and sautéed vegetables provide sufficient liquid to bring most cookers to pressure. Use any boneless beef steaks or fillets that are thin enough (or can be pounded) to be rolled.

Note: This recipe cannot be halved; it may be doubled provided the total volume of the ingredients does not exceed two-thirds of the pressure cooker's capacity.

1 small bunch flat-leaf parsley, chopped

½ cup grated Pecorino Romano cheese

¼ cup pine nuts, chopped

¼ cup raisins, soaked in hot water, drained, and chopped

¼ teaspoon freshly grated nutmeg

1 teaspoon salt

3 garlic cloves

1½ pounds thinly sliced center-cut top round of beef (8 to 10 steaks)

6 ounces thinly sliced pancetta, bacon, or prosciutto (8 to 10 slices)

2 tablespoons olive oil

1 small yellow onion, diced

1 medium carrot, diced

1 medium celery stalk, diced

½ cup dry white wine

2 cups chopped fresh tomatoes (or one 14.5-ounce can), with their juices

1 tablespoon tomato paste

½ cup water (for electric pressure cooker only)

Mashed potatoes (page 83), for serving (optional)

1. Mix the parsley, cheese, pine nuts, raisins, nutmeg, and salt in a small bowl. Finely chop 2 of the garlic cloves and add them to the bowl and mix until combined.

2. Lightly pound the steaks to be ⅛ inch thick if they are not already this thin. Lay them flat and place a slice of pancetta on each. Divide the parsley mixture over them. Beginning at a narrow end, roll up each steak, and then secure by tying with kitchen string or weaving a toothpick or two through the open edge.

3. Heat the pressure cooker base on medium heat, add the oil, and heat briefly. Add the onion, carrot, and celery and sauté until the onion begins to soften. Push the vegetables aside in the cooker and, working in batches if necessary, add the rolled steaks and cook, turning, until brown on all sides, about 7 minutes. To deglaze the cooker, pour in the wine and cook until it evaporates completely, scraping up any browned bits from the bottom as it does. Add the chopped tomatoes, with their juices, the tomato paste, and the water, if using, and stir to mix.

4. Close and lock the lid of the pressure cooker. Cook at high pressure (see "Get *Hip* About the Pressure," page 13) for 20 minutes/stovetop or 24 to 26 minutes/electric (or nonstandard stovetop). When the time is up, open the pressure cooker with the 10-Minute Natural Release method (see page 15).

5. Using a slotted spoon, delicately transfer the meat to a serving platter and cover. Chop the remaining garlic clove and mix it into the hot sauce in the cooker. Serve the meat over a pillow of mashed potatoes with a generous helping of sauce, or reserve the sauce to serve on pasta.

Variations

Apulian Pork Rolls

Bombette Pugliesi are meat rolls made using pork steaks instead of beef. They are usually grilled, but they can be made the same way the Neapolitan Beef Rolls are. Follow the method described in that recipe, replacing the beef with thin-cut boneless pork steaks and the Pecorino Romano with Caciocavallo cheese. Omit the parsley, pine nuts, raisins, nutmeg, salt, and 2 garlic cloves used to make the filling in step 1, but do sprinkle a little chopped parsley over the pancetta before rolling up the *bombette*. Pressure cook for only 15 minutes/stovetop cooker or 18 to 20 minutes/electric or nonstandard stovetop cooker.

Roman Veal Rolls

To make *Saltinbocca alla Romana,* follow the method described in the Neapolitan Beef Rolls recipe, replacing the beef with veal, the pancetta with prosciutto, and the chopped tomatoes and tomato paste with 1 cup salt-free Chicken Stock (page 48), and omitting the parsley, cheese, pine nuts, raisins, nutmeg, salt, and 2 garlic cloves used to make the filling in step 1. To fasten each roll, lay a sage leaf over the open edge and weave a toothpick through. Pressure cook for only 15 minutes/stovetop cooker or 18 to 20 minutes/electric or nonstandard stovetop cooker.

Braised Whole Chicken

Serves 4 to 6

Yes, you can cook a whole chicken in the pressure cooker and it will be ready in just minutes. The tricky parts are making sure the chicken will fit and getting it out without it falling apart. "Sitting" the chicken on its rump allows the largest possible bird to fit in a stockpot-type cooker and also ensures that the tougher dark meat is in the boiling cooking liquid and in contact with the hottest part of the pressure cooker, while the tender breast meat is up and away and steaming. Measure your cooker before you shop for a chicken, and take your tape measure to the market!

Note: This recipe can be halved (cook just half a chicken) provided there is at least 1 cup of liquid in the pressure cooker (or your cooker's minimum liquid requirement minus ¼ cup). It cannot be doubled; to make more, prepare two batches.

> One 3- to 4-pound whole chicken
> 4 fresh rosemary sprigs
> 3 fresh sage sprigs
> 3 fresh thyme sprigs
> 1 lemon
> 2 tablespoons olive oil
> 2 teaspoons salt
> 1 teaspoon freshly ground black pepper
> 1 tablespoon vegetable oil
> 1 bay leaf
> ¾ cup water, beer, or stock, or
>   as needed

1. Rinse the chicken inside and out and pat dry with paper towels. If there are giblets or the neck, you can use them to flavor the braise, so rinse them off too, and set them aside.

2. Reserve 1 rosemary sprig for a garnish. Pull or snip the leaves from the 3 remaining sprigs and also from the sage and thyme sprigs; chop all the herb leaves. Grate the zest from the lemon; set the lemon aside. Mix the chopped herbs, lemon zest, olive oil, salt, and pepper in a small bowl and then rub the mixture all over the outside and inside of the chicken.

3. Heat a large sauté pan over medium-high heat, add the vegetable oil, and heat briefly. Add the chicken and cook until browned on all sides, about 5 minutes per side.

4. Squeeze the juice from the lemon and strain it into a measuring cup. Add water (or beer or stock) to equal 1 cup (or the minimum amount required by your cooker to reach pressure minus ¼ cup—the chicken will release a lot of juice so the liquid needed to bring this dish to pressure is a little less than usual) and pour into the pressure cooker base. Add the bay leaf to the cooker, along with the chicken giblets and neck if using.

5. If you have a trivet, support the chicken on it (see "Use the Trivet to Skewer the Chicken," page 175). Lower the chicken into the pressure cooker and pour in any juices remaining in the sauté pan.

6. Close and lock the lid of the pressure cooker. Cook at high pressure (see "Get *Hip* About the Pressure," page 13) for 20 minutes/stovetop or 26 to 28 minutes/electric (or nonstandard stovetop). When the time is up, open the pressure cooker with the Normal Release method (see page 15).

7. Lift or slide the chicken out of the cooker and transfer to a serving platter; cover tightly with aluminum foil and let rest while you prepare the sauce. Or if you would like the skin to be crisp and golden, heat the broiler and place the chicken under it for a few minutes right before serving.

8. Meanwhile, return the pressure cooker base to high heat and boil the contents until reduced to a sauce consistency, about 5 minutes. Chop the leaves from the remaining rosemary sprig. Pour the sauce through a fine-mesh strainer over the chicken and sprinkle with the reserved rosemary.

Variations

Honey-Orange Whole Chicken

Follow the Braised Whole Chicken recipe, replacing the lemon with 2 oranges, using a small bunch of fresh thyme instead of the mix of herbs, and mixing 1 tablespoon honey into the herb-oil rub.

Spicy Cumin Whole Chicken

A tasty dish inspired by my Lebanese neighbor, Lamia, and her cooking. Follow the Braised Whole Chicken recipe, but replace the rosemary, sage, and thyme with 5 finely minced garlic cloves, 2 teaspoons dried oregano, 2 teaspoons ground cumin, 1 teaspoon ground cinnamon, and 1 teaspoon cayenne pepper.

Use the Trivet to Skewer the Chicken

Pulling the nicely cooked bird up out of the cooker in one piece provides one of the few (and undocumented) uses for that funny metal triangle that usually comes with the pressure cooker: the trivet. Insert the trivet partway into the tail cavity of the chicken, so its two bottom "feet" extend beyond the body, and lower the chicken on the trivet, tail first, into the cooker. After cooking, instead of pulling the chicken out by a tender wing that might break off, just insert the hooked handle of a kitchen utensil through the neck cavity to grab the "tip" of the trivet and lift!

If you don't have a trivet, carefully slide the cooked chicken out of the pressure cooker onto the serving platter, and then pour the liquids back in the pressure cooker to be reduced.

Pork Chops with Apples

Serves 4

This is a classic salty-sweet combination, in which the apples disintegrate into the sauce leaving only their flavor behind.

Note: This recipe can be either halved or doubled provided there is at least 1 cup of liquid in the pressure cooker (or your cooker's minimum liquid requirement) and the total volume of the ingredients does not exceed two-thirds of the cooker's capacity.

4 bone-in pork chops (loin or shoulder),
    cut ¾ inch thick
½ teaspoon salt
½ teaspoon freshly ground black pepper
½ cup all-purpose flour
1 tablespoon extra-virgin olive oil or
    vegetable oil
1 tablespoon butter
1 large white onion, thinly sliced
2 to 3 tart apples (such as Granny
    Smith), cored and sliced
¾ cup beer or salt-free Chicken Stock
    (page 48), or as needed

1. Sprinkle the pork chops with the salt and pepper. Put the flour in a plate; dip the chops into it and shake off the excess (too much flour in the pressure cooker will prevent it from reaching pressure).

2. Heat the pressure cooker base on medium heat, add oil and butter and cook until the butter has melted. Working in batches if necessary, add the chops and cook until brown on one side only. Transfer the chops to a plate. Add the onion to the cooker and sauté until just beginning to turn golden, about 7 minutes.

3. Spread the apples over the onions, and then arrange the pork chops, browned side up, on top, overlapping as needed.

4. Pour the beer into a 2-cup measuring cup. Add to it any juice from the plate that held the chops. If necessary, add more beer to equal the minimum amount required by your cooker to reach pressure. Pour this liquid into the cooker.

5. Close and lock the lid of the pressure cooker. Cook at high pressure (see "Get *Hip* About the Pressure," page 13) for 5 minutes/stovetop or 7 to 8 minutes/electric

(or nonstandard stovetop). When the time is up, open the pressure cooker with the Normal Release method (see page 15).

6. Using tongs, transfer the pork chops to a serving platter and cover tightly with foil. Using an immersion blender, puree the onion-apple mixture in the cooker. Return the cooker to medium heat and cook the puree until it has thickened to sauce consistency. Pour the puree over the chops and serve.

Variation

Pork Chops with Prunes and Cream

Follow the Pork Chops with Apples recipe, replacing the apples with 1 cup pitted prunes and the beer with Vegetable Stock (page 49). To finish, add ¼ cup heavy cream to the reduced puree and then simmer about 1 minute more.

Moroccan Lamb Tagine

Serves 4 to 6

The use of dried fruits and nuts along with lots of spices is a trademark of Moroccan cooking, with results more tangy than sweet.

Note: This recipe can be either halved or doubled provided there is at least 1 cup of liquid in the pressure cooker (or your cooker's minimum liquid requirement) and the total volume of the ingredients does not exceed two-thirds of the cooker's capacity.

1 teaspoon freshly ground
    black pepper

1 teaspoon ground ginger

1 teaspoon ground turmeric

1 teaspoon ground cumin

1 teaspoon ground cinnamon

¼ cup vegetable oil

2½ pounds boneless lamb shoulder, cut
    into 2-inch pieces

10 ounces pitted prunes or a mix of
    apricots and raisins (1½ cups)

2 yellow onions, coarsely chopped

1 cup salt-free Vegetable Stock, or your
    cooker's minimum liquid amount
    (page 49)

1 bay leaf

1 cinnamon stick

1 teaspoon salt

4 ounces shelled almonds (with or
    without skins, your choice)

3 tablespoons honey

1 tablespoon sesame seeds

1. In a large bowl, mix the pepper, ginger, turmeric, cumin, and ground cinnamon with 2 tablespoons of the oil to make a paste. Add the lamb and stir until coated; set aside.

2. Put the prunes (or other dried fruit if using) in a bowl, and add boiling water to cover. Cover the bowl and set aside.

3. Heat the pressure cooker base on medium heat, add the remaining 2 tablespoons oil, and heat briefly. Stir in the onions and let them cook until softened, about 3 minutes. Transfer the onions to a small bowl. Working in batches if necessary, add the meat to the cooker and brown on all sides, about 10 minutes. To deglaze the cooker, stir in the vegetable stock and cook, scraping up any brown bits from the bottom. Return the onions to the cooker and stir in the bay leaf, cinnamon stick, and salt.

4. Close and lock the lid of the pressure cooker. Cook at high pressure (see "Get *Hip* About the Pressure," page 13) for 25 minutes/stovetop or 30 to 35 minutes/electric (or nonstandard stovetop). When the time is up, open the pressure cooker with the 10-Minute Natural Release method (see page 15).

5. Meanwhile, toast the almonds in a dry skillet over low heat. Drain the prunes and add them to the lamb mixture in the cooker. Return the cooker to medium heat and stir in the honey. Simmer, uncovered. until the liquid has reduced to a sauce consistency, about 5 minutes. Fish out and discard the bay leaf and cinnamon stick. Sprinkle with the almonds and sesame seeds and serve.

Variation

Moroccan Chicken Tajine with Preserved Lemons

Follow the Moroccan Lamb Tagine recipe, replacing the lamb with 2 pounds chicken legs and thighs and omitting the prunes. Pressure cook-for just 10 minutes for stovetop and 12 minutes for electric/nonstandard. Serve with wedges of salt-preserved lemons, which you can find in online or in specialty food markets.

Filipino Chicken Adobo

Serves 4 to 6

Adobong Manok, is considered the national dish of the Philippines. Its origins are with the Spanish colonizers—*adobo* is the Spanish word for "marinade"—but Filipinos have happily adapted it as their own. Endless varieties of adobo exist and each region has its own specialty. The sauce is typically made with cane juice vinegar, but white or cider vinegars will do. Additions can include ginger, onions, and—if you like a little spice—crushed red pepper flakes (don't add more than a teaspoonful as their heat grows in the pressure cooker; see "Careful with the Red Pepper Flakes!" (page 105).

I like to serve this chicken dish over steamed white rice (page 137). My Filipina friend in San Francisco, Eleanore, recommends serving a simple tomato or cucumber salad dressed in vinaigrette on the side.

Note: This recipe can be either halved or doubled provided there is at least 1 cup of liquid in the pressure cooker (or your cooker's minimum liquid requirement) and the total volume of the ingredients does not exceed two-thirds of the cooker's capacity.

¼ cup white vinegar
½ cup soy sauce
1 bay leaf
6 to 8 garlic cloves
½ teaspoon freshly ground black pepper
One 5- to 6-pound chicken, cut into 8 pieces
1 tablespoon vegetable oil

½ cup water (for electric pressure cooker only)
Steamed white rice, for serving (optional)

1. Mix the vinegar, soy sauce, garlic, bay leaf, and pepper in a casserole. Add the chicken, turning to coat each piece with the marinade. Cover tightly and refrigerate for 2 to 4 hours. Remove the chicken pieces from the marinade and pat dry with paper towel; reserve the marinade.

2. Heat the pressure cooker base on high heat, add the oil and heat briefly. Working in batches if necessary, arrange the chicken, skin side down, and cook until browned on one side only, about 7 minutes. Arrange all the chicken pieces, skin side up, in the cooker and pour in the reserved marinade, including the bay leaf, and add the water if using.

3. Close and lock the lid of the pressure cooker. Cook at high pressure (see "Get *Hip* About the Pressure," page 13) for 12 minutes/stovetop or 16 to 18 minutes/ electric (or nonstandard stovetop). When the time is up, open the pressure cooker with the Normal Release method (see page 15).

4. Transfer the chicken to a plate and cover tightly with aluminum foil. Return the pressure cooker base to medium heat and simmer, uncovered, until the cooking juices have reduced by half, about 5 minutes. Fish out and discard the bay leaf, and return the chicken to the cooker, turning to coat well with the sauce.

Variation

Filipino Pork Adobo

Follow the Filipino Chicken Adobo recipe, replacing the chicken with stewing pork (shoulder or leg), cut into 1-inch pieces.

Spanish Pimento Braised Chicken

Serves 4 to 6

Pimento is the Spanish name for Spain's local peppers—they are a bit longer and pointier than the common boxy pepper we've come to know. If not available, red bell peppers make a great substitute in this recipe for *Pollo con Pimentos.* I make this with drumsticks, but you may use any chicken pieces you like. Spaniards don't puree the sauce, or even add lemon juice, but something magical happens to the sauce when you add lemon juice to the remaining chicken fat and then puree— they emulsify and make a creamy sauce.

Note: This recipe can be either halved or doubled provided there is at least 1 cup of liquid in the pressure cooker (or your cooker's minimum liquid requirement) and the total volume of the ingredients does not exceed two-thirds of the cooker's capacity.

6 chicken drumsticks
2 teaspoons salt
1 teaspoon freshly ground black pepper
1 tablespoon vegetable oil
1 yellow onion, coarsely chopped
1 small bunch flat-leaf parsley, leaves and stems finely chopped separately
2 medium red bell peppers, stemmed seeded, and coarsely chopped
1 bay leaf
4 garlic cloves
½ cup water (electric pressure cookers use 1 cup)

1 tablespoon freshly squeezed lemon juice

1. Sprinkle the chicken with the salt and black pepper. Heat the pressure cooker base on medium heat, add the oil and heat briefly. Add the chicken and cook until brown on all sides, about 3 minutes per side. Transfer the chicken to a plate. Add the onion, parsley stems, and bell peppers to the cooker and sauté just until the onion begins to soften. Stir in the bay leaf and 3 of the garlic cloves. Arrange the chicken on top of the vegetable mixture and pour in the water,

2. Close and lock the lid of the pressure cooker. Cook at high pressure (see "Get *Hip* About the Pressure," page 13) for 12 minutes/stovetop or 14 to 16 minutes/ electric (or nonstandard stovetop). When the time is up, open the pressure cooker with the Normal Release method (see page 15).

3. Transfer the chicken to a serving platter and cover tightly with aluminum foil. Return the pressure cooker base to high heat and simmer the vegetable mixture, uncovered, for 5 minutes to reduce its liquid. Fish out and discard the bay leaf. Finely chop the remaining garlic clove and stir it into the vegetables along with the lemon juice. Using an immersion blender, puree the mixture. Drizzle the puree over the chicken, sprinkle with the parsley leaves, and serve.

Variation

Tuscan Chicken with Mushrooms

To make *Pollo ai Funghi Toscani,* follow the Spanish Pimiento Braised Chicken recipe, replacing the red peppers with ½ pound each button mushrooms and pearl onions, and using balsamic vinegar instead of lemon juice, and omitting the garlic. Slice the mushrooms and peel the onions before cooking. When you transfer the chicken to the serving platter after pressure cooking, use a slotted spoon to lift out about half the mushrooms and onions and spread them over the chicken. Puree the remaining mushrooms and onions in the pressure cooker after adding the vinegar.

Italian Braised Veal Shanks

Serves 4

An amazingly tender braise of veal shanks, *Ossobuco alla Milanese*, or *os bus* in Milanese dialect, was first written about in the 1600s. There is some controversy as to whether this dish should contain tomato, or not. The original recipe does not, and some Italian families from the region (including my own from nearby Pavia) insist that it should remain so. The "official" recipe for this dish filed in Milano's city hall in 2007 includes a spoonful of tomato paste, but Italians—stubborn to change tradition—still distinguish their *ossobuco* recipes as *bianco* "white" (without tomato, given here) or *rosso* "red."

Ossobuco literally translated means "hole in the bone" because of the ease in which the nutritious marrow may be extracted and eaten. There are two ways to eat it. The marrow may be pulled or coaxed out with a special little fork, toothpick, or skewer. The less elegant, but more effective,

way to extract marrow is to pick up the bone, plug one end of the bone with the tip of your finger and suck the marrow out of the other end by lightly lifting the finger just a bit to break the suction. Serve it over Basic Polenta (page 152) or Risotto with Saffron and Peas (page 144).

Note: This recipe can be either halved or doubled provided there is at least 1 cup of liquid in the pressure cooker (or your cooker's minimum liquid requirement) and the total volume of the ingredients does not exceed two-thirds of the cooker's capacity.

4 veal shank slices, 1½ to 2 inches thick
½ cup all-purpose flour
2 tablespoons unsalted butter
½ cup dry white wine
1 cup salt-free double-strength meat stock, more as needed (see page 47)
2 teaspoons salt
¼ teaspoon freshly ground black pepper

Gremolata
1 small bunch flat-leaf parsley
1 lemon
2 garlic cloves

1. Make small perpendicular cuts at intervals around the edge of each piece of veal to keep the meat from curling, and then tie a length of kitchen string tightly around it. Put the flour in a shallow dish and dip each veal piece into it, shaking off the excess (too much flour in the pressure cooker will prevent it from reaching pressure).

2. Heat the pressure cooker base on medium heat, add the butter, and cook until it has melted. Working in batches if necessary, add the veal and brown well on both sides, about 7 minutes. Transfer the veal to a plate. To deglaze the cooker, pour in the wine, and cook until almost completely evaporated, scraping up all of the brown bits stuck to the bottom. Arrange all the veal in one layer in the cooker and add the 1 cup of stock (or the minimum liquid amount required by your cooker to reach pressure). Sprinkle in the salt and pepper.

3. Close and lock the lid of the pressure cooker. Cook at high pressure (see "Get *Hip* About the Pressure," page 13) for 35 minutes/stovetop or 40 to 45 minutes/electric (or nonstandard stovetop). When the time is up, open the pressure cooker

with the 10-Minute Natural Release method (see page 15).

4. Meanwhile, to make the gremolata, chop the parsley leaves (discard the stems). Grate the zest from the lemon (reserve the lemon for another use). Finely mince the garlic. Mix all the ingredients together in a small bowl.

5. When the cooker is open, using a spatula or wide spoon, carefully lift out the veal, taking care that it doesn't fall apart, and transfer to individual plates; snip the string and discard. Taste and add more salt

Italian Braised Veal Shanks

or pepper to the cooking liquid if you wish, and spoon it liberally over the veal. Dust with gremolata and serve.

Variations

Tomato-Braised Veal Shanks

To make *Ossobuco alla Fiorentina,* follow the recipe for Italian Braised Veal Shanks, replacing the white wine with red, and adding 3 medium chopped tomatoes and their juices to the cooker before adding the meat stock; the combined liquids should come halfway up the side of the meat. Instead of making gremolata, chop a mix of fresh parsley and sage to sprinkle on top after cooking.

Braised Veal Shanks with Peas

To make *Ossobuco alla Romana,* follow the recipe for Italian Braised Veal Shanks, substituting olive oil for the butter and adding 1 yellow onion, 1 carrot, 1 celery stalk, and 1 cup frozen peas, using veal shank sliced to only ¾ inch thick, and omitting the gremolata. Before browning the meat, finely chop the onion, carrot, and celery and sauté them until softened; then push to the side while you brown the meat. Sprinkle the peas over the veal and stock just before pressure cooking, and then pressure cook for only 20 minutes/stovetop cooker or 22 to 24 minutes/ electric (or nonstandard stovetop) cooker.

Braised Sliced Turkey Shanks

It's a big to-do to get a whole turkey in Italy to celebrate the American Thanksgiving (they're mostly sold in parts), so I made up this recipe and call it *Ossobuco all'Americana.* Follow the recipe for Italian Braised Veal Shanks, replacing the veal with 2 turkey legs that have been cut into 2-inch-thick slices (have your butcher do this) and the meat stock with chicken or turkey stock. Add 1 cup dried cranberries, and omit the gremolata. Sprinkle the cranberries over the turkey and stock just before pressure cooking. Pressure cook for 20 minutes/stovetop cooker or 22 to 24 minutes/electric (or nonstandard stovetop) cooker.

Boiled and Stewed Meats

Boiling and stewing in the pressure cooker are much more forgiving than braising—they usually involve tough cuts of meat and they can take a little more or less liquid. The only thing to watch out for is not adding *too much* liquid. There is no need to be precise, but in general you should cover the meat at least halfway or up to three-quarters with cooking liquid (not completely or more as in conventional cooking) to allow for the meat itself to release some of its juices. Meat is 60 to 70 percent water, depending on the cut, so for every 2 pounds of meat you'll get almost an extra cup of cooking liquid! To make up for the fact that the pressure cooker has almost no evaporation during cooking, the concentrated flavor achieved in making a stew in the conventional way can be achieved by reducing the cooking liquid *after* pressure cooking.

Florentine Veal or Beef Roast

Serves 4 to 6

Stracotto alla Fiorentina is, like many Italian boiled meats, a recipe that can make two meals. The meat is a main dish, of course, and the tomato-y cooking liquid is ideal to reuse as a base for soups, a pasta sauce, or the liquid in a risotto.

This recipe is my pressure cooker adaptation of Pellegrino Artusi's *La Scienza in Cucina—L'arte di Mangiar Bene (Science in the Kitchen—The Art of Eating Well)*—a classic compendium of Italian recipes first published 1891 and still used today. The meat is nice served over Basic Polenta (page 152) or Spumante Risotto (page 143).

Note: This recipe can be either halved or doubled provided the liquids (tomatoes and stock) cover the meat halfway. If halving, use at least 1 cup of liquid (or your cooker's minimum requirement); if doubling, make sure the total volume of the ingredients does not exceed two-thirds of the cooker's capacity.

One 2- to 3-pound beef or veal shoulder roast or round roast
3 teaspoons salt
1 teaspoon freshly ground black pepper
¼ cup all-purpose flour
1 tablespoon unsalted butter
1 tablespoon olive oil
4 ounces pancetta or bacon, diced
1 onion, coarsely diced
1 carrot, coarsely diced
2 celery stalks, diced
4 cups stewed tomatoes (two 14.5-ounce cans)

2 tablespoons dried porcini mushrooms (about 1 ounce)

1 cup salt-free meat stock, or as needed (see page 47)

Polenta (page 152) or Spumante Risotto (page 143), for serving (optional)

1. Wrap and tie the roast with kitchen string to help it hold its shape. Sprinkle the meat all over with 1 teaspoon of the salt and the pepper. Put the flour in a shallow dish and dip the roast into it to coat all sides, shaking off the excess (too much flour in the pressure cooker will prevent it from reaching pressure).

2. Heat the pressure cooker base on high heat. Add the butter and oil and cook until the butter has melted. Add the roast and cook, turning, to brown all

sides, about 5 minutes per side. Transfer the roast to a plate. Add the pancetta and sauté just until starting to crisp. Then stir in the onions, carrot, and celery and sauté until the onion is translucent. Add the tomatoes, mushrooms, and the remaining 2 teaspoons salt and cook, gently scraping up any delicious brown bits from the bottom of the cooker until they are incorporated. Return the roast to the cooker and, if needed, add stock so the roast is halfway covered. Spoon some of the tomato mixture over the top.

3. Close and lock the lid of the pressure cooker. Cook at high pressure (see "Get *Hip* About the Pressure," page 13) for 45 minutes/stovetop or 50 to 60 minutes/ electric (or nonstandard stovetop). When the time is up, open the pressure cooker

Florentine Veal or Beef Roast

with the Natural Release method (see page 15); this should take 10 to 15 minutes for a stovetop cooker or 20 to 30 minutes for an electric cooker.

4. Remove the roast from the cooker and slice. Serve immediately with half of the sauce. Reserve the rest of sauce to serve over pasta or for another use.

Coq au Vin

Serves 4 to 6

Coq au Vin, or "wine-stewed chicken," is a true French comfort food, originally developed to tenderize tough, old roosters *(coqs),* but it works just as well made with chicken. This dish has a colorful background including a mention in the 1906 cookbook by Edmond Richardin *La cuisine Française: L'art du Bien Manger* (France's answer to Artusi). In it, the author claims that Julius Cesar himself served this dish to the Gauls (the people in the territories of Northern Europe including what later became known as France)! Though I can't imagine a Roman emperor serving anything to anyone, I *can* imagine the network of roads built across the Roman Empire being the perfect vehicle for not just commerce of goods but also recipe exchange—as you'll see in the Northern Italian variation (page 187), which uses the same technique but a different cut of meat. Plan ahead to serve this dish—it requires a day or two to marinate before cooking for the most flavorful results.

Note: This recipe can be either halved or doubled provided there is at least 1 cup of liquid in the pressure cooker (or your cooker's minimum liquid requirement) and the total volume of the ingredients does not exceed two-thirds of the cooker's capacity.

1 large onion, coarsely chopped
2 celery stalks, coarsely chopped
1 large carrot, coarsely chopped
1 large garlic clove, smashed
1 teaspoon whole black peppercorns, in tea ball or wrapped in cheesecloth
One 750-ml bottle French Burgundy or Pinot Noir wine
One 5- to 6-pound chicken, cut into 8 parts (or 4 thighs and 4 drumsticks)
1 tablespoon olive oil
6 ounces pancetta or thick-cut bacon slices, diced
1 pound assorted fresh wild mushrooms (or farmed cremini and stemmed shiitake), thickly sliced
2 cups peeled large pearl onions (or 8 halved shallots or 3 quartered large onions of any type)
4 tablespoons unsalted butter
3 shallots, chopped
1 bunch flat-leaf parsley
8 fresh thyme sprigs
1 bay leaf
3 teaspoons salt
2 tablespoons all-purpose flour

1. To make a marinade, add the onion, celery, carrot, garlic, and peppercorns to the pressure cooker base and pour in the wine. Set the uncovered cooker on high heat and bring the contents to a boil and let boil for about 10 minutes until the wine is reduced by half. Turn off the heat and let the marinade cool.

2. Put the chicken in a large bowl or casserole, pour in the marinade, and turn the chicken to coat well. Cover tightly and refrigerate overnight or up to 2 days. If the chicken is not fully submerged, turn it over about halfway through the marinating.

3. When ready to cook, lift the chicken pieces from the marinade and pat dry with paper towels. Strain the marinade, reserving the vegetables and wine separately.

4. Heat the pressure cooker base on medium heat, add the oil, and heat briefly. Add the pancetta and sauté until crispy. Using a slotted spoon, transfer the pancetta to a large bowl; if there are more than 2 tablespoons fat remaining in the cooker, remove the excess. Add the chicken to the cooker and cook, turning, to brown all sides, about 8 minutes total. Transfer to a plate and set aside.

5. Stir the mushrooms into the cooker and sauté until they just begin to turn golden, about 5 minutes. Using a slotted spoon, transfer the mushrooms to the bowl with the pancetta. Stir the pearl onions into the cooker and sauté until just starting to turn golden, about 5 minutes, then transfer them to the bowl with the mushrooms and pancetta. Cover the bowl. Melt 2 tablespoons of the butter in the cooker and add the reserved vegetables from the marinade and the chopped shallots and

Coq au Vin

sauté, scraping up the brown bits from the bottom of the cooker.

6. Meanwhile, reserve 4 sprigs from the parsley bunch; chop the remainder and set it aside. Also reserve 4 of the thyme sprigs. Tie the parsley sprigs, remaining thyme sprigs, and bay leaf together in a little bundle or wrap in cheesecloth.

7. Add the chicken to the pressure cooker (if using the parts from a whole chicken, place the wings, thighs, and legs in contact with the base of the cooker and the breasts on top), along with the remaining wine from the marinade, herb bundle, and salt.

8. Close and lock the lid of the pressure cooker. Cook at high pressure (see "Get *Hip* About the Pressure," page 13) for 10 minutes/stovetop or 12 to 14 minutes/electric (or nonstandard stovetop). When the time is up, open the pressure cooker with the 10-Minute Natural Release method (see page 15).

9. Fish out and discard the herb bundle and peppercorns. If you wish, transfer the chicken to a plate and then strain and defat the cooking liquid. Return the chicken and liquid to the cooker; discard the vegetables. Stir the pancetta, mushrooms, and pearl onions into the cooker. Return the uncovered cooker to medium heat and bring the contents to a simmer.

10. Melt the remaining 2 tablespoons butter in a small saucepan, sprinkle in the flour, and stir with a whisk or fork until the mixture is just starting to get some color, about 5 minutes. Stir the roux into the simmering contents of the pressure cooker, raise the heat to medium, and bring the contents to a slow boil, stirring delicately until the sauce has thickened.

11. Spoon the chicken onto a serving platter, tumble the vegetables and sauce from the pressure cooker on top,

and sprinkle with the reserved parsley. Decorate the coq au vin with small pieces of the reserved thyme sprigs just before serving.

Variations

Piedmont Boiled Beef Roast

South of the French Alps is the northern region of Italy called *Piemonte*. There they cook beef in a similar way to Coq au Vin, and their *Brasato al Barolo Piemontese* is a classic, dark, juicy roast that has been marinated and cooked in a bottle of Barolo, the local wine. To make it, follow the Coq au Vin recipe, replacing the chicken with a 3-pound beef shoulder or rump roast, and the Burgundy wine with Barolo. Omit the pancetta, mushrooms, and pearl onions, and pressure cook for 50 minutes/stovetop cooker or 60 to 70 minutes electric (or nonstandard stovetop) cooker.

French Beef Stew

To make *Boeuf Bourguignon,* follow the Coq au Vin recipe, replacing the chicken with 3 pounds stewing beef and adding 2 more carrots: Leave these additional carrots whole and place them on top of the beef mixture just before closing the cooker. Pressure cook for 15 minutes/stovetop cooker or 18 to 20 minutes electric (or nonstandard stovetop) cooker. Slice the whole carrots and mix into the stew before serving.

Filipino Oxtail Stew

Serves 4 to 6

Kare Kare is a traditional Filipino dish. It is made with two pressure cooking steps. In the first, the oxtails are cooked until almost tender. Then they are patted dry, browned in oil, and then pressure cooked again, this time with vegetables. The cook is free to use whatever vegetables are in season, but bok choy, Asian eggplant, and green beans are traditional additions. Serve the stew over steamed rice—Perfect Long-Grain White Rice (page 137) is a good choice.

Note: This recipe can be either halved or doubled provided the liquid fully covers the meat. If halving, use at least 1 cup of liquid (or your cooker's minimum requirement); if doubling, make sure the total volume of the ingredients does not exceed two-thirds of the cooker's capacity.

2 pounds oxtails

3 cups water, or as needed

2 teaspoons salt

3 tablespoons vegetable oil

1 large onion, thinly sliced

2 to 3 garlic cloves

4 ounces shelled peanuts, pureed to a paste in a blender

1 eggplant, coarsely diced, or 2 Asian eggplants, cut into rounds

1 bok choy, leaves separated and trimmed (optional)

½ pound green beans

Perfect Long-Grain White Rice (page 137), for serving (optional)

1. Place the oxtails in the pressure cooker base. Pour in just enough water to cover the meat (or at least the minimum amount required by your cooker to reach pressure). Add the salt.

2. Close and lock the lid of the pressure cooker. Cook at high pressure (see "Get *Hip* About the Pressure," page 13) for 35 minutes/stovetop or 40 to 45 minutes/ electric (or nonstandard stovetop). When the time is up, open the pressure cooker with the Normal Release method (see page 15). The oxtails will not yet be completely tender; this isokay.

3. Using tongs, transfer the oxtails to a plate and pat them dry with paper towels. Pour the broth into a bowl, defat it, and set aside.

4. Heat the pressure cooker base on medium heat, add the oil, and heat briefly. Working in batches if needed, add the oxtails and cook until brown on all sides, about 5 minutes. Using tongs, transfer the oxtails to a plate. Add the onion and garlic to the cooker and sauté until wilted. Return the oxtails to the cooker, pour in enough of the reserved broth to cover (or the minimum amount required by your cooker to reach pressure), and dribble the peanut paste on top of the meat. Lay the green beans, eggplant, and bok choy, if using, on top.

5. Close and lock the lid of the pressure cooker. Cook at high pressure (see "Get *Hip* About the Pressure," page 13) for 5 minutes/all cooker types. When the time is up, open the pressure cooker with the 10-Minute Natural Release method (see page 15).

6. Stir the stew to mix; taste and add more salt if you wish. Serve immediately.

Mexican Pulled Pork

Serves 6 to 8

This flavorful preparation of pork, known colloquially as *carnitas*, can be served in tacos, burritos, tamales, sliders (small bread buns), or lettuce wraps! Accompany it with Black Bean and Corn Salsa Salad (page 99) or whatever side seems appealing at the time.

Note: This recipe can be either halved or doubled provided the liquid fully covers the meat. If halving, use at least 1 cup of liquid (or your cooker's minimum requirement); if doubling, make sure the total volume of the ingredients does not exceed two-thirds of the cooker's capacity.

> 4 pounds boneless pork shoulder roast or leg (fresh, not smoked), cut into 4-inch chunks
> Water, as needed
> 1 bay leaf
> 5 to 6 garlic cloves, in their skins and lightly smashed
> 3 teaspoons ground cumin
> 1 tablespoon fresh marjoram leaves, lightly crushed
> 1 teaspoon crushed red pepper flakes
> 1 tablespoon salt
> 1 teaspoon whole black peppercorns
> 2 tablespoons raw or brown sugar
> Tacos or another wrapper, for serving (optional)
> Black Bean and Corn Salsa Salad (page 99), for serving (optional)

1. Place the meat in the pressure cooker base. Pour in just enough water to cover (or at least the minimum amount required by your cooker to reach pressure). Drop in the bay leaf, garlic, cumin, marjoram, red pepper flakes, salt, peppercorns, and sugar.

2. Close and lock the lid of the pressure cooker. Cook at high pressure (see "Get *Hip* About the Pressure," page 13) for 45 minutes/stovetop or 50 to 60 minutes/electric (or nonstandard stovetop). When the time is up, open the pressure cooker with the Natural Release method (see page 15); this should take 10 to 15 minutes for a stovetop cooker or 20 to 30 minutes for an electric cooker.

3. Using tongs, transfer the meat from the cooker to a rimmed baking sheet. Using two forks, pull each piece into strips. Heat the broiler. Spread out the pulled pork evenly on the baking sheet and broil until it is just beginning to char. Alternatively, fry the pulled pork in small batches in skimmed pork fat or vegetable oil until the edges begin to crisp. Serve, dividing it evenly among wrappers if you wish.

4. Strain and defat the cooking liquid in the pressure cooker base and reserve for another use or, if you wish, return it to the cooker base and heat, uncovered, until reduced to a sauce consistency. Serve with your broiled carnitas.

Variations

BBQ Pulled Pork Sliders

Follow the Mexican Pulled Pork recipe, mixing ½ to 1 cup of your favorite barbecue sauce into the meat on the baking sheet before broiling. To make the sliders, abundantly stuff small dinner rolls or Chinese Steamed Buns (page 159) with the meat so that it's spilling out the sides a bit.

Mexican Shredded Chicken

To make *Carnitas de Pollo,* follow the Mexican Pulled Pork recipe, replacing the pork with 4 whole chicken legs (thighs and drumsticks—the bones will be easy to separate from the cooked meat) and pressure cooking for 15 minutes/stovetop cooker or 18 to 20 minutes electric (or nonstandard stovetop) cooker.

BBQ Pulled Pork Sliders

Cuban Pulled Beef

Serves 6 to 8

Ropa Vieja, meaning "old stuff," is a Cuban dish made with beef, similar to Mexican Pulled Pork, *(carnitas)* but it is pressure cooked twice: once with no seasonings aside from salt and pepper and then again after shredding. It isn't broiled or fried, but is instead pressure cooked again in a *sofrito* of onions, peppers, garlic, and tomato puree. Serve with steamed rice. Good choices are Perfect Long-Grain Rice (page 137) and Cuban Refried Beans (page 104).

Note: This recipe can be either halved or doubled provided the liquid fully covers the meat. If halving, use at least 1 cup of liquid (or your cooker's minimum requirement); if doubling, make sure the total volume of the ingredients does not exceed two-thirds of the cooker's capacity.

2 to 3 pounds flank steak or round steak or chuck steak

2 teaspoons salt

1 teaspoon freshly ground black pepper

1 tablespoon vegetable oil

1 yellow onion, coarsely chopped

1 green bell pepper, stemmed, seeded, and coarsely chopped

1 red bell pepper, stemmed, seeded, and coarsely chopped

2 garlic cloves, chopped

1 cup tomato puree, or as needed

1 cup fresh shelled peas (optional)

Perfect Long-Grain Rice (page 137) or Cuban Refried Beans (page 104), for serving (optional)

1. Place the meat in the pressure cooker base. Pour in just enough water to cover the meat (or at least the minimum amount required by your cooker to reach pressure). Add the salt and black pepper.

2. Close and lock the lid of the pressure cooker. Cook at high pressure (see "Get *Hip* About the Pressure," page 13) for 45 minutes/stovetop or 50 to 60 minutes/electric (or nonstandard stovetop). When the time is up, open the pressure cooker with the 10-Minute Natural Release method (see page 15).

3. Using tongs, transfer the meat from the cooker to a rimmed baking sheet. Using two forks, pull it into strips. Pour ½ cup of the cooking liquid into a measuring cup; pour the rest of the liquid into another container and reserve for another use.

4. Heat the pressure cooker base on medium heat, add the oil, and heat briefly. Stir in the onion, green and red bell peppers, and garlic and sauté until the onion is just starting to soften. Spoon the meat back into the cooker and stir in the tomato puree, the peas if using, and the ½ cup of the cooking liquid (add more cooking liquid as needed if the 1½ cups combined tomato puree and cooking liquid do not equal your cooker's minimum requirement).

5. Close and lock the lid of the pressure cooker. Cook at high pressure (see "Get *Hip* About the Pressure," page 13) for 10 minutes/all cooker types. When the time is up, open the pressure cooker with the Normal Release method (see page 15).

6. Tumble the pulled beef into a large bowl and serve.

Fish and Seafood

Fish in the pressure cooker is a bit of a controversy. While the steam can produce luscious fish, just a few seconds too many in the pressure cooker and the fish can be nearly disintegrated. But this does not mean you should not pressure cook fish!

There are two secrets to making perfectly steamed fish in the pressure cooker: low pressure and a little added protection. The lower temperature at low pressure buys the cook extra time between when the fish is perfect and it is overcooked. Shielding the fish with foil, parchment paper, or veggies further protects this delicate ingredient.

Hip cooks know that fish recipes can play a delicious role in pressure cooker repertoire when prepared with care.

Low pressure. Most seafood dishes are cooked at low pressure to ensure delicate cooking. Should your pressure cooker lack a low pressure setting (sometimes called 1, or the first line of a pressure signal), go ahead and cook at high pressure, but simply cut the recommended low pressure cooking time in half. For example, a recipe that calls for 6 minutes at low pressure requires only 3 minutes at high pressure.

Protect it. Delicate fish needs protection from the super-heated steam in the pressure cooker. This can be done with veggies, parchment paper, or aluminum foil. Make sure any parchment is securely fastened so it does not interfere with the workings of the pressure cooker. The protection also facilitates lifting the fish out of the steamer basket with no risk of it falling apart before it gets to the plate.

Double trouble. Overpacking fish in a steamer basket results in overcooked edges and undercooked centers. To double a steamed fish recipe, use two steamer baskets and stack them on top of each other.

Which Fish?!?

Recipes calling for a "white fish fillet" can be made with cod, flounder, grouper, halibut, orange roughy, red snapper, sole, tilapia, or trout.

The designation of "sustainably fished and farmed" seafood is a moving target, and some species (particularly tuna, salmon, and swordfish) could be endangered in one part of the world but not in another. For the latest information, including a free printable shopping guide, visit the Monterey Bay Aquarium's "Seafood Watch" program (www.seafoodwatch.org).

Steamy Seafood

Shellfish is steamed in the pressure cooker in the same way it is in conventional cooking, but the high temperature manages to get all of the shells open at once instead of a few here or a few there.

Clams in White Wine

Serves 4 to 6

Vongole al vino bianco, or "clams in white wine," can be served as an appetizer, or used to dress freshly boiled spaghetti for the classic Italian dish *Spaghetti alle Vongole* —"spaghetti with clams." When pressure cooked, clams open in the steam and release their briny liquid into the cooking liquid, which can then be concentrated and used as a delicate sauce. This classic preparation can also be made with mussels, steamer clams, razor clams, and cockles. See "Purging Clams" (this page), before beginning.

Note: This recipe can be either halved or doubled provided there is at least 1 cup of liquid in the pressure cooker (or your cooker's minimum liquid requirement) and the total volume of the ingredients does not exceed two-thirds of the cooker's capacity; divide the clams between 2 stacked steamer baskets if doubling.

2 pounds live small clams, purged
1 tablespoon olive oil
3 garlic cloves, crushed
1 cup dry white wine, plus more as needed
1 small bunch flat-leaf parsley, chopped

1. Arrange the clams in the steamer basket and set aside.

2. Heat the pressure cooker base on medium heat, add the oil, and heat briefly. Add the garlic and sauté until it just begins to take on some color. Pour in the wine, adding enough to equal your cooker's

Purging Clams

Clams and other shellfish that dwell in the muddy bottom of the sea may contain a bit of sand or dirt that would not be welcome in a finished dish and so need to be purged. Mussels do not need purging as they grow on rocks or on ropes that are held vertically in the sea.

To purge, place live shellfish in a very large bowl of cold saltwater (make your own using ⅓ cup of salt to a gallon of water). Let them purge for about 30 minutes, drain, and then repeat two or three times until the water is free of sand.

If not using the shellfish right away, place in a bowl, cover loosely with a damp paper towels, and refrigerate to use the next day.

minimum liquid requirement. Insert the steamer basket full of clams.

3. Close and lock the lid of the pressure cooker. Cook at low pressure (see "Get *Hip* About the Pressure," page 13) for 5 minutes/all cooker types. When the time is up, open the pressure cooker with the Normal Release method (see page 15).

4. Invert the cooker cover on your countertop and set the steamer basket on it, shaking the basket as you lift it to allow all the clam liquid to drip down into the cooking liquid. Discard any unopened clams. Cover the steamer basket with aluminum foil and set aside to keep warm. Return the cooker base to medium heat and boil the liquid until reduced by half. Tumble the clams back into the pressure cooker and stir to combine well and warm through.

5. Spoon the clams and some sauce into individual bowls and sprinkle with the parsley.

Stuffed Mussels

Serves 8 to 10 as an appetizer

This recipe makes a lovely appetizer! When serving, be sure to also have a common bowl available for discarding the empty shells. See "Cleaning Mussels" (this page) before beginning.

Note: This recipe can be either halved or doubled provided there is at least 1 cup of liquid in the pressure cooker (or your cooker's minimum liquid requirement) and the total volume of the ingredients does not

Cleaning Mussels

Debeard the mussels right before cooking. To do this, hold the mussel with the round end away from you and pull on the stringy "beard," sliding it along the edge of the shell and pulling outward to remove it. Then clean the shells by scrubbing with a nylon brush or scrubby sponge.

exceed two-thirds of the cooker's capacity; divide the mussels between 2 stacked steamer baskets if doubling.

2 pounds live mussels, debearded and
    scrubbed
⅔ cup bread crumbs
½ cup tomato puree
½ cup grated Pecorino Romano cheese
2 tablespoons olive oil
2 garlic cloves, finely minced
1 bunch flat-leaf parsley, finely
    chopped
1 teaspoon salt
¼ teaspoon
    freshly ground black pepper

1. Add 1 cup of water (or the minimum amount required by your cooker to reach pressure) to the pressure cooker base. Place the mussels in the steamer basket and lower it into the cooker.

2. Close and lock the lid of the pressure cooker. Cook at low pressure (see "Get *Hip* About the Pressure," page 13) for 1 minute/ all cooker types. When the time is up, open the pressure cooker with the Normal Release method (see page 15).

3. Invert the cooker cover on your countertop and set the steamer basket on it, shaking the basket as you lift it to allow all the mussel liquid to drip down into the cooking liquid. Discard any unopened mussels. Reserve the cooking liquid to use as a base for a seafood soup.

4. Preheat the oven to 325°F. Place a rimmed baking sheet on your work surface. Pull the shells of each mussel apart, placing the half that holds the mussel on the baking sheet and discard the empty half.

5. To make the stuffing, place the bread crumbs, tomato puree, cheese, oil, garlic, 2 tablespoons of the parsley, and the salt and pepper in a small bowl and stir together until well combined. Spoon a small amount onto each mussel and lightly tap it into the shell; do not pack. Bake the mussels until the stuffing is golden, 7 to 10 minutes. Sprinkle with the remaining parsley and serve.

Spanish Mussels

Serves 4 to 6 as an appetizer

This dish is not only delicious but also visually stunning. The black shells open to reveal a bright orange mussel in a blue cradle, topped with ruby-red tomatoes. See "Cleaning Mussels" (page 196) before beginning.

Note: This recipe can be either halved or doubled provided there is at least 1 cup of liquid in the pressure cooker (or your cooker's minimum liquid requirement) and the total volume of the ingredients does not exceed two-thirds of the cooker's capacity; divide the mussels between 2 stacked steamer baskets if doubling.

Stuffed Mussels

2 pounds live mussels, debearded and
    scrubbed
1 cup chopped tomatoes, with their juices
Water, as needed
2 tablespoons olive oil
2 garlic cloves, finely minced
½ teaspoon crushed red pepper flakes
1 small bunch flat-leaf parsley, finely
    chopped

1. Place the mussels in the steamer basket and set aside. Place the tomatoes and their juices in a 2-cup measuring cup; add water to equal your cooker's minimum liquid requirement.

2. Heat the pressure cooker base on medium heat, add the oil, and heat briefly. Stir in the garlic and red pepper flakes and sauté until the garlic begins to turn golden. Then, moving quickly, stir in the tomatoes and water. Lower the steamer basket with the mussels into the cooker.

3. Close and lock the lid of the pressure cooker. Cook at low pressure (see "Get *Hip* About the Pressure," page 13) for 1 minute/ all cooker types. When the time is up, open the pressure cooker with the Normal Release method (see page 15).

4. Lift the steamer basket from the cooker and tumble the mussels into a large serving platter or individual appetizer plates; spoon the cooked tomatoes over them. Sprinkle with the parsley and serve.

Swordfish with Lemon and Capers

Serves 2 to 3

Lidia Bastianich bakes this dish in the oven, but the pressure cooker can make this Southern Italian dish even faster.

Note: This recipe can be either halved or doubled provided there is at least 1 cup of liquid in the pressure cooker (or your cooker's minimum liquid requirement) and the total volume of the ingredients does not exceed two-thirds of the cooker's capacity; divide the fish between 2 stacked steamer baskets if doubling.

1 swordfish steak, about the size
    of your steamer basket and
    ¾ inch thick
3 tablespoons olive oil
½ teaspoon sea salt
Pinch freshly ground black pepper
2 teaspoons dried oregano, crushed
1 lemon, half thinly sliced, juice of other
    half squeezed
2 tablespoons capers, drained

1. Add 1 cup of water (or the minimum amount required by your cooker to reach pressure) to the pressure cooker base; set aside.

2. Line the steamer basket with wax paper and dab with about 1 tablespoon of the oil. Place the swordfish on the paper and sprinkle with the salt, pepper, and oregano. Cover the steak with the lemon slices and swirl the remaining 2 tablespoons oil over them. Lower the steamer basket into the pressure cooker.

3. Close and lock the lid of the pressure cooker. Cook at low pressure (see "Get *Hip* About the Pressure," page 13) for 5 minutes/all cooker types. When the time is up, open the pressure cooker with the Normal Release method (see page 15). Check the fish for doneness; it should easily flake when teased with a fork. If necessary, cook at low pressure for 1 more minute.

5. Lift the steamer basket out of the cooker and slide the steak onto a serving plate. Spritz with the lemon juice and serve, cutting a wedge from the steak for each dinner guest.

White Fish Fillets Cradled in Greens

Serves 3

Cradling fish fillets in slices of cabbage or a nest of kale, lettuce, or spinach leaves keeps the fillets intact, and makes a side dish to boot. Choose fish fillets that together will fit in your steamer basket in one layer.

Note: This recipe can be either halved or doubled provided there is at least 1 cup of liquid in the pressure cooker (or your cooker's minimum liquid requirement) and the total volume of the ingredients does not exceed two-thirds of the cooker's capacity; divide the fish between 2 stacked steamer baskets if doubling.

> **8 ounces fresh spinach (baby spinach is nice)**
> **12 ounces white fish fillets (about 3)**
> **1 teaspoon Dijon mustard**
> **1 shallot, finely chopped**

1. Add 1 cup of water (or the minimum amount required by your cooker to reach pressure) to the pressure cooker base; set aside.

2. Line the steamer basket with half of the spinach and arrange the fish fillets on top. Gently coat the top of each fillet with a small dab of mustard, sprinkle with the chopped shallots, and cover with the remaining spinach. Lower the steamer basket into the pressure cooker.

3. Close and lock the lid of the pressure cooker. Cook at low pressure (see "Get *Hip* About the Pressure," page 13) for 5 minutes/all cooker types. When the time is up, open the pressure cooker with the Normal Release method (see page 15).

4. Invert the cooker cover on your countertop and set the steamer basket on it. Using an offset spatula, delicately transfer each fillet and the spinach to a platter. Serve immediately.

Salmon Steaks with Asparagus and Capers

Serves 2 to 3

You may use salmon steaks or fillets with equal success in this recipe; when purchasing, choose pieces that together will fit in your steamer basket in one layer. If using fillets, place them, skin side down, in the basket. Asparagus has such a short season, so if you can't find it fresh, substitute thinly sliced artichokes, green beans, or halved Brussels sprouts for the spears—as I did in the photo below. If you happen to have salt-packed capers, go ahead and use them, but rinse them off and add a squirt of fresh lemon juice to them.

Note: This recipe can be either halved or doubled provided there is at least 1 cup of liquid in the pressure cooker (or your cooker's minimum liquid requirement) and the total volume of the ingredients does not exceed two-thirds of the cooker's capacity; divide the fish between 2 stacked steamer baskets if doubling.

> 2 to 3 salmon steaks or fillets
> Olive oil
> ½ teaspoon salt
> ¼ teaspoon freshly ground black
>   pepper
> 8 ounces thick white (or green)
>   asparagus, woody ends removed
> 2 tablespoons capers, drained

1. Add 1 cup of water (or the minimum amount required by your cooker to reach pressure) to the pressure cooker base; set aside.

2. Cut rectangles of wax paper to match the size of each salmon piece. Lightly oil the paper, top with the salmon, and place in the steamer basket. Sprinkle with the salt and pepper. Lower the basket into the pressure cooker.

3. Slice the asparagus spears in half crosswise and scatter on top of the salmon. Swirl just a bit of oil on top of everything.

4. Close and lock the lid of the pressure cooker. Cook at low pressure (see "Get *Hip* About the Pressure," page 13) for 5 minutes/all cooker types. When the time is up, open the pressure cooker with the Normal Release method (see page 15). Check the fish for doneness (the flesh should readily flake when teased with a fork). If necessary, cook at low pressure for 1 more minute.

5. Invert the cooker cover on your counter and set the steamer basket on it. Arrange the salmon and asparagus on individual plates and sprinkle with the capers; serve.

Salmon Steaks with Asparagus and Capers

White Fish Fillets with Lemon and Herbs

Serves 3

This recipe is great with fresh fish, even better when made with anonymous frozen white fish fillets (defrosted, of course!). Choose fish fillets that together will fit in your steamer basket in one layer.

Note: This recipe can be either halved or doubled provided there is at least 1 cup of liquid in the pressure cooker (or your cooker's minimum liquid requirement) and the total volume of the ingredients does not exceed two-thirds of the cooker's capacity; divide the fish between 2 stacked steamer baskets if doubling.

1 generous bunch fresh thyme
3 lemons, 2 thinly sliced and 1 cut into wedges
12 ounces white fish fillets (about 3)
1 tablespoon olive oil
4 garlic cloves, minced
1 teaspoon salt
1 teaspoon ground white pepper

1. Add 1 cup of water (or the minimum amount required by your cooker to reach pressure) to the pressure cooker base; set aside.

2. Separate 3 or 4 sprigs from the thyme bunch and set aside. Pluck the leaves from the rest of the sprigs, mince them, and set aside.

3. Line the steamer basket with half the lemon slices and lay the fish fillets on top.

Mix the oil and garlic in a cup and then divide evenly among the fillets, gently rubbing it over each. Sprinkle the fillets with the salt and pepper, lay a sprig of thyme on each, and then cover with the remaining lemon slices. Lower the steamer basket into the pressure cooker.

4. Close and lock the lid of the pressure cooker. Cook at low pressure (see "Get *Hip* About the Pressure," page 13) for 5 minutes/all cooker types. When the time is up, open the pressure cooker with the Normal Release method (see page 15).

5. Invert the cooker cover on your countertop and set the steamer basket on it. Using an offset spatula, delicately transfer the fillets to a platter or individual plates. Sprinkle the minced thyme over the fish; serve with the lemon wedges.

Variation

White Fish Fillets with Tomatoes and Olives

Follow the White Fish Fillets with Lemon and Herbs recipe, replacing the lemon slices with thick tomato slices. Use only a few thyme sprigs (for step 3); replace the rest of the thyme with chopped fresh basil leaves. Sprinkle ½ cup chopped pitted black olives and the basil over the cooked fish just before serving.

Stewy Seafood

Boiling fish in the pressure cooker infuses it with the flavor of the other ingredients and also distributes the flavor of the fish through the whole dish.

Coconut Curry Poached White Fish

Serves 4 to 6

Here's an excellent way to use anonymous frozen white fish filets. You can add them frozen without changing the pressure cooking time though the cooker will take a minute or two extra to reach pressure. If you like, serve over steamed rice of your choice—there are many options in the grains chapter, page 133.

Note: This recipe can be either halved or doubled provided there is at least 1 cup of liquid in the pressure cooker (or your cooker's minimum liquid requirement) and the total volume of the ingredients does not exceed two-thirds of the cooker's capacity.

1 tablespoon vegetable oil
1 tablespoon minced garlic
1 tablespoon peeled and minced fresh ginger
½ teaspoon crushed red pepper flakes
2 tablespoons curry powder
3 medium zucchini, sliced into ½-inch-thick rounds
1 cup unsweetened coconut milk
½ cup water
1 pound fresh or frozen white fish fillets, cut into large squares
3 fresh cilantro sprigs, finely chopped

1. Heat the pressure cooker base on medium heat, add the oil, and heat briefly. Stir in the garlic and ginger and sauté for about 30 seconds. Stir in the red pepper flakes, curry powder, and zucchini and mix well. Sauté the zucchini, undisturbed, for 1 minute more. Mix in the coconut milk and water. Place the fish squares in this poaching mixture.

2. Close and lock the lid of the pressure cooker. Cook at low pressure (see "Get *Hip* About the Pressure," page 13) for 1 minutes/all cooker types. When the time is up, open the pressure cooker with the 10-Minute Natural Release method (see page 15).

3. Using a soup ladle, scoop spoonfuls of fish, vegetables, and poaching liquid into individual bowls and sprinkle with the cilantro.

Tomato-Stewed Calamari

Serves 4 to 6

Calamari in umido, or "stewed calamari," is a classic Italian preparation that usually requires nearly an hour's simmering on the stovetop. The pressure cooker can give soft silky calamari in about 10 minutes. It can be served by itself as a rich stew or as a topping for freshly cooked pasta.

Note: This recipe can be either halved or doubled provided there is at least 1 cup of liquid in the pressure cooker (or your cooker's minimum liquid requirement) and the total volume of the ingredients does not exceed two-thirds of the cooker's capacity.

2 tablespoons olive oil (everyday quality)

½ teaspoon crushed red pepper flakes

2 oil-packed anchovies

2 garlic cloves, smashed

1½ pounds calamari, cleaned, with "hats" sliced into rings

½ cup dry white wine

2 cups chopped tomatoes, with their juices

1½ cups water

1 bunch flat-leaf parsley, finely chopped

1 teaspoon salt

½ teaspoon freshly ground black pepper

1 tablespoon good-quality extra-virgin olive oil

1. Heat the pressure cooker base on medium heat, add the everyday olive oil, and heat briefly. Stir in the red pepper flakes, anchovies, and garlic and swish around until the garlic just begins to turn golden and the anchovies fall apart. Stir in the calamari and sauté for 2 to 3 minutes. To deglaze the cooker, pour in the wine and cook, stirring occasionally, until it evaporates almost completely. Add the tomatoes, water, half of the parsley, and the salt and black pepper and mix well.

2. Close and lock the lid of the pressure cooker. Cook at high pressure (see "Get *Hip* About the Pressure," page 13) for 10 minutes/stovetop or 13 to 15 minutes/ electric (or nonstandard stovetop). When the time is up, open the pressure cooker

Cleaning Calamari

To clean calamari, first tug lightly to detach the head from the "hat." Pull carefully, as most of the innards that are attached to the head will come out with it. Hold the hat under running water and gently peel off the skin on the outside; then fill with water to remove anything that might still be stuck in there. Gently tug out the cartilage quill that runs vertically through the hat; discard. Next, place the head on a cutting board, and cut off the tentacles above the eyes— discard them and anything attached. Finally, remove the beak from the tentacles by gently squeezing it out from behind; discard it.

with the Normal Release method (see page 15).

3. Toss in the rest of the parsley, swirl with the extra-virgin olive oil, and serve.

Spanish Stuffed Calamari

Serves 4 to 6

Calamares rellenos de Andalucía is a stunning dish that uses only the "caps" of the calamari. Freeze the tentacles to use later, or dip in a paste of flour and beer and then deep-fry them and use as garnish.

Note: This recipe can be either halved or doubled provided there is at least 1 cup of liquid in the pressure cooker (or your cooker's minimum liquid requirement) and the total volume of the ingredients does not exceed two-thirds of the cooker's capacity.

Filling

¼ cup olive oil

2 large carrots, grated

2 large yellow onions, finely chopped

1 cup plain dried bread crumbs

2 hard-boiled eggs (page 55), crumbled

1 small bunch flat-leaf parsley, finely chopped

1 teaspoon salt

¼ teaspoon freshly ground black pepper

1 large egg, lightly beaten

1 pound calamari, cleaned

Sauce

2 tablespoons olive oil

1 yellow onion, chopped

1 carrot, grated

1 cup chopped tomatoes, with their juices

1 cup salt-free Vegetable Stock (page 49)

Large pinch saffron (or 1 packet saffron powder)

1. To make the filling, heat the pressure cooker base on medium heat, add the oil, and heat briefly. Stir in the carrots and onions and sauté until soft, about 3 minutes. Turn off the heat and mix in the bread crumbs and hard-boiled eggs, half of the parsley, and the salt and pepper. When the mixture has cooled, mix in the beaten egg.

2. Using a small spoon, stuff the calamari caps with the filling and fold and fasten the open end of each with a toothpick.

3. To make the sauce, first clean and dry the pressure cooker base and then heat it on medium heat. Add the oil and heat briefly; then stir in the onion and carrot and sauté until softened. Add the stuffed calamari and pour in the tomatoes and stock.

4. Close and lock the lid of the pressure cooker. Cook at high pressure (see "Get *Hip* About the Pressure," page 13) for 10 minutes/stovetop or 13 to 15 minutes/electric (or nonstandard stovetop). When the time is up, open the pressure cooker with the Normal Release method (see page 15).

5. Return the cooker to medium heat. Delicately mix in the saffron and simmer the stew, uncovered, for 5 minutes.

6. Serve the calamari hot, either whole or cut into slices, with a good drizzle of the sauce and sprinkle with the remaining chopped parsley.

Poached Octopus Salad

Serves 4 to 6

This is a common antipasto in Italy and is especially popular during the summer, when it is served chilled. This recipe also forms the base of an excellent Octopus Carpaccio, for which a recipe follows.

Note: This recipe can be either halved or doubled provided there is at least 1 cup of liquid in the pressure cooker (or your cooker's minimum liquid requirement) and the total volume of the ingredients does not exceed two-thirds of the cooker's capacity.

One 2-pound octopus

4 cups water, plus more as needed

1 whole garlic bulb

2 bay leaves

1 tablespoon whole black peppercorns

1 tablespoon sea salt

4 tablespoons olive oil

4 teaspoons white vinegar

2 garlic cloves, finely minced

1 bunch flat-leaf parsley, finely chopped

1. To clean the octopus, cut the head from the tentacles, slit it in half, and turn it inside out to empty and discard its contents. Slice off the segment with the eyes and discard. Then remove the beak where all of the tentacles meet. Rinse the cleaned octopus under cold running water.

2. Cut off the top of the garlic bulb to expose the tops of all the cloves. Add the 4 cups water, the garlic bulb, bay leaves, peppercorns, and salt to the pressure cooker base and bring to a boil on high heat. Lower in the octopus tentacles, dipping the tips and pulling them out, and then dipping a little further and pulling out (this will curl the tentacles), until you finally drop in the whole lot. Then add the head. If the pieces are not completely covered by water, pour in more until they are.

3. Close and lock the lid of the pressure cooker. Cook at high pressure (see "Get *Hip* About the Pressure," page 13) for 15 minutes/stovetop or 18 to 20 minutes/ electric (or nonstandard stovetop). When the time is up, open the pressure cooker with the 10-Minute Natural Release method (see page 15). Check the octopus for tenderness by seeing if a fork will easily pierce the thickest part of the flesh. If it does not, pressure cook for a few minutes more.

4. Drain the octopus in a strainer set over a bowl; reserve the cooking liquid

Octopus Carpaccio

for another use such as the Risotto with Mixed Seafood (page 145) or the Octopus Carpaccio, below. Slice the octopus into bite-size pieces and add to a clean bowl; discard the garlic bulb, bay leaves, and peppercorns.

5. Place the oil, vinegar, and minced garlic in a small jar, cover tightly, and shake to blend. Pour this dressing over the octopus and stir to mix. If not serving the salad immediately, cover tightly and refrigerate up to 24 hours. Sprinkle with parsley right before serving.

Variation

Octopus Carpaccio

Before beginning, choose a vessel to use as a mold. A cylindrical container like a large can or a tall measuring cup will give you round slices like those in the photo (previous page), but a small loaf pan will work, too. Prepare the Poached Octopus Salad recipe, but omit the oil-vinegar-minced-garlic dressing, and do not slice the octopus in bite-size pieces after cooking as directed in the main recipe. Line your chosen container with plastic wrap, and arrange the cooked octopus in it. Pour in about 1 cup of the strained cooking liquid. Lay a piece of plastic wrap directly on the octopus and place the container in your sink. Press a similar sized container into the one filled with octopus, and fill this second container with weighty items like canned food. Place the whole package in the refrigerator to chill overnight. The next day, unmold the octopus loaf and cut it into thin slices. Arrange the slices on a serving platter with some thin lemon slices; squirt with lemon juice and sprinkle with chopped parsley just before serving.

Mixed Fish Stew

Serves 4 to 6

You can use any seafood or shellfish, or a combination of both, in this recipe; so let your preferences or the options at the market be your guide. Shellfish goes in the steamer basket to make it easier to pull out and distribute into the bowls when serving. Because the feet are short on the steamer basket, the shellfish will be immersed in the stew and not steamed above it. Be sure to purge any clams before cooking (see "Purging Clams," page 195).

Note: This recipe can be either halved or doubled provided there is at least 1 cup of liquid in the pressure cooker (or your cooker's minimum liquid requirement) and the total volume of the ingredients does not exceed two-thirds of the cooker's capacity.

3 tablespoons olive oil
4 garlic cloves, minced
4 oil-packed anchovies
½ cup dry white wine
2 pounds assorted seafood (fish fillets, shellfish, shrimp, etc.)
2 cups Seafood Stock (page 50), or water
1 cup chopped tomatoes, with their juices
1 cup tomato puree
2 teaspoons salt
1 bunch flat-leaf parsley, finely chopped

1. Heat the pressure cooker base on medium heat, add the oil, and heat briefly. Stir in the garlic and anchovies and sauté until the garlic is golden and the anchovies have dissolved. To deglaze the cooker, pour in the wine and cook, stirring occasionally, until it has evaporated almost completely. Next, add all of the fish, but not any shellfish, to the pressure cooker and pour in the stock, chopped tomatoes, and tomato puree. Sprinkle with the salt. Arrange any shellfish in the steamer basket and lower it into the pressure cooker.

2. Close and lock the lid of the pressure cooker. Cook at low pressure (see "Get *Hip* About the Pressure" (page 13) for 5 minutes/all cooker types. When the time is up, open the pressure cooker with the Normal Release method (see page 15).

3. If you included shellfish, invert the cooker cover on your countertop and set the steamer basket on it, shaking the basket as you lift it to allow any lingering liquid to drip down into the stew; discard any unopened shellfish. Ladle the stew into individual bowls, and then top with the shellfish if using. Sprinkle with the chopped parsley and serve.

One-Pot Meals

In pressure cooking, "one-pot meal" escapes the common meaning of mixing everything *together* and serving it as *one* dish. Instead, with the steamer basket and foil packets called into service, several recipes can be stacked and cooked at once, but in just one pot. The tall, slender 6- or 8-quart cooker is perfectly suited for this vertical approach, with plenty of space for meat, veggies, and even dessert!

I first heard about this method from Lorna Sass's blog (pressurecookingwithlornasass.word press.com) where she included a recipe from her book, *Pressure Perfect*. Lorna made a complete meal by boiling potatoes in the base of the cooker, steaming a meat loaf on top, and adding a foil packet of carrots. Lorna's recipe inspired my quest to find all of the possible combinations of boiling, steaming, and packeting that would produce a complete meal made in just one pot.

Stack It. A second steamer basket or a trivet (see page 10) is helpful when cooking two or more recipes together in the pressure cooker. You can use the first steamer basket to either steam or lift a heat-proof bowl above the base and the second to add another layer. And once you've placed food in one steamer basket, you can place a second basket on top and then put a foil packet in it; this prevents the packet from covering the food below and blocking the steam that should be cooking it. Before you begin, ensure everything fits by stacking all of the pressure cooker accessories in the pressure cooker. In a pinch, if you need to elevate something, aluminum foil can come to the rescue: crush it into three golf-ball size pieces and space them out evenly to hold up a heat-proof dish or foil packet.

Match it. Generally, the best way to select foods or recipes that will be good one-pot combinations is to look for things with matching pressure cooking times. In this chapter are a number of examples that combine recipes from elsewhere in the book, and also some versatile veggie combos to be cooked in foil that work with many other recipes. Plus there are Pressure Cooking Timetables at the end of the book that give the basic cooking times for many ingredients.

Root it. Most root vegetables, such as potatoes and beets, are very forgiving about their cooking times and can be cooked for almost twice the recommended cooking time with little downside—especially if the goal is a puree or mash.

Size it. Whether vegetables are whole, sliced, or diced affects their cooking time. For example, a whole medium potato needs 10 minutes to pressure cook, but a diced one only 5 minutes. So choose the size of the vegetable according to the cooking time of the accompanying ingredients (like legumes or meats).

Foil it. Wrapping or covering delicate ingredients with aluminum foil extends the time they can remain in the pressure cooker. They will cook much more slowly than if they were boiled or steamed directly in the super-heated steam.

Phase it in. In the case where sizing and foiling won't work—as for pasta—then pressure cooking of the longer-cooking ingredients can be interrupted and the more delicate ingredient can be added, and then either pressure cooked more or finished in an uncovered boil.

Patience. Making a one-pot meal with multiple elements fills the pressure cooker quite a bit. This means that it could take a little longer than usual for the cooker to reach pressure, and then for the pressure to come down after cooking.

Favorite One-Pot Meal Combinations

Here are a few of my favorite ways to combine dishes in order to get dinner on the table for the whole family with the bare minimum amount of work and cleanup that would be involved if all of these things were cooked separately.

BBQ Pork Ribs with Spinach-Bean Salad and Black Fudge and Walnut Brownie

Serves 4 to 6

This one-pot meal is an excuse for cooking some especially delicious items that one would ordinarily assume take too much time to make for an everyday dinner. This meal is a treat from beginning to end! Read both recipes through before starting so you can see how to coordinate the finishing steps.

Have at the ready ingredients and instructions for:

Black Fudge and Walnut Brownies
(page 234)
BBQ Pork Ribs with Spinach-Bean Salad
(page 165)

1. Complete steps 1 and 2 of the brownie recipe (batter mixed and in the prepared heat-proof bowl), but do not put water or the steamer basket in the pressure cooker base and do not lower the batter-filled bowl into the cooker—just set the bowl aside.

2. Complete steps 1 and 2 of the ribs and salad recipe (ribs prepped and in the steamer basket, beans in the cooker base).

3. Lower the steamer basket with the ribs into the pressure cooker (do not cover the ribs) and then balance the bowl with the brownie batter on top of the ribs, using a foil sling (see page 11), and do not cover the bowl;.

4. Close and lock the lid of the pressure cooker. Cook at high pressure (see "Get *Hip* About the Pressure," page 13) for 20 minutes/stovetop or 21 to 25 minutes/electric (or nonstandard stovetop). When the time is up, open the pressure cooker with the 10-Minute Natural Release method (see page 15).

5. Lift the bowl with the brownie out of the pressure cooker and transfer to a wire rack. Lift the basket of ribs out of the cooker and then complete the ribs and salad as directed in the recipe. Meanwhile, cool the brownie and remove from the bowl as directed in its recipe.

6. Serve the ribs and bean salad as the main course, followed by the brownies for dessert.

Drunken Cowboy Chili, and
Chunky Maple Syrup Cornbread

Drunken Cowboy Chili, Chunky Maple Syrup Cornbread, and Corn Salsa

Serves 4 to 6

Chili and cornbread are a classic combination—and now you can have both ready quickly and at the same time! Read all three recipes through before starting so you can see how to coordinate the steps.

Have at the ready ingredients and instructions for:

Corn Salsa Packet (page 215)
Chunky Maple Syrup Cornbread (page 157)
Drunken Cowboy Chili (page 105)

1. Prepare the Corn Salsa Packet so it's ready to pressure cook and set aside. Complete steps 1 and 2 of the cornbread recipe (bowl prepped, dry ingredients mixed, wet ingredients mixed), but do not put water or the steamer basket in the pressure cooker base.

2. Complete steps 1 and 2 of the chili recipe (mixed and sautéed in the cooker base, ready to pressure cook). Lower the steamer basket into the cooker on top of the chili. Complete step 3 of the cornbread recipe, placing the batter-filled bowl in the basket, using a foil sling, (see page 11), and do not cover the bowl. Then rest the salsa packet across the rim of the bowl, making sure the packet doesn't completely cover the bowl.

3. Close and lock the lid of the pressure cooker. Cook at high pressure (see "Get *Hip* About the Pressure," page 13) for 25 minutes/stovetop or 28 to 30 minutes/electric (or nonstandard stovetop). When the time is up, open the pressure cooker with the Natural Release method (see page 15); this should take 10 to 15 minutes for a stovetop cooker, 20 to 30 minutes for an electric cooker.

4. Remove the packet from the cooker and tumble the salsa into a small bowl; sprinkle with the chopped fresh cilantro and add a squeeze of lime. Turn on the broiler. Lift the bowl of cornbread out of the cooker and turn it out onto a heat-proof plate; slide under the broiler for a few minutes until the top is crunchy and golden. Lift the steamer basket out of the cooker. Serve the chili in individual bowls with a wedge of cornbread, passing the salsa at the table.

Hip Foil Packet Recipes

For an easy side-dish component to a one-pot meal, simply gather a few ingredients with seasonings and enclose in a little foil packet; then place in the cooker along with the other components of the meal. Here are a few versatile examples. These recipes are not particularly faster made this way than by a conventional cooking method, but they are designed to be cooked in conjunction with recipes made in the cooker base or steamer basket—they take advantage of the existing heat and steam and save you from dirtying a second pot. Usually a foil packet is placed above a steamer basket or heat-proof bowl, but if you are making a more liquid, stewy-type recipe, the packets can be floated on top like a little boat.

Any of the following packets can be included in a one-pot meal for which the pressure cooking time of the other recipes is 10 to 20 minutes.

To fashion a packet, place the ingredients in the middle of a rectangle of aluminum foil. Bring the 2 long edges of the foil up and fold over; then roll each end closed toward the middle.

Spicy Green Bean Packet

Place 2 cups green beans, 1 teaspoon dried oregano, ½ teaspoon crushed red pepper flakes, and ½ teaspoon garlic powder on a foil rectangle; drizzle with 1 tablespoon olive oil and seal.

Curried Cauliflower Packet

Place 2 cups cauliflower florets sliced into 1-inch pieces on a foil rectangle. Sprinkle with 1 teaspoon curry powder, ½ teaspoon garlic powder, and ¼ teaspoon ground ginger. Top with 2 tablespoons butter and seal. When finished cooking, mix well.

Three Veg Packet

Place 1 cup broccoli florets, 1 diced carrot, and ½ cup shelled fresh or frozen peas on a foil rectangle. Drizzle with olive oil and seal.

Peas and Mint Packet

Place 2 cups shelled fresh or frozen peas, 1 tablespoon dried mint leaves, and 1 tablespoon butter on a foil rectangle and seal.

Balsamic Bells Packet

Cut 3 large bell peppers into ¼-inch slivers, place on a foil rectangle and seal. When finished pressure cooking, dress with 1 finely chopped garlic clove mixed with 1 tablespoon balsamic vinegar.

Corn Salsa Packet

Coarsely chop 1 green bell pepper and finely chop half a yellow onion. Place 1 cup fresh or frozen corn kernels, the peppers, onions, and ½ teaspoon ground cumin on a foil rectangle and seal. When finished pressure cooking, sprinkle with chopped fresh cilantro and add a squeeze of lime juice.

Maple-Glazed Carrot Packet

Cut 3 thick carrots in half crosswise; then cut the bottom sections lengthwise in half and the top sections lengthwise into quarters. Place the carrots on a foil rectangle; drizzle with 1 tablespoon maple syrup and seal.

Coq au Vin with Mashed Potatoes and Bread Pudding with Brandy Sauce

Serves 4 to 6

Who would have thought that a French and a British classic could be pressure cooked together? The rustic bread pudding recalls coq au vin's farmhouse origins. The potatoes are a nice, tangy break from these two very rich dishes. They use my favorite substitution of yogurt in place of sour cream, for the same tang but without the fat. Read both recipes through before starting so you can see how far in advance to start the chicken and how to coordinate the steps.

Have at the ready ingredients and instructions for:

Bread Pudding with Brandy Sauce
(page 239)
Coq au Vin (page 185)

Also have ready:

2 potatoes, cut into chunks
½ cup plain fat-free yogurt
½ teaspoon salt
¼ teaspoon ground white pepper

1. Complete steps 2, 3, and 4 of the bread pudding recipe (fruit soaked, pudding mixed, soaked, and in the prepared bowl), but do not lower the pudding-filled bowl into the cooker—just set the bowl aside. Place the potatoes in the steamer basket and set aside.

2. Prepare the coq au vin recipe through step 7, up to the point where it is ready to pressure cook. Before closing the cooker, insert the potato-filled steamer basket and rest it on the chicken. Then lower the pudding-filled bowl into the cooker and rest it on the potatoes, using a foil sling (see page 11); and do not cover the bowl;.

3. Close and lock the lid of the pressure cooker. Cook at high pressure (see "Get *Hip* About the Pressure," page 13) for 10 minutes/stovetop or 12 to 14 minutes/electric (or nonstandard stovetop). When the time is up, open the pressure cooker with the 10-Minute Natural Release method (see page 15).

4. Lift the bowl with the pudding out of the cooker, transfer to a wire rack, and cover with aluminum foil. Then lift the steamer basket out of the cooker; tumble the potatoes into a large bowl and mash them with the yogurt, salt, and pepper.

5. Complete the coq au vin as directed in its recipe. Serve with the potatoes. When ready to serve the dessert, make the brandy sauce as directed in the bread pudding recipe, pour over the pudding, and serve the pudding cut into wedges.

Meat Loaf Ring with Cauliflower-Potato Mash and Maple-Glazed Carrots

Serves 4 to 6

An updated version of the Lorna Sass classic. And super-easy to do as "one-pot" as the carrot and meat loaf recipes are completely prepared before you put them in the cooker—no moving back and forth between recipes here.

Have at the ready ingredients and instructions for:

Maple-Glazed Carrot Packet (page 215)
Meat Loaf Ring, without the gravy
(page 168)

Also have ready:

2 pounds russet potatoes, peeled and
halved
2 cups white cauliflower florets
1 tablespoon unsalted butter
1 teaspoon salt

1. Prepare the Maple-Glazed Carrot Packet so it's ready to pressure cook and set aside. Mix and shape the Meat Loaf Ring as directed in its recipe, placing it in the steamer basket, and set aside.

2. Add 1 cup of water (or the minimum required by your cooker to reach pressure), the potatoes, and cauliflower to the pressure cooker base. Lower the steamer basket with the meat loaf into the cooker and place on top of the vegetables. Then rest the carrots packet across the top of the steamer basket.

3. Close and lock the lid of the pressure cooker. Cook at high pressure (see "Get *Hip* About the Pressure," page 13) for 8 minutes/stovetop or 9 to 10 minutes/ electric (or nonstandard stovetop). When the time is up, open the pressure cooker with the 10-Minute Natural Release method (see page 15).

4. Remove the packet from the cooker and tumble the carrots into a small bowl. Set the upturned lid of the cooker on your countertop. Lift the basket of meat loaf out of the cooker and place it on the lid; cover the basket with aluminum foil. Mash the cooking liquid, potatoes, and cauliflower together in the base of the cooker (if you added more than 1 cup water, pour off the excess so you get a nice thick mash); then mash in the butter and salt.

5. Cut the meat loaf ring into wedges and serve each with a mound of the mashed vegetables, passing the carrots at the table.

Farro Risotto with Radicchio and Gorgonzola, Potato-Stuffed Onions, and Peas and Mint

Serves 4 to 6

This combination is a contrast in colors. The brown farro with the red radicchio, white onions, and green peas. If you've been having a hard time "eating the rainbow," this combination shows how many vegetables can be stuffed in a single meal. Read all three recipes through before starting so you can see how to coordinate the steps.

Have at the ready ingredients and instructions for:

Peas and Mint Packet (page 215)
Potato-Stuffed Onions (page 89)
Farro Risotto with Radicchio and
    Gorgonzola (page 146)

1. Prepare the Peas and Mint Packet so it is ready to pressure cook as directed in its recipe; set aside. Complete steps 2 and 3 of the stuffed onions recipe (so they are stuffed and in the steamer basket); set aside.

2. Complete steps 1 and 2 of the risotto recipe (chopped, mixed, and sautéed, ready to pressure cook). Lower the onion-filled steamer basket into the pressure cooker on top of the risotto. Then rest the peas packet across the top of the steamer basket.

3. Close and lock the lid of the pressure cooker. Cook at high pressure for 9 minutes/all cooker types. When the time is up, open the pressure cooker with the Normal Release method (see page 15).

4. Remove the packet from the cooker and tumble the peas into a small bowl; mix well. Set the upturned lid of the cooker on your counter. Lift the basket out of the cooker and set it on the lid. Add the red radicchio and the Gorgonzola to the risotto in the cooker base, mixing until the radicchio has wilted and the cheese melted. Using tongs, place an onion on each dinner plate, spoon some risotto and peas onto each, and serve.

Will the Dessert Taste Like the Other Ingredients?

In one-pot meals where the dessert remains uncovered during pressure cooking, you might be concerned the dessert will end up tasting like the meat cooking below. No fear! The steam from the cooking liquid of the recipe that is boiling below will have about 1/1600 the flavor concentration of that liquid. In other words, the steam in the pressure cooker is *nearly* tasteless and your brownie won't taste like curry!

Florentine Veal Roast, Bain-Marie Buttered Barley and Herbs, and Spicy Green Beans

Serves 4 to 6

With this meal we combine the north of Italy (Florence, namesake of the meat) with the south (spicy beans). Read all three recipes through before starting so you can see how to coordinate the steps.

Have at the ready ingredients and instructions for:

Spicy Green Bean Packet (page 215)
Bain-Marie Buttered Barley and Herbs (page 151)
Florentine Veal or Beef Roast (page 183)

Also have ready:

2 large all-purpose potatoes

1. Prepare the Spicy Green Beans Packet so it's ready to pressure cook and set aside. Mix the Bain-Marie Barley and place it in a heat-proof bowl as directed in its recipe; set aside.

2. Complete steps 1 and 2 of the veal roast (so it is in the cooker base with the sauce). Pierce the potatoes with a fork and then place on opposite sides of the roast so they will support the steamer basket in a fairly level position. Place the basket on the potatoes and lower the barley-filled bowl into it, using a foil sling (see page 11); do not cover the bowl. Then rest the beans packet on the rim of the bowl, making sure the packet doesn't completely cover the bowl.

3. Close and lock the lid of the pressure cooker. Cook at high pressure (see "Get *Hip* About the Pressure," page 13) for 45 minutes/stovetop or 50 to 60 minutes/electric (or nonstandard stovetop). When the time is up, open the pressure cooker with the Natural Release method (see page 15); this should take 10 to 15 minutes for a stovetop cooker; 20 to 30 minutes for an electric cooker.

4. Remove the packet from the cooker and tumble the beans into a small bowl. Lift the barley-filled bowl out of the cooker, and lift out the steamer basket. Transfer the potatoes to a small bowl and break them up with a fork. Lift the roast from the cooker and slice. Ladle about half the sauce into a serving boat or pitcher (reserve the rest of the sauce for another use). Serve immediately, ladling the sauce over the meat and potatoes.

Mexican Shredded Chicken, Bain-Marie Brown Rice with Salted Peanuts, and Corn Salsa

Serves 4 to 6

The recipes in this meal can be used together to stuff a burrito, taco, or quesadilla! Read all three recipes through before starting so you can see how to coordinate the steps.

Have at the ready ingredients and instructions for:

Corn Salsa Packet (page 215)
Bain-Marie Brown Rice with Salted
    Peanuts (page 151)
Mexican Shredded Chicken (page 190)

1. Prepare the Corn Salsa Packet so it's ready to pressure cook and set aside. Mix the brown rice and place it in a heat-proof bowl as directed in its recipe; set aside.

2. Place the water and other ingredients for the shredded chicken in the pressure cooker base as directed in its recipe. Place the steamer basket in the cooker on top of the chicken and lower the rice-filled bowl into it, using a foil sling (see page 11); do not cover the bowl. Then rest the salsa packet across the rim of the bowl, making sure the packet doesn't completely cover the bowl.

3. Close and lock the lid of the pressure cooker. Cook at high pressure (see "Get *Hip* About the Pressure," page 13) for 15 minutes/stovetop or 18 to 20 minutes/ electric (or nonstandard stovetop). When the time is up, open the pressure cooker with the Natural Release method (see page 15); this should take 10 to 15 minutes for a stovetop cooker or 20 to 30 minutes for an electric cooker.

4. Remove the packet from the cooker and tumble the salsa into a small bowl. Lift the rice-filled bowl out of the cooker. Cover both bowls and keep warm. Lift the basket out of the cooker. Shred and finish the chicken as described in its recipe. Serve the chicken accompanied by the rice, with a side of salsa.

Cannellini in Tomato-Sage Sauce with Veal-Stuffed Artichoke Halves

Serves 4 to 6

This one-pot meal is Italian through-and-through. It uses the "phase it in" method because artichokes don't need as much time to cook as the cannellini beans in tomato sauce. Read both recipes through before starting so you can see how to coordinate the steps.

Have at the ready ingredients and instructions for:

Cannellini in Tomato-Sage Sauce (page 102)
Veal-Stuffed Artichokes Halves (page 86)

1. Complete steps 1, 2, and 3 of the cannellini recipe but pressure cook for only 10 minutes (for all cooker types) and then open the cooker with the 10-Minute Natural Release method (see page 15).

2. While the beans are cooking, complete steps 2 and 3 of the artichoke recipe (stuffing mixed, artichokes stuffed). After opening the cooker, place the steamer basket in it, on top of the beans. Delicately lower the artichokes, stuffed side up, into the basket.

3. Close and lock the lid of the pressure cooker. Cook at high pressure (see "Get *Hip* About the Pressure," page 13) for 8 minutes/stovetop or 10 minutes/electric (or nonstandard stovetop). When the time is up, open the pressure cooker with the Normal Release method (see page 15).

4. Lift the steamer basket out of the cooker. One at a time, delicately slide a large serving spoon under each artichoke and then, using tongs, transfer it to a serving platter; cover and keep warm. Then complete the beans as directed in their recipe. Sprinkle the artichokes with the reserved parsley. Serve the artichokes accompanied by the beans.

Zone it!

The pressure cooker has three heat zones and they can be used to the cook's advantage to pressure cook a complete meal.

The hottest zone is at the base of the cooker—where the bottom of the pot touches the heat source—usually this is where the longest-cooking ingredient, or recipe, is boiled.

The second heat zone is right above the liquid—in a steamer basket or heat-proof bowl, where an ingredient or recipe steams above the liquid in the base.

The last heat zone is at the top, near the lid—created with the help of a little aluminum foil. This is the spot for delicate ingredients with shorter cooking times that have been wrapped in foil to protect them and slow their pressure cooking time.

Taking advantage of these different heat zones allows for several items with different cooking times to be pressure cooked *together*.

Desserts

The pressure cooker can produce silky-smooth custards, crack-free cheesecakes, and other delicious, easy desserts. Even though its heat is not dry, like that of an oven, the pressure cooker's steamy heat can cook a wide variety of cakes, cupcakes, and even puddings. You'll learn how to make all of these desserts, along with some updated pressure cooker classics such as fruit compote (with a little surprise) and apple sauce.

Making desserts in the pressure cooker not only saves time and energy; making sweets in the pressure cooker keeps your oven off, house cool, and desserts coming!

223

Get *Hip* About Desserts Under Pressure

Uncover-up. With the exception of custards, desserts are pressure cooked *uncovered* to achieve fluffy and moist results. Plus, direct contact with the super-heated steam inside the pressure cooker will speed up cooking. Just be careful when opening the cooker that liquid condensed on the lid does not drip on your perfectly pressure cooked dessert.

Stay the course. Do not fluctuate pressure or let your pressure cooker go into over-pressure or lose pressure while cooking the custards, or they will form bubbles and overcook.

Time it to size. The smaller the dessert forms, the shorter time they will take to cook and vice-versa. A cake or large custard could need 20 to 25 minutes at high pressure to fully cook to the center, but a ramekin or teacup only 5 minutes with the *same* batter. But size isn't the only thing that affects cooking time. Aluminum and stainless steel containers will cook their contents a little faster than ceramic, silicone, or Pyrex. So be aware that the timing of a particular recipe may need to be adjusted according to the size and material of your heat-proof bowl or ramekins.

No more than half full for fruits. Fruit that steams in a heat-proof bowl does not foam much. However, fruit cooked directly in the pressure cooker base will expand and foam a lot, so when cooking this way, never fill the pressure cooker more than half full with fruit, liquid, and other ingredients. Some pressure cookers have a little mark with "½" written next to it. If not, eyeball it.

Watch the height: Make sure any containers such as ramekins or bowls and the fruit that fills them don't interfere with the workings of the cooker or the lid—don't fill above the max.

Pyramid style. If the steamer basket won't accommodate all of the ramekins, make a second level by offsetting a second layer on the edges of the layer below, like a pyramid.

Fresh and Dried Fruits

Fruit can easily be made into, or play a major role in, dessert. Fresh fruit can become so tender that it's easily broken with a spoon. Dried fruits plump to their original shape under pressure. It's really amazing to see what was a shriveled raisin or flat cranberry looking plump and round when it comes out of the pressure cooker!

Peach and Vanilla Compote

Serves 4 to 6

Serve this warm, fresh out of the cooker, or chilled. This compote makes an excellent topping for the Yogurt Cake (without the glaze) (page 235) and is delicious on its own or simply topped with a dollop of fresh whipped cream.

Note: This recipe can be either halved or doubled provided there is at least 1 cup of liquid in the pressure cooker (or your cooker's minimum liquid requirement) and the total volume of the ingredients does not exceed half the cooker's capacity.

    1 vanilla bean
    1 cup sugar
    1 cup water
    4 or 5 ripe fresh peaches or nectarines,
       pitted and sliced into wedges
    Fresh whipped cream, for serving
       (optional)

1. Halve the vanilla bean lengthwise and scrape the seeds into the pressure cooker base. Add the bean pod as well. Add the sugar and water; heat on medium heat, delicately stirring the contents until the sugar has completely dissolved. Add the peaches and their juice and stir to coat evenly.

2. Close and lock the lid of the pressure cooker. Cook at high pressure (see "Get *Hip* About the Pressure," page 13) for 1 minute/ all cooker types. When the time is up, open the pressure cooker with the 10-Minute Natural Release method (see page 15).

3. Fish out and discard the vanilla bean pod. Spoon the compote into individual bowls and serve, or allow to cool before serving.

Pink Apple-Cranberry Compote

Serves 4 to 6

The skin stays on the apples here to help them keep their shape and stop them from turning to mush as they cook.

Note: This recipe can be either halved or doubled provided there is at least 1 cup of liquid in the pressure cooker (or your cooker's minimum liquid requirement) and the total volume of the ingredients does not exceed half the cooker's capacity.

1 lemon
½ cup dried cranberries
½ cup sugar
One 1-inch fresh ginger, peeled
1 teaspoon olive oil
1 cup water
1 pound apples, cored, and coarsely chopped

1. Grate the zest from the lemon and add to the pressure cooker base. Squeeze the lemon juice through a sieve into the cooker. Add the cranberries, sugar, ginger, oil, and water. Heat the cooker base on medium heat, delicately stirring the contents until the sugar is completely dissolved. Add the apples and stir to coat evenly.

2. Close and lock the lid of the pressure cooker. Cook at high pressure (see "Get *Hip* About the Pressure," page 13) for 2 minutes/all cooker types. When the time is up, open the pressure cooker using the Slow Normal Release method (see page 15).

3. Spoon the compote into individual bowls and serve warm.

Variation

Pink Apple-Cranberry Sauce

Follow the Pink Apple-Cranberry Compote recipe but open the cooker using the 10-Minute Natural Release method (see page 15). Then puree the contents of the cooker with an immersion blender, making the apple peels disappear into the mixture.

Dried Apricot Compote on Ricotta Cheese

Serves 4 to 6

This is a great way to plump up tired, shriveled, dried apricots. Serve piled on a small mound of ricotta, as in this recipe, or towered onto a cracker with a round of goat cheese. Use a really good-quality cheese—it is dessert and you'll appreciate it! Serve warm in the winter and chilled in the summer, and whatever temperature you prefer anytime in between.

Note: This recipe can be either halved or doubled provided there is at least 1 cup of liquid in the pressure cooker (or your cooker's minimum liquid requirement) and the total volume of the ingredients does not exceed half the cooker's capacity.

1 cup dried apricots
½ cup golden raisins
1 cup orange juice
1 cup water
1 lemon
1 cinnamon stick
½ teaspoon whole black peppercorns
½ teaspoon whole cloves
1 pound fresh ricotta cheese
2 teaspoons pine nuts

1. Add the apricots, raisins, orange juice, and water to the pressure cooker base. Grate the zest from the lemon into the cooker, and then squeeze the juice and strain it into the cooker. Place the cinnamon, peppercorns, and cloves in a tea ball (or wrap and tie them in cheesecloth) and put into the cooker. Swish everything around to mix well.

2. Close and lock the lid of the pressure cooker. Cook at high pressure (see "Get *Hip* About the Pressure," page 13) for 5 minutes/all cooker types. When the time is up, open the pressure cooker using the 10-Minute Natural Release method (see page 15).

3. Remove the spice-filled tea ball from the cooker. Divide the ricotta among individual dessert plates or bowls, shaping it into mounds with an indentation in the middle. Pour the fruit compote on top and sprinkle with the pine nuts just before serving (if you wish, decorate with the cinnamon sticks from the tea ball).

Dried Apricot Compote on Ricotta Cheese

Balsamic Syrup-Poached Figs

Serves 4 to 6

You can use fresh figs of any color for this dessert. They can be ripe, but in truth, this is a great use for figs that are still a little *too* firm.

Note: This recipe can be either halved or doubled provided there is at least 1 cup of liquid in the pressure cooker (or your cooker's minimum liquid requirement) and the total volume of the ingredients does not exceed half the cooker's capacity.

> 5 tablespoons balsamic vinegar
> ½ cup water
> 1 cup sugar
> 1 pound small fresh figs, halved vertically
> One 4-ounce cylinder fresh goat cheese, sliced into ¼-inch-thick rounds
> 1 fresh mint sprig

1. Add the vinegar, water, and sugar to the pressure cooker base, and heat on medium heat, stirring delicately, until the sugar has completely dissolved. Tumble the figs into the pressure cooker and stir to coat evenly.

2. Close and lock the lid of the pressure cooker. Cook at high pressure (see "Get *Hip* About the Pressure," page 13) for 2 minutes/all cooker types. When the time is up, open the pressure cooker using the Normal Release method (see page 15).

3. Position a goat cheese round (or rounds, if the figs are large or the cheese is small) on each dessert plate. Using two

spoons, delicately lift the figs from the pressure cooker and position them on the cheese rounds.

4. Return the uncovered pressure cooker to high heat and simmer the vinegar mixture until reduced by about half and slightly syrupy. Meanwhile, pluck the leaves from the mint sprig. Drizzle the syrup over each serving of figs and cheese, garnish with the mint leaves, and serve.

Amaretti-Stuffed Apples

Serves 4 to 6

When testing this recipe, some apples held their shape, while others practically disintegrated. When I went back to the veggie mart to inquire, I discovered that some apple varieties had been in cold storage from *last* year. Visually the older apples were as shiny and colorful as the freshly picked (or shipped) ones. This distinction is not important when making applesauce—where puree is the goal anyway. But if the goal is for the apples to hold their shape, it can only be met with *truly* fresh apples. To distinguish fresh apples from stored, look carefully at their stems: Brown, shriveled dry stems indicate an apple that has been stored in a controlled environment for as much as a year. Stems with a green tip signify a truly fresh apple.

You can make this recipe with pears, peaches, or apricots instead of apples without changing the pressure cooking time. And if you like, use gingersnaps instead of the amaretti cookies. If you wish to make your own lemon marmalade, follow the Blood Orange Marmalade recipe on page 262.

Note: This recipe can be either halved or doubled provided there is at least 1 cup of liquid in the pressure cooker (or your cooker's minimum liquid requirement).

4 to 6 very small apples, preferably Granny Smith
4 to 6 tablespoons lemon marmalade, or your favorite preserves
1¼ cups crumbled amaretti cookies
½ cup crushed walnuts
3 teaspoons turbinado (raw) sugar
4 tablespoons cold unsalted butter, chopped
Vanilla ice cream, for serving

1. Add 2 cups of water to the pressure cooker base and set aside.

2. Slice the apples in half lengthwise and then use a melon baller to scoop out the core from each half. Leave the stem on—it looks pretty. Paint the cut surface of each with a little of the marmalade to keep it from oxidizing.

3. Add 1 cup of the cookie crumbs, the walnuts, and sugar to a small bowl and mix in the butter until well combined. Spoon the mixture onto each apple half, filling the cavity and covering the top. Arrange the apples in the steamer basket. If you run out of room, you can either make a second row, offset on the first pyramid-style, or hold the extras to cook as a second batch. Lower the steamer basket into the pressure cooker.

4. Close and lock the lid of the pressure cooker. Cook at high pressure (see "Get *Hip* About the Pressure," page 13) for 5 minutes/all cooker types. When the time

is up, open the pressure cooker using the Normal Release method (see page 15).

5. Using two spoons, delicately lift the apples from the pressure cooker and position 2 halves on each dessert plate. Serve with a dollop of vanilla ice cream and a sprinkling of the remaining cookie crumbs.

Chai-Spiced Apricot Crisp

Serves 4 to 6

The crystallized ginger, cinnamon, and white pepper make this crisp a little "hot" and spicy! If making for a sensitive eater, omit the ginger and pepper. This recipe permits some freedom with the choice of spices, other good additions and variations include nutmeg, cloves, star anise, vanilla bean or extract, almond extract, lemon zest, orange zest, and mulling-spice blends.

You can make this recipe with apples, pears, peaches, nectarines, or plums instead of apricots without changing the pressure cooking time.

Note: This recipe can be either halved or doubled provided there are 2 cups of water in the pressure cooker (or your cooker's minimum liquid requirement).

5 tablespoons cold unsalted butter
2 pounds fresh apricots, pitted and diced
½ cup finely ground bread crumbs
½ cup turbinado (raw) sugar
½ cup plain whole-milk yogurt
1 tablespoon chopped crystallized ginger

⅛ teaspoon ground cardamom
¼ teaspoon ground cinnamon
Pinch ground white pepper
6 tablespoons granulated sugar
Vanilla ice cream, for serving

1. Add 2 cups of water to the pressure cooker base; insert the steamer basket and set aside.

2. Chop 3 tablespoons of the butter and place in a 4-cup heat-proof bowl; add the apricots, half the bread crumbs, the turbinado sugar, yogurt, ginger, cardamom, cinnamon, and pepper; mix well. Using a foil sling (see page 11), lower the bowl into the pressure cooker; do not cover the bowl.

3. Close and lock the lid of the pressure cooker. Cook at high pressure (see "Get *Hip* About the Pressure," page 13) for 10 minutes/stovetop or 11 to 15 minutes/electric (or nonstandard stovetop). When the time is up, open the pressure cooker using the Normal Release method (see page 15).

4. Meanwhile, chop the remaining 2 tablespoons butter. Turn on the broiler.

5. When the cooker is open, lift the heat-proof bowl out of the cooker. Moving quickly, sprinkle the granulated sugar and remaining ¼ cup bread crumbs over the apricot mixture, then scatter the chopped butter over the top. Place the heat-proof bowl under the broiler until the top of the crisp is caramelized and turns golden brown, about 5 minutes. Serve warm in small bowls with a scoop of vanilla ice cream.

Cakes

The pressure cooker gives an unexpected bonus to cake baking. The process is much faster than usual because there is no need to preheat the oven and the results are absolutely moist, not soggy!

There are two things to be vigilant about when pressure cooking cakes: If you've baked conventionally, you may already know that working with baking powder or soda is a race to quickly mix them with the liquid ingredients and pour the mix into the dry ingredients before all of their bubbles fizz—but with the pressure cooker you also need to have the cooker, steamer basket, and any needed accessories at the ready as well. The second is to remember that condensation forms inside the lid during pressure cooking; while this usually isn't a problem, of course you don't want dribbles of wet condensation to fall onto a cake as you remove the lid. To prevent this, confidently turn and lift the lid, then offset it from the cooker and tilt it so as to direct the condensation away from the dessert.

Upside-Down Polenta and Almond Cake with Caramelized Lemon Slices

Serves 6 to 8

This is my adaptation of the Northern Italian dessert *Amor di Polenta,* which means "love of polenta" and is a simple pound cake–type loaf that is dusted with powdered sugar. I could not help combining this beautiful yellow cake with lemons to enhance the flavor and give it a pretty topping. You can use common corn flour or the finely ground polenta flour known as *fioretto,* or for a more rustic texture, the coarsely ground polenta flour known as *bramata.* And, yes, being raised in Northern Italy as a child means that I *love* polenta too!

Note: This recipe can be halved provided there are 2 cups of water in the pressure cooker base. It cannot be doubled; to make more, make two batches.

2 tablespoons turbinado (raw) sugar
2 lemons
1 cup corn flour
2/3 cup all-purpose flour
1/2 cup finely chopped almonds
2 large eggs
1 cup granulated sugar

½ cup olive oil, plus more for the bowl

1 teaspoon pure vanilla extract

2 teaspoons baking powder

½ teaspoon baking soda

1. Add 2 cups of water to the pressure cooker base; insert the steamer basket and set aside.

2. Line a wide, shallow 4-cup heat-proof bowl with wax paper, and lightly oil the paper. Scatter the turbinado sugar evenly across the bottom of the bowl. Using a mandoline, very thinly slice one of the lemons and then arrange the slices decoratively over the sugar. Set the bowl aside.

3. Whisk together the corn flour, all-purpose flour, and almonds in a small bowl. Grate the zest from the remaining lemon, then squeeze its juice into a cup. Using a fork, mix together the eggs and granulated sugar in another small bowl until you no longer feel the grit of the sugar. Mix in the oil, lemon zest and juice, and vanilla. Stir in the flour mixture, mixing until well combined. Then sprinkle on the baking powder and baking soda through a strainer and incorporate with a quick, thorough

Upside-Down Polenta
and Almond Cake with
Caramelized Lemon Slices

stir. Pour the batter into the prepared bowl. Using a foil sling (see page 11), lower the bowl into the pressure cooker; do not cover the bowl.

4. Close and lock the lid of the pressure cooker. Cook at high pressure (see "Get *Hip* About the Pressure," page 13) for 20 minutes/stovetop or 24 to 25 minutes/electric (or nonstandard stovetop). When the time is up, open the pressure cooker using the 10-Minute Natural Release method (see page 15).

5. Lift the bowl out of the pressure cooker and check the cake for doneness (see "Check Cakes for Doneness," page 236); transfer the bowl to a wire rack to rest for 5 minutes. Then invert a serving plate over the bowl and flip the bowl and plate over together. Lift the bowl off the cake; carefully peel off the paper. Serve the cake warm or at room temperature, cut into wedges.

Chinese Sponge Cake

Serves 6 to 8

This cake is conventionally steamed without pressure, but when you steam it in the pressure cooker, it will be ready in half the usual time. Generally served and consumed plain, it is the perfect base for any of the fruit compotes given earlier in this chapter!

Note: This recipe can be halved provided there are 2 cups of water in the pressure cooker base. It cannot be doubled; to make more, make two batches.

Oil, for the bowl
2 large eggs
1 large egg white
½ cup sugar
1 teaspoon vanilla extract
½ cup cake flour, sifted
1 teaspoon baking powder

1. Add 2 cups of water to the pressure cooker base; insert the steamer basket and set aside. Line a wide, shallow 4-cup heat-proof bowl with wax paper, and lightly oil the paper.

2. In a small bowl, using the whisk attachment of an immersion blender or electric mixer, whip together the eggs, egg white, and sugar. Add the vanilla and whisk until foamy and pale yellow, about 5 minutes. In a separate bowl, whisk together the flour and baking powder until well blended. Then sprinkle the flour mixture through a sifter or fine-mesh strainer over the egg mixture, delicately folding together until combined. Pour the batter into the prepared bowl. Using a foil sling (see page 11), lower the bowl into the pressure cooker; do not cover the bowl.

3. Close and lock the lid of the pressure cooker. Cook at high pressure (see "Get *Hip* About the Pressure," page 13) for 15 minutes/stovetop or 18 to 20 minutes/electric (or nonstandard stovetop). When the time is up, open the pressure cooker using the Normal Release method (see page 15).

4. Lift the bowl out of the pressure cooker and check the cake for doneness (see "Check Cakes for Doneness," page 236); transfer the bowl to a wire rack to rest for 5 minutes. Then invert a serving plate over the bowl and flip the bowl and plate over together. Lift the bowl off the cake; carefully peel off the paper. Serve the cake warm or at room temperature, cut into wedges or diamonds.

Black Fudge and Walnut Brownies

Serves 6 to 8

I can never keep chocolate around the house long enough to cook with it— everyone in my family has a sweet radar to detect the "cooking" chocolate stashed in the deep recesses of my baking drawer.

However, the little box of cocoa powder gets shoved to the side and remains undisturbed and at the ready for action like this recipe.

Eschewing butter for extra-virgin olive oil results in an extremely dark—almost black—fudge brownie, one that gets a little extra oomph from the olive oil too—so use the good stuff. Enjoy these brownies warm or cooled!

Note: This recipe can be halved provided there are 2 cups of water in the pressure cooker base. It cannot be doubled; to make more, make two batches.

Black Fudge and
Walnut Brownies

2 large eggs

1 cup granulated sugar

½ cup extra-virgin olive oil, plus more
for the bowl

⅔ cups unsweetened cocoa powder

¼ teaspoon salt

½ teaspoon vanilla extract

½ cup all-purpose flour

½ cup chopped walnuts

Powdered sugar, for dusting

1. Add 2 cups of water to the pressure cooker base; insert the steamer basket and set aside. Line a wide, shallow 4-cup heat-proof bowl with wax paper, and lightly oil the paper.

2. In a small bowl whisk together the eggs and granulated sugar until you no longer feel the grit of the sugar. Then whisk in the oil, cocoa powder, salt, and vanilla until well combined. Sprinkle the flour over the mixture a little at a time, mixing in with a fork. When well combined stir in the walnuts. Pour the batter into the prepared bowl. Using a foil sling (see page 11), lower the bowl into the pressure cooker; do not cover the bowl.

3. Close and lock the lid of the pressure cooker. Cook at high pressure (see "Get *Hip* About the Pressure," page 13) for 20 minutes/stovetop or 24 to 25 minutes/electric (or nonstandard stovetop). When the time is up, open the pressure cooker using the 10-Minute Natural Release method (see page 15).

4. Lift the bowl out of the pressure cooker and transfer to a wire rack. The brownie will be somewhat flexible and almost jiggly and pudding-like—but a toothpick inserted in the middle should come out clean; the brownie will firm up as it cools. If the toothpick does not come out clean, pressure cook the brownie for a few more minutes (see "Check Cakes

for Doneness," page 236). Let the brownie stand for 5 minutes, then lift it out of the bowl by gently tugging on the wax paper. Invert the brownie on a plate and peel up and remove the wax paper. Serve warm or let cool further.

5. When ready to serve, dust the brownie with powdered sugar and cut into wedges or squares.

Yogurt Cake with Yogurt Glaze

Serves 6 to 8

This is my absolutely favorite cake. It's not particularly fussy and there is no need for any special equipment beyond a fork and one mixing bowl. You can skip the glaze if you like, but I think it really dresses up the cake.

Note: This recipe can be halved provided there are 2 cups of water in the pressure cooker base. It cannot be doubled; to make more, make two batches.

⅔ cup plain whole-milk yogurt

1 large egg

3 tablespoons olive oil, plus more for the
bowl

1 teaspoon almond extract or vanilla
extract

½ cup granulated sugar

1 cup all-purpose flour, plus more for
dusting the bowl

1½ teaspoons baking powder

½ teaspoon baking soda

Glaze

¼ cup sliced almonds

1 tablespoon yogurt (any type, plain or flavored), more as needed

1 cup powdered sugar, or more as needed

1. Add 2 cups of water to the pressure cooker base; insert the steamer basket and set aside. Lightly oil a wide, shallow 4-cup heat-proof bowl and dust it with flour, knocking out the excess.

2. Put the yogurt, egg, oil and almond extract in a small bowl and mix with a fork. Add the sugar and mix until well combined. Using a fine-mesh strainer, sprinkle the flour, followed by the baking powder and baking soda, over the yogurt mixture and mix together until well blended. Pour the batter into the prepared bowl. Using a foil sling (see page 11), lower the bowl into the pressure cooker; do not cover the bowl.

3. Close and lock the lid of the pressure cooker. Cook at high pressure (see "Get *Hip* About the Pressure," page 13) for 15 minutes/stovetop or 18 to 20 minutes/ electric (or nonstandard stovetop). When the time is up, open the pressure cooker using the 10-Minute Natural Release method (see page 15).

4. Lift the bowl out of the pressure cooker and check the cake for doneness (see "Check Cakes for Doneness," this page); transfer the bowl to a wire rack to cool.

5. Meanwhile make the glaze: Toast the almonds in a dry skillet over low heat and set aside to cool. Put the yogurt in a 2-cup measuring cup and gradually add the powdered sugar, mixing well with a fork. At first the glaze will seem pasty, but then the sugar will begin to melt and the texture will change, so keep stirring even though at first it may seem like it's not ever going to become liquid. The goal is to achieve a thick creamlike texture. If the glaze seems too wet, add a little more sugar, if too dry add just a touch more yogurt.

6. Invert a serving plate over the bowl and flip the bowl and plate over together. Lift the bowl off the cake. Pour the glaze on the center of the cake and let it run down the sides. Sprinkle the almonds over the glaze. Serve the cake cut into wedges, either immediately, while the glaze is sticky, or refrigerate first to harden the glaze.

Check Cakes for Doneness

Test pressure cooked cakes for doneness by inserting a toothpick in the center of the cake and removing it—it should come out clean. If it doesn't, return the cake to the cooker and pressure cook for a few more minutes. Don't forget, the cooking time will vary a bit depending on the shape and material of the baking dish, so testing a recipe before serving to guests is smart.

Blackberry Swirl Cheesecake

Serves 4 to 6

Although it's been said that the best way to pressure cook a cheesecake is in a springform pan, I have found otherwise. I've tried several styles and qualities of springform pans and they have always left my cake with a soggy bottom unless wrapped and rewrapped carefully and completely. I say, why bother? Although you don't need to use a straight-sided baking dish the bottom does need to be flat; this ensures that once removed from the dish, the crumb crust and filling will sit flat on the serving plate.

Note: This recipe can be halved provided there are 2 cups of water in the pressure cooker base. It cannot be doubled; to make more, make two batches.

> 1 cup fresh blackberries
> ½ cup powdered sugar
> 4 tablespoons unsalted butter
> 1 cup crushed graham crackers
> 14 ounces cream cheese (one 8-ounce and two 3-ounce packages)
> ½ cup granulated sugar
> Freshly grated zest from 1 lemon
> Freshly grated zest from half an orange
> 2 large eggs

1. Add 2 cups of water to the pressure cooker base; insert the steamer basket and set aside. Cut a piece of wax paper to fit the bottom of a wide, flat-bottomed 4-cup baking dish; also cut a strip sized to fit the sides of the dish. Line the dish with the paper.

2. Puree the blackberries and powdered sugar in a blender and set aside.

3. Melt the butter in a medium saucepan on medium heat. Remove the pan from the heat and mix in the crushed crackers. Scoop the mixture into the prepared baking dish and, using the back of your hand, push it into a flat, thin, even layer that covers the bottom of the dish, and, if there is enough, partway up the sides. Put the dish in the refrigerator to chill, uncovered, while you prepare the filling.

4. In a medium bowl, using an electric mixer on medium speed, mix together the cream cheese, granulated sugar, and lemon and orange zests. Add the eggs and mix into a smooth batter, about 5 minutes.

5. Remove the dish with the crust from the refrigerator. Slowly pour the batter over the crust, spreading level. To add the blackberry swirl, pour the puree into a squirt bottle (or food storage bag with one corner clipped off) and with it draw a spiral from the center out on top of the batter. Then use a toothpick or skewer to drag radiating lines from the center to the edge of the dish. Using a foil sling (see page 11), lower the dish into the pressure cooker; do not cover the dish.

6. Close and lock the lid of the pressure cooker. Cook at high pressure (see "Get *Hip* About the Pressure," page 13) for 20 minutes/all cooker types. When the time is up, open the pressure cooker using the 10-Minute Natural Release method (see page 15).

7. Lift the dish out of the pressure cooker and check the cake for doneness (see "Check Cakes for Doneness," page 236); transfer the dish to a wire rack.

Let the cake cool, uncovered, for about 30 minutes. Then cover the dish with plastic wrap and refrigerate until ready to serve, for at least 4 hours.

8. Work quickly and delicately to unmold the chilled cake: Invert a plate over the dish and flip the dish and plate over together. Lift the dish off the cake and then peel off the wax paper circle on the base and the strip on the sides. Then invert a serving plate on the cake and gently flip all three components over together; lift off the top plate. Serve the cake cold, cut into wedges.

Variations

Classic New York Cheesecake

Follow the Blackberry Swirl Cheesecake recipe, omitting the blackberries. Use only 1 tablespoon powdered sugar, mixing it with ½ cup sour cream to make a topping; spread the topping over the cake just before serving.

Chopped Chocolate Cheesecake

Follow the Blackberry Swirl Cheesecake recipe, omitting the blackberries and powdered sugar. Instead, chop three or four 1-ounce squares semisweet baking chocolate (or an equivalent chocolate bar) and stir into the batter before pouring onto the crust.

Bread Puddings

The classic, perfectly cooked, fluffy bread pudding is oven-baked, uncovered, in a bain-marie (in a pan half-submerged in water), and so we will use an equivalent process in the pressure cooker—with equally excellent results. You can use all sorts of bread, from a French baguette to packaged sandwich loaf; the key to making the bread fully absorb the custard mixture is that it must be one or two days old or lightly dried in the oven—it should have a consistency that is slightly softer than dry toast.

Bread Pudding with Brandy Sauce

Serves 4 to 6

The sauce has a very fancy taste that belies the peasant ingenuity that first turned dry, leftover bread into a dessert! If you don't want to add the liquor, you can get a similarly exciting sauce by replacing it with a teaspoon of almond extract. However you decide to make the sauce, be sure to smother the pudding with it!

Note: This recipe can be halved provided there are 2 cups of water in the pressure cooker base. It cannot be doubled; to make more, make two batches.

¾ cup chopped mixed dried fruit
16 ounces stale or oven-dried bread (about three-quarters of a French baguette or 8 to 10 sandwich slices), cut into ½-inch pieces
2 large eggs
1 cup granulated sugar
2 cups milk (any type)
1 tablespoon freshly grated lemon, orange, or mandarin orange zest
½ teaspoon ground cinnamon
¼ teaspoon freshly grated nutmeg
1 tablespoon unsalted butter, chopped, plus more as needed
1 tablespoon turbinado (raw) sugar

Brandy Sauce
2 tablespoons unsalted butter
2 tablespoons all-purpose flour
1 cup milk (any type)
3 tablespoons granulated sugar
3 tablespoons brandy or rum

1. Add 2 cups of water to the pressure cooker base; insert the steamer basket and set aside.

2. Place the dried fruits in a small heat-proof bowl and cover with boiling water. Set aside to soak for 10 minutes; then drain. Meanwhile, liberally butter a 4- to 5-cup heat-proof bowl and set it aside.

3. In a large bowl, whisk together the eggs and granulated sugar until the sugar has dissolved and the mixture is pale yellow. Whisk in the milk, citrus zest, cinnamon, and nutmeg and combine well. Stir in the bread and dried fruit and let stand for about 20 minutes, stirring again about every 5 minutes to ensure that all the bread is thoroughly soaked and the fruit coated.

4. Tumble the bread mixture into the prepared bowl, scraping any liquid remaining in the mixing bowl over the top. Dot with the butter and sprinkle with the turbinado sugar. Using a foil sling (see page 11), lower the bowl into the pressure cooker; do not cover the bowl.

5. Close and lock the lid of the pressure cooker. Cook at high pressure (see "Get *Hip* About the Pressure," page 13) for 10 minutes/stovetop or 13 to 15 minutes/electric (or nonstandard stovetop). When the time is up, open the pressure cooker using the 10-Minute Natural Release method (see page 15).

6. Lift the bowl out of the cooker and transfer to a wire rack; quickly cover it with aluminum foil and set aside.

Bread Pudding with Brandy Sauce

7. To make the brandy sauce, melt the butter in a small saucepan on medium heat. Whisk in the flour and let cook until the flour begins to turn golden, and then whisk in the milk and granulated sugar. Simmer for about 5 minutes, whisking constantly, until thickened. Remove the pan from the heat and whisk in the brandy.

8. Pour the sauce over the pudding, and serve right from the bowl, making sure there is a good dousing of sauce on each portion.

Variation

Pear-and-Ginger Bread Pudding

Follow the Bread Pudding with Brandy Sauce recipe, replacing the mixed dried fruits with 2 cored and diced fresh pears (no need to soak them) and the citrus zest with 1 tablespoon finely chopped crystallized ginger. Omit the brandy sauce or serve it, as you prefer.

Bread and Butter Pudding

Serves 4 to 6

If you are able to find white Muscat raisins, use them! They have an especially sweet, musky flavor that makes this classic dessert extra-special.

Note: This recipe can be halved provided there are 2 cups of water in the pressure

cooker base. It cannot be doubled; to make more, make two batches.

½ cup white Muscat raisins or golden raisins, or a mix of both
4 tablespoons unsalted butter, plus more as needed, at room temperature
16 ounces stale or oven-dried bread, sliced (about three-quarters of a French baguette or 8 to 10 sandwich slices)
2 large eggs
½ cup granulated sugar
1 cup milk (any type)
½ cup heavy cream
1 teaspoon vanilla extract
Freshly grated zest from half a lemon
¼ teaspoon freshly grated nutmeg
¼ teaspoon ground cinnamon
1 tablespoon rum (optional)
2 tablespoons butter
2 tablespoons turbinado (raw) sugar
Sweetened whipped cream, for serving

1. Add 2 cups of water to the pressure cooker base; insert the steamer basket and set aside.

2. Place the raisins in a small heat-proof bowl and cover with boiling water. Set aside to soak for 10 minutes; then drain. Meanwhile, liberally butter a 4- to 5-cup heat-proof bowl and set it aside. Butter the bread slices on one side and then stack them and cut into approximately 1-inch pieces; set aside.

3. In a large bowl, whisk together the eggs and granulated sugar until the sugar is dissolved and the mixture is pale yellow. Whisk in the milk, cream, and vanilla and combine well. Whisk in the lemon zest, nutmeg, cinnamon, and rum if using. Stir in the bread and raisins and let stand for about 20 minutes, stirring again about every 5 minutes to ensure that all the bread is thoroughly soaked and the raisins coated.

4. Tumble the bread mixture into the prepared bowl, scraping any liquid remaining in the mixing bowl over the top. Using a foil sling (see page 11), lower the bowl into the pressure cooker; do not cover the bowl.

5. Close and lock the lid of the pressure cooker. Cook at high pressure (see "Get *Hip* About the Pressure," page 13) for 10 minutes/stovetop or 13 to 15 minutes/ electric (or nonstandard stovetop). When the time is up, open the pressure cooker using the 10-Minute Natural Release method (see page 15).

6. Lift the bowl out of the cooker and transfer to a wire rack. Turn on the broiler. Quickly spread 2 tablespoons of butter over the top of the pudding and dust with the turbinado sugar. Slide the pudding under the broiler until golden, about 5 minutes.

7. Serve the pudding from the bowl, cut into wedges, and place a dollop of whipped cream on each serving.

Variations

Nutella Bread Pudding

Follow the Bread and Butter Pudding recipe, but instead of buttering the bread, spread Nutella on the slices. Proceed with the rest of the recipe as directed (the egg mixture will get dark and chocolaty; this is okay).

Marmalade Bread Pudding

Follow the Bread and Butter Pudding recipe, slathering each buttered slice with a layer of marmalade before cutting into pieces and soaking; then proceed as directed.

Flans, Pots, and Crèmes

This family of recipes is called custards because each contains milk or cream, eggs, and sugar—but in varying proportions that result in different degrees of creaminess. Recipes with more egg whites will be a little stiffer than the recipes with more milk fat, which will lean toward creamy.

These custards are traditionally oven-baked in bain-marie—in ramekins half-submerged in a "bath" of water. This usually involves negotiating large pans of boiling water in and out of the oven. In the pressure cooker, the same ingredients and ramekins are simply set in a basket above the boiling water and steamed, with no worries that the bath will evaporate and need topping up and making the whole procedure not only faster but also easier.

Three-Ingredient Honey Flans

Yields six 4-ounce custards

I developed this recipe for my in-store pressure cooker demonstrations. I wanted a flan that is as delicious fresh out of the pressure cooker as it is chilled. It also had to be not at all fussy to make, with just three ingredients for the custard, plus a crushed cookie topping. The honey serves as both a flavor *and* sweetener, eliminating the need for sugar and the conventional step for infusing milk with spice of some sort. Use a dark, flavorful honey to get the most bang of flavor. My favorite: chestnut honey, but any dark-colored, full-flavored honey will do.

Note: This recipe can be either halved or doubled, provided there are 2 cups of water in the pressure cooker base. If doubling, stack the ramekins pyramid-style or cook in two batches.

2 large eggs
⅓ cup dark honey
1 cup whole milk
8 amaretti cookies or gingersnaps, finely crushed, for sprinkling

1. Add 2 cups of water to the pressure cooker base; insert the steamer basket and set aside.

2. Break one of the eggs into a 4-cup measuring cup; separate the other egg, adding the yolk to the measuring cup and reserving the white for another use. Add the honey to the eggs and whisk together until well combined, then whisk in the milk. Pour the mixture through a fine-mesh strainer into six 4-ounce ramekins; cover each tightly with aluminum foil. Arrange the ramekins in the steamer basket, making sure they are level.

3. Close and lock the lid of the pressure cooker. Cook at high pressure (see "Get

Hip About the Pressure," page 13) for 5 minutes/all cooker types. When the time is up, open the pressure cooker using the 10-Minute Natural Release method (see page 15).

4. Check the flan for doneness (see "Check Custards for Doneness," page 246). Lift the ramekins out of the cooker. Remove the foil and sprinkle crushed cookies over each flan and serve warm. Or if you prefer to serve them chilled, hold off on the crushed cookies. Instead, let the flans cool for about 30 minutes, then cover with plastic wrap and refrigerate. Add the crushed cookies just before serving.

Variation

Maple Syrup Flans

Follow the Three-Ingredient Honey Flans recipe, replacing the honey with maple syrup and the cookies with crumbled pecan toffee (or toasted pecans and brown sugar).

Hazelnut Chocolate Pots de Crème

Yields six 4-ounce custards

Turning Nutella—a hazelnut-chocolate spread—into a flan is a little classier than serving your guests a jar and a spoon (even though this is probably how they eat it at home) or slathering on a slice of bread as we do because it's Italy's "peanut

Choose a Sweet Size

All of the flan and custard recipes may be made in six 4-ounce ramekins or four 6-ounce ramekins. For a change of pace, cook them in teeny-tiny espresso cups. You should be able to make 10 petite servings from these same recipes—yielding a small decadence perfect to serve after a rich pressure cooked meal. Cut the pressure cooking time in half for these small cups.

butter." Since for the pots de crème I dilute the "Nutella-ness" a bit with the milk and cream, I put a little bit back with the extra cocoa powder. You get the same Nutella flavor, but in a silky smooth flan.

Note: This recipe can be either halved or doubled provided there are 2 cups of water in the pressure cooker base. If doubling, stack the ramekins pyramid-style or cook in two batches.

1 cup whole milk
1 cup heavy cream
1½ cups Nutella (one 13-ounce jar)
2 tablespoons unsweetened cocoa powder
6 large egg yolks
3 tablespoons sugar
¼ cup chopped hazelnuts, for sprinkling

1. Add 2 cups of water to the pressure cooker base; insert the steamer basket and set aside.

Hazelnut Chocolate
Pots de Crème

2. Add the milk, cream, Nutella, and cocoa powder to a small, heavy-bottomed saucepan. Warm over low heat, stirring occasionally, until the Nutella dissolves and the mixture is blended, about 5 minutes. Turn off the heat and let cool, 20 to 30 minutes.

3. In a 4-cup measuring cup, whisk together the egg yolks and sugar until the sugar has dissolved. Add the milk mixture, whisking just enough to combine; do not whip. Pour the mixture through a fine-mesh strainer into six 4-ounce ramekins; cover each tightly with aluminum foil. Arrange in the steamer basket, making sure they are level.

4. Close and lock the lid of the pressure cooker. Cook at high pressure (see "Get *Hip* About the Pressure," page 13) for 5 minutes/all cooker types. When the time is up, open the pressure cooker using the 10-Minute Natural Release method (see page 15).

5. Check the custard for doneness (see "Check Custards for Doneness," this page). Lift all the ramekins out of the cooker, remove the foil, and set aside to cool for 30 to 45 minutes. Cover the custards tightly with plastic wrap and refrigerate until chilled. Sprinkle with the chopped hazelnuts just before serving.

Check Custards for Doneness

To see if your custard or flan is cooked enough, lift one ramekin from the cooker; remove the foil and jiggle the custard a bit. It should be nearly solid, not liquid; it will continue to cook while cooling and solidify further when chilled. If you are unsure, you can insert a toothpick in the middle of the custard; if it comes out clean it means the custard is ready. If the toothpick does not come out clean, return the ramekin to the cooker and pressure cook for 2 minutes more.

Vanilla Pots de Crème

Yields six 4-ounce custards

These little custards serve as a blank yet tasty canvas for whatever fruit may be in season. Slice or chop the fruit decoratively according to its type. For example mandarins can be thinly sliced crosswise, berries can be added whole, and peaches can be chopped.

Note: This recipe can be either halved or doubled provided there are 2 cups of water in the pressure cooker base. If doubling, stack the ramekins pyramid-style or cook in two batches.

> 6 large egg yolks
> ⅔ cup sugar
> 1 cup whole milk
> 1 cup heavy cream
> 1 teaspoon vanilla extract
> Seasonal fruit, for serving

1. Add 2 cups of water to the pressure cooker base; insert the steamer basket and set aside.

2. In a large bowl, whisk together the

egg yolks and sugar until the sugar has dissolved. Add the milk, cream, and vanilla, whisking just enough to combine; do not whip. Pour the mixture through a fine-mesh strainer into six 4-ounce ramekins; cover each tightly with aluminum foil. Arrange in the steamer basket, making sure they are level.

3. Close and lock the lid of the pressure cooker. Cook at high pressure (see "Get *Hip* About the Pressure," page 13) for 5 minutes/all cooker types. When the time is up, open the pressure cooker using the 10-Minute Natural Release method (see page 15).

4. Check the custard for doneness (see "Check Custards for Doneness," page 246). Lift all the ramekins out of the cooker; remove the foil. Serve the pots de crème warm, topped with seasonal fruit. Or if you prefer to serve them chilled, let them cool for 30 to 45 minutes, then cover tightly with plastic wrap and refrigerate until chilled. Add the fruit when serving.

Variations

Coffee Cream Puddings

Follow the Vanilla Pots de Crème recipe, replacing the milk with brewed American coffee (or 1 espresso shot diluted with milk to equal 1 cup), the vanilla extract with almond extract, and the fruit with sweetened whipped cream. Dust the whipped cream with cocoa powder.

Sacher Torte Pots de Crème

A pudding inspired by the original Sacher Torte from Vienna, Austria. Follow the Vanilla Pots de Crème recipe, omitting the seasonal fruit and adding 6 tablespoons unsweetened cocoa powder with the milk and cream. Also add 6 teaspoons apricot preserves, placing 1 teaspoonful in each ramekin before pouring in the custard mixture. Dust each pot de crème with cocoa powder before serving.

Crème Brûlée

Yields six 4-ounce custards

This is one of the most entertaining custards to eat because of the simplicity of its contrasting sensations. The custard is creamy and cold while the caramelized sugar topping is hard as glass and still a little bit warm. You tap on the "glass" with the back of your spoon until it cracks and then plunge the spoon down into the crème, getting a little bit of both in each spoonful.

> 6 Vanilla Pots de Crème (page 246), Coffee Cream Puddings, or Sacher Torte Pots de Crème, chilled (this page)
> 6 tablespoons turbinado raw sugar or granulated sugar

1. When ready to serve the dessert, turn on the broiler or have ready a kitchen blowtorch. If using the broiler, arrange the ramekins of custard on a baking sheet. Sprinkle the sugar evenly over the top of each ramekin, tapping the ramekin until the sugar settles in an even layer.

2. Place under the broiler or heat the tops with the blowtorch until the sugar has melted into a smooth layer and has caramelized, about 3 minutes; when removed from the heat, the tops will harden.

Preserves and Juicing

Jams and marmalades rely upon sugar, time, and the heat of cooking to break down fruit and coax it to release its precious juice. The pressure cooker accomplishes both of these tasks in a flash. Strawberries burst open to release their juices after just a minute under pressure and tough citrus peels only need to boil *minutes* under pressure to turn them from tough leathery strips to silky ribbons. This "flash" cooking for berries and quick softening for citrus peels not only saves time but also locks in their color and flavor.

Halve, mandoline, and whirl. The most time-consuming part of making preserves is cutting the fruits to the required size. In pressure cooking, most fruits need only be halved to remove their pits and then the pressure cooker will do the rest. For marmalades, a mandoline cuts citrus quickly and finely. For a more refined result, simply whirl everything with an immersion blender *after* pressure cooking!

No more than half, plus a tad of oil. Fruit is notoriously foamy—and the foam can squirt super-heated sugar right out the pressure cooker valve! So *never* exceed the half-full mark of the pressure cooker, and *always* add a teaspoon or so of olive oil to reduce foaming.

Delay the mash. While conventional jam recipes may recommend mashing the fruit at the *beginning* of the process, in pressure cooking, it's best to do this *after*. This ensures that there are no small pieces to clog the valves *and* that the crushed fruit does not rest on the bottom of the cooker and scorch.

Organic-ise. Many of the jam recipes include the skin or zest of a fruit. When this is the case, I prefer to go with organic (or backyard grown) fruit to ensure the best flavor and least amount of chemicals. A neighborhood tree is the best source of very fresh, ripe local produce—offer a jar or two of preserves in exchange for harvesting your neighbor's neglected fruit tree!

Sugar power?!? When making desserts and jams directly in the pressure cooker base, sugar can count as a liquid, too! Before pressure cooking make sure sugar is completely dissolved—you'll know you're there when you no longer feel the "grit" of the sugar at the base of the cooker while stirring.

Sweeten it down. I prefer my jams to taste very fruity, not sugary, so most of my recipes use less sugar than is traditional, and call for "low or no-sugar" pectin, which is specially formulated to firm up jam that is made without much sugar or with a sugar substitute. You can adjust the sugar of any of these recipes to taste; just use more or less as you prefer. When adding very little sugar, to ensure that the preserves will still jell, be sure to use low or no-sugar pectin. Refer to the pectin package to see how much you need for the quantity of fruit you are using.

Cooking Times

In this chapter, cooking times are the same regardless of which type cooker you are using—standard and nonstandard stovetop models and electric ones all take the same time to produce jams and conserves. Most of the recipes use the Natural Release method (see page 14), and the longer time an electric pressure cooker needs for this release extends the cooking enough to compensate for the fact that the cooker used a lower temperature and pressure than a standard stovetop model.

Most of the jam recipes in this chapter cannot be halved because the fruit's juice and the liquid from the sugar need to be enough for the cooker to reach pressure. However, the small pressure pan that comes in a pressure cooker set (usually 3 liters or less) needs *less* liquid to reach pressure and is ideal for making a half recipe, so if you have one of these smaller pans, go ahead. The same cooking times and rules apply—do not fill the pressure pan more than halfway.

Sterilize for Storage

To sterilize jars and lids for jam storage, cover them in cold water and bring to a rolling boil; then boil for 15 minutes. Alternatively, run them through the dishwasher at the highest setting.

Pour hot jam into a hot jar freshly pulled out of the water with tongs or a sterilized jar lifter, or just removed from the dishwasher and handled with a clean kitchen towel.

The recipes in this section are designed as "refrigerator" jams that should be kept chilled; to make your pressure cooked jams shelf stable, follow the processing directions given with any conventional jam recipe or with the canning equipment.

Pulpy Stone Fruits

Jams are the perfect antidote for what to do with slightly over-ripe or not particularly nice-looking fruits—the ones that can be rescued from the back of the refrigerator or had at a bargain price as seconds at local orchards.

Plum and Ginger Spread

Yields about 3 cups spread

Plums can be both sweet and tangy; add a little peppery fresh ginger, and the result is a versatile spread that can be used both as a jam and a condiment for a cheese platter, or as a marinade or sauce for meat or poultry. Here's a *hip* tip for prepping the plums: Cut around each vertically, using the indent as a guide, then twist the halves apart. Use a melon baller to scoop out the pit. The weight ratio is 1:1; pitted plums to sugar.

Note: This recipe cannot be halved. It can be doubled provided the total volume of the ingredients does not exceed half the pressure cooker's capacity.

2 pounds fresh plums, halved and pitted
About 2 pounds sugar (see step 1)
½ cup freshly squeezed lemon juice
   (about 2 lemons)
One 1-inch piece fresh ginger, peeled and
   cut into 3 chunks
2 teaspoons olive oil

1. Weigh the cut-up plums (see "Weigh for Sugar and Measure for Pectin!,"

page 253), and then weigh an equal amount of sugar.

2. Heat the pressure cooker base on low heat (keep warm setting for electric cookers). Add the plums, sugar, lemon juice, ginger, and oil and stir to mix well. Cook, without stirring, until all of the sugar has dissolved and liquefied, about 5 minutes.

3. Close and lock the lid of the pressure cooker. Cook at high pressure (see "Get *Hip* About the Pressure," page 13) for 5 minutes/all cooker types. When the time is up, open the pressure cooker using the Natural Release method (see page 15); this should take 10 to 15 minutes for a stovetop cooker or 20 to 30 minutes for an electric cooker.

4. Fish out and discard the ginger, or if you prefer, keep it for a more savory kick. Use an immersion blender to puree the plum mixture in the cooker. Then return the cooker base to low heat ("keep warm" setting for electric cookers) and simmer the contents gently for 15 to 20 minutes, or until the jam sets (see "Has It Set Yet?," page 256).

5. Pour the spread into sterilized jars (see "Sterilize for Storage," page 251), or to freeze, into plastic food storage containers. Cover and refrigerate for up to 5 weeks, or freeze for up to 1 year.

Peach and Cardamom Preserves

Yields about 3 cups preserves

Peaches also go well with cinnamon, but cardamom pods give these preserves an exotic kick. I like to keep the skin on and then puree after pressure cooking—this creates a rustic, full-flavored spread. For a more refined jam, peel the peaches before pressure cooking them and instead of pureeing, just lightly crush them with a wooden spoon before adding the pectin. The weight ratio is 2:1; pitted peaches to sugar.

Note: This recipe cannot be halved. It can be doubled provided the total volume of the ingredients does not exceed half the pressure cooker's capacity.

> 2 pounds fresh peaches, pitted and coarsely sliced
> About 1 pound sugar (see step 1)
> 2 teaspoons ghee or vegetable oil
> 3 cardamom pods, lightly crushed
> ½ cup freshly squeezed lemon juice (about 2 lemons)
> Low or No-sugar pectin (follow package instructions)

1. Weigh the cut-up peaches (see "Weigh for Sugar and Measure for Pectin!" (this page), note the weight and volume, and then weigh half that amount of sugar.

2. Heat the pressure cooker base on medium heat; add the ghee and heat briefly. Add the cardamom and fry until the pods begin to release their aroma. Turn the heat

Weigh for Sugar and Measure for Pectin!

The best jams are created with a precise weight-based ratio of fruit to sugar; with pectin added to make the jam jell. In Europe, the pectin packages specify how much to add based on the weight of the fruit, so once you've weighed the fruit, it's easy to know how much pectin to add. But in the States, the pectin is specified based on the volume of the fruit, not the weight. Here's the method for working around this:

Use a digital scale. Weigh the fruit in a 4-cup measuring cup. Simply put the measuring cup on the scale and hit "tare" or "0," and then pile in the cut-up fruit. Write down the weight of the fruit in order to calculate the amount of sugar as directed in the recipe, and also its volume so you can calculate the pectin as directed on the package (some recipes may have more than 4 cups fruit, so just keep track of the total). Then weigh the determined amount of sugar in the same way, in a clean, dry measuring cup or bowl. (Actually, if it makes sense for your recipe, you can just put the pressure cooker base on the scale, hit tare, and then pour in the sugar to reach the determined weight.) This system will ensure a perfect jam no matter how much fruit you have on hand—or on which continent you happen to live.

to low, add the peaches, sugar, and lemon juice, and stir to mix well. Cook, without stirring, until all of the sugar has dissolved and liquefied, about 10 minutes.

3. Close and lock the lid of the pressure cooker. Cook at high pressure (see "Get *Hip* About the Pressure," page 13) for 3 minutes/all cooker types. When the time is up, open the pressure cooker using the Natural Release method (see page 15); this should take 10 to 15 minutes for a stovetop cooker, 20 to 30 minutes for an electric cooker.

4. Fish out and discard the cardamom pods. Use an immersion blender to puree the peach mixture in the cooker. Then return the cooker base to medium heat and bring the contents to a rolling boil. Stir in the pectin and boil, stirring constantly, for 3 to 5 minutes, or until the preserves set (see "Has It Set, Yet?," page 256).

5. Pour the preserves into sterilized jars (see "Sterilize for Storage," page 251), or to freeze, into plastic food storage containers. Cover and refrigerate for up to 5 weeks, or freeze for up to 1 year.

Apricot and Honey Jam

Yields about 3 cups jam

Honey can be substituted in equal weight for the sugar in any of the recipes in this chapter—but its delicate flavor is particularly well matched with apricots. The lighter the honey's color the more delicate its flavor. The weight ratio is 2:1; pitted apricots to honey.

Note: This recipe cannot be halved. It can be doubled provided the total volume

of the ingredients does not exceed half the pressure cooker's capacity.

> **2 pounds fresh apricots, pitted and quartered**
> **About 1 pound light-color honey (see step 1)**
> **½ cup freshly squeezed lemon juice (about 2 lemons)**
> **2 teaspoons olive oil**
> **Low or No-sugar pectin (follow package instructions)**

1. Weigh the cut-up apricots (see "Weigh for Sugar and Measure for Pectin!," page 253), note the weight and volume, and then weigh half that amount of honey.

2. Heat the pressure cooker base on low heat (keep warm setting on electric cookers). Add the apricots, honey, lemon juice, and oil and stir to mix well. Cook, without stirring, until all of the honey has liquefied, about 5 minutes.

3. Close and lock the lid of the pressure cooker. Cook at high pressure (see "Get *Hip* About the Pressure," page 13) for 3 minutes/all cooker types. When the time is up, open the pressure cooker using the Natural Release method (see page 15); this should take 10 to 15 minutes for a stovetop cooker, 20 to 30 minutes for an electric cooker.

4. Using an immersion blender, puree the apricot mixture in the cooker. Then heat the cooker base on medium heat and bring the contents to a rolling boil. Stir in the pectin and boil, stirring constantly, for 3 to 5 minutes, or until the jam sets (see "Has It Set Yet?," page 256).

5. Pour the jam into sterilized jars (see "Sterilize for Storage," page 251), or to freeze, into plastic food storage containers. Cover and refrigerate for up to 5 weeks, or freeze for up to 1 year.

Cherry Preserves

Yields about 3 cups preserves

Cherries are a glorious combination of sweet and tart and, like the plum spread, this jam is as well matched with both sweets and braised meats. The weight ratio is 2:1; pitted cherries to sugar.

Note: This recipe cannot be halved. It can be doubled provided the total volume of the ingredients does not exceed half the pressure cooker's capacity.

2 pounds fresh cherries, pitted and halved
About 1 pound sugar (see step 1)
½ cup freshly squeezed lemon juice (about 2 lemons)
2 teaspoons olive oil
Low or No-sugar pectin (follow package instructions)

1. Weigh the halved cherries (see "Weigh for Sugar and Measure for Pectin!," page 253), note the weight and volume, and then weigh half that amount of sugar.

2. Heat the pressure cooker base on low heat (keep warm setting on electric

cookers). Add the cherries, sugar, lemon juice, and oil and stir to mix well. Cook, without stirring, until all of the sugar has dissolved and liquefied, about 10 minutes.

3. Close and lock the lid of the pressure cooker. Cook at high pressure (see "Get *Hip* About the Pressure," page 13) for 3 minutes/all cooker types. When the time is up, open the pressure cooker using the Natural Release method (see page 15); this should take 10 to 15 minutes for a stovetop cooker, 20 to 30 minutes for an electric cooker.

4. Using a potato masher, lightly crush the cherries in the cooker Then heat the cooker base on medium heat and bring the contents to a rolling boil. Stir in the pectin and boil, stirring constantly, for 3 to 5 minutes, or until the preserves set (see "Has It Set Yet?," this page).

5. Pour the preserves into sterilized jars (see "Sterilize for Storage," page 251), or to freeze, into plastic food storage containers. Cover and refrigerate for up to 5 weeks, or freeze for up to 1 year.

Has It Set Yet?

When making preserves, instructions will often direct to cook "until jam consistency" or until it sets. How to tell?

As soon as you open the pressure cooker, take a small spoonful of the mixture and dot it on a cold ceramic plate. Count to 10, and then tilt the plate. If the mixture doesn't run, it has set. If it runs, simmer it, uncovered, for a bit longer or sprinkle it with a tad of "no or low-sugar" pectin to hurry the process along. (Put a small plate in the freezer just as you're starting to make your jam so it's ready for your tests when you are.)

Burstin' Berries

Typically, berry jam ingredients need to macerate overnight before cooking to coax the juices out and the sugar in. This process can vary anywhere from 6 to 24 hours. The pressure cooker eliminates this step in an instant. The berries practically "burst" open to release their juice and the fruit is quickly infused with a sugar and juice mixture.

1-Minute Strawberry and Rose Petal Jam

Yields about 3 cups jam

I have included two versions of this recipe. The main recipe uses "Low or No-Sugar Pectin", which is a jelling agent and gives you a jam similar to what you would find in a conventional grocery store. The variation that follows uses no pectin—and results in a very dark, concentrated, "tangy" old-style strawberry jam. If you include the rose petals, make sure they are fresh and pesticide free, and store the jam in jars—the petals won't freeze nicely. The weight ratio is 1:2; trimmed strawberries to sugar.

Note: This recipe cannot be halved. It can be doubled provided the total volume of the ingredients does not exceed half the pressure cooker's capacity.

2 pounds fresh strawberries, hulled and halved
About 1 pound sugar (see step 1)
4 tablespoons freshly squeezed lemon juice (about 2 lemons)

2 teaspoons olive oil
2 teaspoons rose water
Low or No-Sugar Pectin (follow package instructions)
Fresh rose petals, rinsed and strained (optional)

1. Weigh the trimmed strawberries (see "Weigh for Sugar and Measure for Pectin!," page 253), note the weight and volume, and then weigh half that amount of sugar.

2. Heat the pressure cooker base on low heat (keep warm setting on electric cookers). Add the strawberries, sugar, lemon juice, and oil and stir to mix well. Cook, without stirring, until all of the sugar has dissolved and liquefied, about 10 minutes.

3. Close and lock the lid of the pressure cooker. Cook at high pressure (see "Get *Hip* About the Pressure," page 13) for 1 minute/ all cooker types. When the time is up, open the pressure cooker using the Natural Release method (see page 15); this should take 10 to 15 minutes for a stovetop cooker, 20 to 30 minutes for an electric cooker.

4. Stir the rose water into the strawberries in the cooker and then, if you wish, use a potato masher to push down on the fruit a few times to break it up a little more. Then heat the cooker base on medium heat and bring the contents to a rolling boil. Stir in the pectin and boil, stirring constantly, for 3 to 5 minutes, or until the jam sets (see "Has It Set Yet?," page 256).

5. Pour the jam into sterilized jars (see "Sterilize for Storage," page 251), or to freeze, into plastic food storage containers. If you wish to include the rose petals, drop a few into the bottom of the jar and in the middle of the jam as you pour. The petals will be instantly sterilized by the heat of the jam. Cover and refrigerate for up to 5 weeks, or freeze for up to 1 year.

Variation

Pectin-free Strawberry Jam

This recipe yields only about 1 cup of super-tangy intensely flavored jam. Follow the 1-Minute Strawberry and Rose Petal Jam recipe, using only 1 teaspoon rose water and omitting the pectin. After pressure cooking the mixture, return the cooker base to low heat ("keep warm" setting for electric cookers) and simmer gently, uncovered, for 15 to 20 minutes, or until the jam sets (see "Has It Set Yet?," page 256). Then complete the recipe as written.

1-Minute Strawberry and
Rose Petal Jam

3-Minute Kiwi Preserves

Yields about 3 cups preserves

The black seeds are left out of some kiwi jams, but I like them. They say "kiwi" at a glance. The weight ratio is 2:1; peeled kiwis to sugar.

Note: This recipe cannot be halved. It can be doubled provided the total volume of the ingredients does not exceed half the pressure cooker's capacity.

> 2 pounds fresh kiwis, peeled and
>   coarsely chopped
> About 1 pound sugar (see step 1)
> 1 lemon
> 2 teaspoons olive oil
> Low or No-Sugar Pectin (follow package
>   instructions)

1. Weigh the chopped kiwis (see "Weigh for Sugar and Measure for Pectin!," page 253), note the weight and volume, and then weigh half that amount of sugar. Grate the zest from the lemon and squeeze its juice (there should be about ¼ cup juice).

2. Heat the pressure cooker base on low heat (keep warm setting on electric cookers). Add the kiwis, sugar, lemon zest and juice, and oil and stir to mix well. Cook, without stirring, until all of the sugar has dissolved and liquefied, about 10 minutes.

3. Close and lock the lid of the pressure cooker. Cook at high pressure (see "Get *Hip* About the Pressure," page 13) for 3 minutes/all cooker types. When the time is up, open the pressure cooker using the Natural Release method (see page 15); this

should take 10 to 15 minutes for a stovetop cooker, 20 to 30 minutes for an electric cooker.

4. If you wish, use a potato masher to push down on the fruit a few times to break it up a little more. Then heat the cooker base on medium heat and bring the contents to a rolling boil. Stir in the pectin and boil, stirring constantly, for 3 to 5 minutes, or until the preserves set (see "Has It Set Yet?," page 256).

5. Pour the preserves into sterilized jars (see "Sterilize for Storage," page 251), or to freeze, into plastic food storage containers. Cover and refrigerate for up to 5 weeks, or freeze for up to 1 year.

Blackberry–Balsamic Vinegar Jam

Yields about 3 cups jam

This jam is nearly black and will be equally at home as a topping for meat or another fruit, or on a cheesecake (see page 237), as well as slathered on a piece of toast. The weight ratio is 2:1; blackberries to sugar.

Note: This recipe cannot be halved. It can be doubled provided the total volume of the ingredients does not exceed half the pressure cooker's capacity.

> 2 pounds fresh blackberries (about
>   3 pints), washed and air-dried
> About 1 pound sugar (see step 1)
> 2 tablespoons balsamic vinegar

2 teaspoons olive oil

Low or No-Sugar Pectin (follow package instructions)

1. If you bought your berries by the pint, weigh them (see "Weigh for Sugar and Measure for Pectin!," page 253). Whether you purchased them by pint or weight, weigh sugar equal to half their weight. Note the volume of the berries so you will be able to calculate the amount of pectin to use.

2. Heat the pressure cooker base on low heat (keep warm setting on electric cookers). Add the blackberries, sugar, vinegar, and oil and stir to mix well. Cook, without stirring, until all of the sugar has dissolved and liquefied, about 10 minutes.

3. Close and lock the lid of the pressure cooker. Cook at high pressure (see "Get *Hip* About the Pressure," page 13) for 3 minutes/all cooker types. When the time is up, open the pressure cooker using the Natural Release method (see page 15); this should take 10 to 15 minutes for a stovetop cooker, 20 to 30 minutes for an electric cooker.

4. If you wish, use a potato masher to push down on the fruit a few times to break it up a little more. Then return the cooker base to medium heat and bring the contents to a rolling boil. Stir in the pectin and boil, stirring constantly, for 3 to 5 minutes, or until the jam sets (see "Has It Set Yet?," page 256).

5. Pour the jam into sterilized jars (see "Sterilize for Storage," page 251), or to freeze, into plastic food storage containers. Cover and refrigerate for up to 5 weeks, or freeze for up to 1 year.

Citrus Marmalades

Citrus fruits need to be treated a little differently from stone fruits and berries. Cooking them with sugar, as you do for preserves made with other fruits, will only toughen the peels. Instead, the peels must first be softened by boiling under pressure, without sugar, and then the sugar can be added to make a marmalade—which is the word for jam containing peel or rind.

The seeds and pith of citrus fruits are filled with natural pectin, so these marmalades will jell naturally and there is no need to add pectin powder to them. So while you won't need to note the volume of the fruit in order to calculate the pectin required, as you do for jam, you'll still need to weigh the fruit in order to know how much sugar to use.

Super-Easy Seedless Mandarin Marmalade

Yields about 5 cups marmalade

Seedless mandarin oranges have a very thin skin with very little pith, this means that they can be used almost whole! Use organic ones to ensure that the peels, which you are going to eat, are truly pesticide-free. The weight ratio is 1:1; mandarins to sugar.

Note: This recipe cannot be halved. It can be doubled provided the total volume of the ingredients does not exceed half the pressure cooker's capacity.

2 pounds seedless mandarin oranges
About 2 pounds sugar (see step 1)
2 lemons
2½ cups water, or as needed
2 teaspoons olive oil

1. Place the oranges on a digital scale and note their exact weight (see "Weigh for Sugar and Measure for Pectin!," page 253). Then weigh an equal amount of sugar; set the sugar aside.

2. Wash the oranges well with a clean "scrubby" sponge; then cut them into quarters and place in the pressure cooker base. Squeeze the juice from the lemons and add to the cooker; place the seeds from the lemons in a tea ball (or tie in cheesecloth) and set aside. Add just enough water to cover the orange quarters to the cooker and stir in the oil.

3. Close and lock the lid of the pressure cooker. Cook at high pressure (see "Get *Hip* About the Pressure," page 13) for 10 minutes/all cooker types. When the time is up, open the pressure cooker using the Natural Release method (see page 15); this should take 10 to 15 minutes for a stovetop cooker, 20 to 30 minutes for an electric cooker.

5. Heat the cooker base on low heat (keep warm setting on electric cookers). Add the sugar and the tea ball with the lemon seeds and stir to mix well. Cook, stirring constantly, until all of the sugar has dissolved and liquefied, about 10 minutes.

6. Remove the tea ball and, using an immersion blender puree the orange mixture in the cooker base. Then turn the heat to high and bring the mixture to a rolling boil; do not cover. Boil, stirring constantly, for 5 minutes, or until the marmalade sets (see "Has It Set Yet?," page 256).

7. Pour the marmalade into sterilized jars (see "Sterilize for Storage," page 251), or to freeze, into plastic food storage containers. Cover and refrigerate for up to 5 weeks, or freeze for up to 1 year.

Blood Orange Marmalade

Yields about 4 cups marmalade

A mandoline, one of my favorite kitchen helpers, makes quick work of prepping the fruit for this marmalade. This method of making marmalade can be used with other types of citrus too, but the ratio of sugar to fruit varies with the acidity and sweetness of the particular citrus, so I've provided a few variations. The ratio is based on weight, not volume, and should be exact, so use a scale and take notes as indicated in the recipe. The weight ratio is 1:1; blood oranges (after trimming) to sugar but for lemons, which are bitter, it's 1:2, while for sweeter kumquats it's 1:1. Make it with lemons to use in the Amaretti-Stuffed Apples, page 228.

Note: This recipe cannot be halved. It can be doubled provided the total volume of the ingredients does not exceed half the pressure cooker's capacity.

2 pounds blood oranges, plus 2 more to squeeze
½ cup water
2 teaspoons olive oil
About 2 pounds sugar (see step 5)

1. Wash the 2 pounds of oranges well with a clean "scrubby" sponge. Cut each in half. Set a mandoline to "thin" and slice them, discarding the ends or any slices that are all pith. Then arrange the slices in short stacks, picking out the seeds as you go. Place the seeds in a tea ball (or tie in cheesecloth) and set aside. Cut each stack of slices into 4 wedges.

2. Put the pressure cooker base on a digital scale and press "tare" or zero, then add the orange pieces and any juices that may have squirted out as you cut them. Write down the weight of the fruit (for example, 28 ounces). Remove the cooker from the scale.

3. Squeeze enough juice from the 2 additional oranges to equal ½ cup. Add it to the pressure cooker along with the water and oil and stir.

4. Close and lock the lid of the pressure cooker. Cook at high pressure (see "Get *Hip* About the Pressure," page 13) for 10 minutes/all cooker types. When the time is up, open the pressure cooker using the Natural Release method (see page 15); this should take 10 to 15 minutes for a stovetop cooker, 20 to 30 minutes for an electric cooker.

5. In the meantime, put a bowl on the scale, set the scale to zero again, and put sugar in the bowl to equal the weight noted for your fruit.

6. When the cooker is open, heat the base on low heat (keep warm setting on electric cookers). Add the sugar and the tea ball with the orange seeds and stir to mix well. Cook, stirring constantly, until all of the sugar has dissolved and liquefied, about 10 minutes. Then turn the heat to high and bring the mixture to a rolling boil; do not cover. Boil, stirring constantly, for 5 minutes, or until the marmalade sets (see "Has It Set Yet?," page 256).

7. Pour the marmalade into sterilized jars (see "Sterilize for Storage," page 251), or to freeze, into plastic food storage containers. Cover and refrigerate for up to 5 weeks, or freeze for up to 1 year.

Variations

Orange and Rosemary Marmalade

Follow the Blood Orange Marmalade recipe, adding 2 fresh rosemary sprigs to the pressure cooker with the oranges and orange juice.

Pink Lemon Marmalade

Follow the Blood Orange Marmalade recipe, using lemons instead of oranges, adding 1 cup chopped, dried cranberries to the pressure cooker along with the lemons and lemon juice, and using sugar equal to twice the weight of the cut-up lemons.

Kumquat Marmalade

Follow the Blood Orange Marmalade recipe, using kumquats instead of oranges and sugar equal to half the weight of the cut-up kumquats. However, slice the kumquats by hand into 3 or 4 rounds (no need to stack and quarter them), and use all of the peel, including the end slices. There will be a lot of seeds, you need use only as many as fill the tea ball and discard the rest.

Juice Extraction

The pressure cooker is the perfect vehicle for extracting fruit or vegetable juice. Instead of mechanically crushing the fruit, delicate pressure is applied by the steam in the cooker, and the process is very quick, preserving most of the nutrients and vitamins of the food. The juice can be used in a soup or braise, as a base for making a jelly, or turned into a syrup that can be used in desserts, drinks, and cocktails!

This process requires quite a few accessories, however if you don't have two steamer baskets but you do have a lowly trivet, it can be used in the base of the cooker in place of a steamer basket. The top item HAS to be a steamer basket because it must contain fruit and strain its juices.

Raspberry Juice and Syrup

This recipe yields about 4 ounces (150 ml or ½ cup) of raspberry extract, which in turn will make about 8 ounces (250 ml or 1 cup) of raspberry syrup. The exact yield will vary, depending on the age of the fruit and how much you can fit in one layer in your steamer basket. You can reserve the juice from several batches and combine it to make a single, larger batch of syrup, just be sure to maintain the ratio of juice to sugar as directed in the step. In case you need an excuse for doing this, check out the recipe for making raspberry popsicles from the syrup (page 267). And feel free to use blackberries instead, equally yum!

Note: This recipe can be halved provided there is at least 1 cup of water in the pressure cooker (or your cooker's minimum liquid requirement). It cannot be doubled, instead, make as many batches as you wish.

1½ pints fresh raspberries, washed and air-dried
About 1 cup sugar, for the syrup (see step 4)

1. Add 1 cup of water (or the minimum amount required by your cooker to reach pressure) to the pressure cooker base. Insert a steamer basket (or trivet) and place a 4-cup heat-proof bowl cradled in a foil sling (see page 11) in it. Place a second steamer basket on top of (or inside) the bowl. Add berries to the top steamer basket, spreading in a single layer. Reserve any remaining berries to use whole in popsicles (page 267) or for another use.

2. Close and lock the lid of the pressure cooker. Cook at high pressure (see "Get *Hip* About the Pressure," page 13) for 12 minutes/all cooker types. When the time is up, open the pressure cooker using the Natural Release method (see page 15); this should take 10 to 15 minutes for a stovetop cooker, 20 to 30 minutes for an electric cooker.

3. Lift the basket with the berries out of the cooker. Then carefully lift out the bowl and pour the extracted juice into a measuring cup. (If you do not want to make syrup, use the juice now or skip to the last step to store it properly.) The berries will still appear plump, but don't be fooled, their precious juice has leaked into the bowl below, and they are filled with water now so do not squeeze them; you can eat them separately if you like but they won't taste very nice anymore.

4. To make a syrup, first note the amount of extracted juice in the measuring cup. Then pour the juice into a small heavy-bottomed saucepan. Measure sugar equal to twice the amount of juice and add it to the saucepan. (For example, if there is ½ cup juice, add 1 cup sugar.) Place the pan over medium heat and stir the mixture constantly until the sugar has completely dissolved, about 5 minutes; the syrup will not be obviously thick while hot but it will thicken as it cools.

5. To store the juice or syrup, pour it into a food storage container and refrigerate until ready to use (up to 3 weeks). Or dilute the syrup with half as much water and make into ice cubes to put in lemonade or iced tea later!

Prickly Pear Juice and Syrup

Prickly pears are a cactus fruit that can be anywhere from yellow to orange to ruby-red inside. Once you get past the prickly part, the fruit has a refreshing flavor that is a

bit of a mix between a banana and a plum. Unfortunately these fruits are packed with large spherical seeds that can either be spit out like small marbles or swallowed—with restraint, as swallowing seeds from more than a few prickly pears can lead to constipation. It requires talent to peel prickly pears without getting any spines into the fruit or yourself. Handle them with newspapers, metal forks (or disposable plastic) or tongs (not silicone-tipped), and don't store them in a plastic tub unless it won't be used for anything else, EVER. Luckily, pressure cooking resolves most of the handling and digestive problems. This recipe allows you to be adventurous without becoming a prickly pear expert because you get all the flavor without the seeds or the perils of peeling. It yields about 4 ounces (150 ml or ½ cup) of prickly pear juice, which in turn will make about 8 ounces (250 ml or 1 cup) of prickly pear syrup. You can reserve the juice from several batches and combine it to make a single, larger batch of syrup, just be sure to maintain the ratio of juice to sugar as directed in the step. The syrup in turn makes a great cordial, for which the recipe follows.

Note: This recipe can be halved provided there is at least 1 cup of water in the pressure cooker (or your cooker's minimum liquid requirement). It cannot be doubled, instead, make as many batches as you wish.

About 6 prickly pears, not peeled
About 1 cup sugar, for the syrup
  (see step 5)

1. Add 1 cup of water (or the minimum amount required by your cooker to reach pressure) to the pressure cooker base. Insert a steamer basket (or trivet) and place a 2-cup heat-proof bowl cradled in a foil sling in it. Place a second steamer basket (not made of silicone) on top of the bowl.

2. Holding them with tongs (not silicone-tipped), or with two forks, carefully cut each pear into 4 wedges and arrange the wedges in a single layer in the top steamer basket. Stop cutting when the layer is complete; set any remaining pears aside for another batch.

3. Close and lock the lid of the pressure cooker. Cook at high pressure (see "Get *Hip* About the Pressure," page 13) for 15 minutes/all cooker types. When the time is up, open the pressure cooker using the Natural Release method (see page 15); this should take 10 to 15 minutes for a stovetop cooker, 20 to 30 minutes for an electric cooker.

4. Lift the top steamer basket out of the cooker and tumble the prickly pears onto several layers of newspaper; wrap the paper around the pears and discard in the trash. Take the steamer basket directly to the sink; rinse well. Carefully lift the bowl out of the cooker and pour the extracted juice into a measuring cup. (If you do not want to make syrup, use the juice now or skip to the last step to store it properly.)

5. To make a syrup, first note the amount of extracted juice in the measuring cup. Then pour the juice into a small heavy-bottomed saucepan. Measure sugar equal to twice the amount of juice and add it to the saucepan. (For example, if there is ½ cup juice, add 1 cup sugar.) Place the pan over medium heat and stir the mixture constantly until the sugar has completely dissolved (about 5 minutes); the syrup will not be obviously thick while hot but it will thicken as it cools.

6. To store the juice or syrup, pour it into a food storage container and refrigerate until ready to use (up to 3 weeks) or freeze.

Prickly Pear Cordial

Makes 1 cordial
(duplicate as desired)

Serve these cordials on a hot summer afternoon, accompanied by your own tale of spiny danger!

6 ounces (¾ cup) chilled sparkling water or sparkling wine
1 tablespoon Prickly Pear Syrup, more if desired
1 sprig lemon thyme

Pour the water into a pretty glass. Stir in the syrup. Tuck in a thyme sprig and serve!

Prickly ... indeed

Handling prickly pears is a tricky affair. You want to house and treat them in temporary containers as their spines will spear and remain embedded in anything. I will never live down accidentally hand-washing my undergarments in a plastic tub exclusively reserved for prickly pears on my newlywed visit to my husband's Southern Italian family. I didn't realize my mistake until I donned said undergarments and now my misadventure is part of the little town's "remember when . . ." snickering lore. When I visit I'm referred to as "Isn't she the one who . . ."

Raspberry Syrup Popsicles

Yields about 8 popsicles,
depending on mold size

Once you've made raspberry syrup, popsicles are a snap to make. Allow time for them to freeze though, overnight if possible. (And if your kids are like mine, you'll want to remind them that checking the status every half hour does not make the popsicles freeze faster!)

2 cups warm water
1 cup Raspberry Juice and Syrup
    (page 264)
Fresh mint leaves
½ cup fresh raspberries (approximately,
    reserved from the syrup making)

Mix the water and syrup in a 4-cup measuring cup or a pitcher (warm water helps the syrup loosen up quickly). Place a couple of mint leaves and 2 or 3 raspberries in each popsicle mold, then pour in the syrup mixture. Close the molds and place in the freezer until solid.

Raspberry Syrup Popsicles

Appendix: *Pressure Cooking Timetables*

The charts on the following pages provide the basic information needed to successfully pressure cook a great variety of foods. For helpful tips on each ingredient group or recipe type, refer to the "Get *Hip* About..." sidebars at the beginning of the recipe chapters. Add your favorite seasoning and enjoy!

DRIED BEANS and LEGUMES

	Stovetop Cooker: Minutes to Cook	Electric Cooker: (or Nonstandard Stovetop): Minutes to Cook	Stovetop Cooker: Minutes to Cook	Electric Cooker: (or Nonstandard Stovetop): Minutes to Cook	Pressure	Release Method	Cooking Method
	DRIED		SOAKED, QUICK-SOAKED (OR FRESH)				
Adzuki	14	18–20	5	6–9	High	Natural	Boil
Anasazi	20	22–24	4	5–7	High	Natural	Boil
Black	25	28–30	4	5–7	High	Natural	Boil
Black-eyed Peas	6	7–8	3	4–5	High	Natural	Boil
Borlotti	20	23–25	7	8–10	High	Natural	Boil
Cannellini	25	28–30	6	7–8	High	Natural	Boil
Chickpeas	35	38–40	13	18–20	High	Natural	Boil
Chickpeas, split	5	6–9	Not necessary		High	Natural	Boil
Corona	25	28–30	8	10–12	High	Natural	Boil
Cranberry	20	23–25	7	8–10	High	Natural	Boil
Fava, dried	25	28–30	10	12–14	High	Natural	Boil
Fava, fresh	6	7–8	Not necessary		High	Normal	Boil
Garbanzo (see Chickpeas)							
Giant White Beans (see Coronas)							
Great Northern	25	28–30	6	7–8	High	Natural	Boil
Green Beans (see Vegetables Timetable)							
Kidney, (see Borlotti)							
Kidney, white (see Great Northern)							
Kidney, red	22	23–25	6	7–8	High	Natural	Boil
Lentils, French green, green, or mini	8	10–12	Not necessary		High	Natural	Boil
Lentils, red or yellow split	1	1	Not necessary		High	Natural	Boil
Lentils, regular	10	12–14	Not necessary		High	Natural	Boil
Lima, baby or large	12	13–15	6	7–8	High	Natural	Boil
Mung	6	7–8	Not necessary				
Navy or Pea or White	18	20–22	6	7–8	High	Natural	Boil
Peanuts, fresh			45	48–50	High	Natural	Boil
Peas, dried, whole	16	19–20	8	10–12	High	Natural	Boil
Peas, green or yellow split	6	7–8	Not necessary		High	Natural	Boil

DRIED BEANS and LEGUMES

	Stovetop Cooker: Minutes to Cook	Electric Cooker: (or Nonstandard Stovetop): Minutes to Cook	Stovetop Cooker: Minutes to Cook	Electric Cooker: (or Nonstandard Stovetop): Minutes to Cook	Pressure	Release Method	Cooking Method
	DRIED		**SOAKED, QUICK-SOAKED (OR FRESH)**				
Pinto (see Borlotti)							
Romano (see Vegetables Timetable)							
Scarlet runner	18	20–22	6	7–8	High	Natural	Boil
Soy, black	35	38–40	20	18–20	High	Natural	Boil
Soy, red (see Adzuki)							
Soy, yellow or beige	35	38–40	20	18–20	High	Natural	Boil
White Beans (see Navy)							

Never fill the pressure cooker more than half full.

Use oil or butter to reduce foaming.

Open with the Natural, Slow Normal, or Cold-Water Quick Release methods (pages 14–15).

FISH and SEAFOOD

	Stovetop Cooker: Minutes to Cook	Electric Cooker: (or Nonstandard Stovetop): Minutes to Cook	Pressure	Release Method	Cooking Method
Calamari	10	13–15	High	Quick, Normal	Boil
Carp	4	4	Low	Quick, Normal	Steam
Clams, canned/jarred	Add after pressure cooking a recipe and then warm through in the uncovered cooker.				NA
Clams, fresh	5	5	Low	Quick, Normal	Steam
Cod	3	3	Low	Quick, Normal	Steam
Crab	2	2	Low	Quick, Normal	Steam
Eel	8	8	High	Quick, Normal	Boil
White Fish, fillet	2	3	Low	Quick, Normal	All
Fish stock	5	7–8	High	Quick, Normal	Boil
White Fish, steak	3	3	Low	Quick, Normal	Steam
Fish, mixed pieces (for Fish Soup)	6	6	Low	Quick, Normal	All
White Fish, whole cleaned	5	5	Low	Quick, Normal	All
Frog's Legs	5	5	High	Quick, Normal	Braise, Boil
Haddock	6	6	Low	Quick, Normal	Steam
Halibut	6	6	Low	Quick, Normal	Steam
Lobster (2 lb/1k)	2	2	Low	Quick, Normal	Steam
Mussels	1	1	Low	Quick, Normal	Steam
Ocean Perch	6	6	Low	Quick, Normal	Steam
Octopus	15	18–20	High	Normal, Natural	Boil
Oysters	4	4	Low	Normal	Steam, Braise
Perch	4	4	Low	Quick, Normal	Steam
Prawns (shrimp)	1	1	Low	Quick, Normal	All
Salmon	5	5	Low	Quick, Normal	Steam
Scallops	1	1	Low	Quick, Normal	Steam
Scampi	4	4	Low	Quick, Normal	Braise, Boil
Shrimp	4	4	Low	Quick, Normal	All
Swordfish	5	5	Low	Quick, Normal	Steam
Trout	8	8	Low	Quick, Normal	Steam

Don't crowd fish in steamer basket.

Almost always use low pressure.

FRUIT	Stovetop Cooker: Minutes to Cook	Electric Cooker: (or Nonstandard Stovetop): Minutes to Cook	Pressure	Cooking Method	Release Method
Apples	1	1	High	Boil	Natural
Apricot	2	2	High	Steam	Normal
Blackberries	1	1	High	Steam	Normal
Blueberries	1	1	High	All	Normal
Cherries	3	3	High	Steam	Normal
Chestnuts	20	30	High	Boil	Natural
Coconut Milk	5	5	Low	Boil	Normal
Cranberries	5	5	High	All	Normal
Figs	3	3	Low/High	Steam, Braise	Normal, Quick
Grapes/Raisins	2	5–7	High	All	Normal
Kumquat, slices	10	13	High	Boil	Natural
Lemon, wedges	10	15	High	Boil	Natural
Orange, wedges	10	15	High	Boil	Natural
Peaches	3	3	High	All	Normal
Pears, sliced	2	2	High	All	Natural
Pears, whole	5	4	High	All	Natural
Plums/Prunes	5	5	High	All	Natural
Quince	10	15	High	Steam	Natural
Raspberries	1	1	High	Steam, Braise	Quick
Strawberries	1	1	High	Steam, Braise	Natural

Never fill pressure cooker more than half-full.

Use oil or butter to reduce foaming.

Open with Natural, Slow Normal, or Cold-Water Quick Release methods (pages 14–15).

GRAINS and PASTA

	Liquid per Cup	Stovetop Cooker: Minutes to Cook	Electric Cooker: (or Nonstandard Stovetop): Minutes to Cook	Pressure	Release Method
Amaranth	2 cups	8	8	High	Normal
Barley, flakes	4½ cups	9	9	High	Normal
Barley, pearled	2 cups	18	20	High	Natural
Barley, whole	2¼ cups	30	35–40	High	Natural
Bread (see specific recipes)				High	Natural
Buckwheat	2 cups	3	3	High	Natural
Bulgur	3 cups	8	8	High	Normal
Cornmeal (see Polenta or Hominy)					
Farro (semipearled)	2 cups	9	9	High	Normal
Hominy	4 cups	10	12–15	High	Normal
Kamut, whole	3 cups	10	10	High	Natural
Tamales/Masa Harina	See recipe p. 000	15	15	High	Normal
Millet	1½ cups	1	1	High	Natural
Oats, rolled	4 cups	10	10	High	Normal
Oats, steel-cut	3 cups	5	5	High	Normal
Pasta	To cover	See "Pressure Cook Pasta to al Dente," page 000		Low	Quick, Normal
Polenta, coarse	4 cups	8	8	High	Quick, Normal
Polenta, fine (not instant)	3 cups	5	5	High	Quick, Normal
Quinoa	1½ cups	1	1	High	10-Minute Natural
Rice, Arborio	2 cups	7	7	High	Quick, Normal
Rice, Basmati	1½ cups	4	4	High	10-Minute Natural
Rice, Basmati (soaked)	1 cup	3	3	High	10-Minute Natural
Rice, Brown	1¼ cups	18	20	High	10-Minute Natural
Rice, Jasmine (rinsed)	1 cup	1	1	High	10-Minute Natural
Rice Pudding	3 cups	10	10	High	Normal
Rice, Romano	2¼ cups	5	5	High	Quick, Normal

GRAINS and PASTA	Liquid per Cup	Stovetop Cooker: Minutes to Cook	Electric Cooker: (or Nonstandard Stovetop): Minutes to Cook	Pressure	Release Method
Rice, White, long-grain	1½ cups	4	4	High	10-Minute Natural
Rice, White, short-grain	1½ cups	8	8	High	10-Minute Natural
Rice, Wild	3 cups	22	24–26	Low	10-Minute Natural
Semolina	3 cups	4	4	Low	Quick, Normal
Spelt Berries (see Farro)					
Wheat Berries	3 cups	30	35–40	High	Natural

Never fill the pressure cooker more than half full.

Use oil or butter to reduce foaming.

Open with Natural, Slow Normal, or Cold-Water Quick Release methods (pages 14–15).

DAIRY, EGGS, MEAT, and POULTRY	Stovetop Cooker: Minutes to Cook	Electric Cooker: (or Nonstandard Stovetop): Minutes to Cook	Pressure	Release Method	Cooking Method
Beef bones, etc. (for stock)	60	70–75	High	Natural	Boil
Beef, brisket	50–55	60–70	High	Natural	Boil
Beef, cubed	15	18–20	High	Normal/Natural	Braise, Boil
Beef, ground	5	8	High	Natural	Boil
Beef, ossobuco	20–25	25–30	High	Natural	Braise
Beef, oxtail	35	40–45	High	Natural	Boil
Beef, ribs	20	23–25	High	Natural	Boil, Braise
Beef, rolls	20	23–25	High	Natural	Boil, Braise
Beef, roast (shoulder, rump, or round)	50–55	60–70	High	Natural	Boil, Braise
Beef, tongue	50–55	60–65	High	Natural	Braise
Boar, cubed	15–20	20–25	High	Normal, Natural	Braise, Boil
Boar, roast	40–45	50–60	High	Natural	Braise, Boil
Cheese (to melt) Note: In ramekins, uncovered	Read specific instructions on www.hippressurecooking.com		High	Natural	Steam
Chicken bones, etc. (for stock)	30–35	40–45	High	Natural	Boil
Chicken, breasts (boneless)	4	4	High	Quick	Steam, Braise
Chicken, liver	3	3	High	Quick	Braise
Chicken, pieces (bone-in)	10	12–14	High	All	Braise
Chicken, whole (up to 4 lbs/2kg)	20	26–20	High	Normal, Natural	Boil, Braise
Cornish Hen, whole	8	10–12	High	Normal	Braise
Deer, saddle	15	18–20	High	Normal	Braise, Boil
Deer, roast	20–30	25–30	High	Natural	Roast
Duck, pieces	8	10–12	High	Normal	Braise
Duck, whole	25–30	30–35	High	Normal, Natural	Roast
Eggs, en cocotte	3–4	3–4	Low	Quick	Steam
Eggs, hard-boiled Note: In steamer basket	See recipe page 55		Low	All	Steam
Eggs, poached	2	2	Low	Normal	Steam
Elk, roast	25–30	30–35	High	Normal, Natural	Braise, Boil
Elk, stew	15–20	20–25	High	Normal, Natural	Braise, Boil

DAIRY, EGGS, MEAT, and POULTRY

	Stovetop Cooker: Minutes to Cook	Electric Cooker: (or Nonstandard Stovetop): Minutes to Cook	Pressure	Release Method	Cooking Method
Goat	15–20	20–25	High	Normal, Natural	Braise, Boil
Goose, pieces	15–20	20–25	High	Normal	Braise
Ham (see Pork)					
Hare	30	35–30	High	Normal, Natural	Braise, Boil
Lamb, chops	3–7	3–7	High	Normal	Braise
Lamb, ground	10	12–15	High	Normal	Boil
Lamb, leg/shank	30	35–40	High	Normal	Braise, Boil
Lamb, roast	20	25–30	High	Natural	Roast
Lamb, shoulder	20	25–30	High	Normal, Natural	Braise, Boil
Lamb, stew	10	12–15	High	Normal, Natural	Braise, Boil
Milk, coconut (see FRUIT TIMETABLE)					
Milk, condensed	Read specific instructions on www.hippressurecooking.com		High	Natural	Boil
Mutton (see Lamb)					
Pheasant	15–20	20–25	High	Normal, Natural	Braise, Boil
Pigeon	20–25	20–25	High	Normal, Natural	Braise, Boil
Pork, stew	15–20	20–25	High	Normal	Boil
Pork, belly	35–40	45–50	High	Normal, Natural	Braise, Boil
Pork, chops or steaks	5	7–8	High	Normal, Quick	Steam, Braise
Pork, cubes	10	10	High	Normal, Natural	Braise, Boil
Pork, loin	5–7	5–7	High	Natural	All
Pork, ribs	20	23–25	High	Normal, Natural	All
Pork, roast (shoulder or leg)	40	55–60	High	Normal, Natural	All
Pork, foot/ham hock (raw)	35–40	45–50	High	Natural	Boil
Pork, sausage (must be pierced)	8–10	8–10	High	Normal, Quick	Steam, Boil
Pork, shank	30–35	35–40	High	Normal, Natural	Braise, Boil
Pork, shoulder	45–50	50–60	High	Natural	Braise, Boil
Pork, stock (bones, etc.)	45–60	60–75	High	Natural	Boil
Pork, ground	5	5	High	Normal	Boil
Quail	7	7	High	Normal	Braise
Rabbit	15–20	20–25	High	Natural	Braise, Boil

DAIRY, EGGS, MEAT, and POULTRY	Stovetop Cooker: Minutes to Cook	Electric Cooker: (or Nonstandard Stovetop): Minutes to Cook	Pressure	Release Method	Cooking Method
Roast Beef, medium	8–10	8–10	High	Normal	Roast
Roast Beef, rare	6–8	6–8	High	Quick	Roast
Roast Beef, well done	10–12	10–12	High	Natural	Roast
Squab (see Pigeon)					
Tripe	15–20	20–25	High	Natural	Boil
Turkey, breast (stuffed/rolled)	20	22–25	High	Normal	Braise, Boil
Turkey, breast sliced	7	7–9	High	Normal	Steam, Braise
Turkey, legs	25–30	35–40	High	Natural	Braise Boil
Turkey, wings	15–20	20–25	High	Natural	Braise, Boil
Veal, chop or steak	5–8	5–8	High	Normal, Quick	Steam, Braise
Veal, ground	5	8	High	Normal	Boil
Ossobuco, veal	35	40–45	High	Normal, Natural	Braise, Boil
Veal, roast (shoulder or rump)	45	50–60	High	Normal, Natural	Braise, Roast
Veal Stock (bones, etc.)	45–60	60–80	High	Natural	Boil
Veal, tongue	40	40	High	Natural	Braise
Venison (see Deer or Boar)					

Boil tough meats, steam delicate meats, and braise everything in between.

VEGETABLES	Stovetop Cooker: Minutes to Cook	Electric Cooker: (or Nonstandard Stovetop): Minutes to Cook	Pressure	Release Method	Cooking Method
Artichoke, hearts	4	4	High	Normal	Steam, Braise
Artichoke, pieces or baby	4	4	High	Normal	Steam, Braise
Artichoke, whole large	9	9	High	Normal	Steam
Artichoke, whole medium	6	6	High	Normal	Steam
Asparagus	2	2	High	Normal	Steam
Beans, fresh shelled	Follow cooking time for soaked beans	Follow cooking time for soaked beans	High	Natural	Boil, Steam, Braise
Beans, green (see Green Beans and Romano)					
Beet Greens	2	4	High	Normal	Steam
Beets, cubed	4	8	High	Natural	Boil, Steam, Braise
Beets, whole (small, med, large)	10, 15, 20	15, 20 ,25	High	Normal	Boil
Bok Choy, leaves and stems	5	5	High	Normal	Boil, Steam, Braise
Broccoli	3	3	High	Normal	Steam, Braise
Brussels Sprouts	3	3	High	Normal	Steam
Cabbage, red, green, Savoy	5	5	High	Normal	Steam, Braise
Capsicums (see Peppers)					
Carrots, sliced	4	4	High	Normal	Steam
Carrots, whole	8	8	High	Normal	Steam, Braise
Cauliflower, florets	3	3	High	Normal	Steam
Cauliflower, whole	6	6	High	Normal	Steam, Braise
Celery, sliced	2	2	High	Normal	Braise, Boil
Chicory	5	7	High	Natural	Boil
Chinese Cabbage (see Bok Choy)					
Collards	6	8	High	Normal	Boil
Corn, kernels	1	1	High	Normal	Boil, Steam, Braise
Corn, on the cob	2-5	2-5	High	Normal	Boil, Steam, Braise
Eggplant	5	5	High	Quick	Steam/Braise

VEGETABLES	Stovetop Cooker: Minutes to Cook	Electric Cooker: (or Nonstandard Stovetop): Minutes to Cook	Pressure	Release Method	Cooking Method
Endive	1	1	High	Quick	Steam
Fennel, thickly sliced	3	3	High	Quick	Steam, Braise
Garlic	5	5	High	Normal	Steam
Green Beans	8	8	High	Normal	Steam, Braise
Greens, chopped	3	5	High	Normal	Boil
Kale, curly	3	3	High	Normal	Boil, Steam, Braise
Kohlrabi, pieces	3	5	High	Quick	Boil, Steam, Braise
Leeks	3	3	High	Quick	Boil, Steam, Braise
Mushrooms, dried	10	15	High	Natural	Boil
Mushrooms, fresh white or cultured	5	5	High	Normal	Braise
Mushrooms, fresh wild	7	7	High	Normal	Boil, Braise
Mustard greens (see Bok Choi)					
Okra	3	3	High	Normal	Boil, Steam, Braise
Onions, cut or whole	3	3	High	Normal	Boil, Steam, Braise
Onions, baby	2	2	High	Normal, Quick	Boil, Steam, Braise
Peas	2	2	High	Normal	Boil, Steam, Braise
Peppers, Bell	3	3	High	Normal	Boil, Steam, Braise
Peppers, small or hot	1	1	High	Normal	Boil, Steam, Braise
Potatoes, baby or fingerling	5	8	High	Natural	Boil, Steam, Braise
Potatoes, quartered	5	8	High	Natural, Normal	Steam, Braise
Potatoes, small, new or red	5	7	High	Natural, Normal	Steam, Braise
Potatoes, whole, medium or large	10–13	13–15	High	Natural, Normal	Boil, Steam, Braise
Pumpkin, sliced	5	5	High	Natural, Normal	Steam, Braise

VEGETABLES	Stovetop Cooker: Minutes to Cook	Electric Cooker: (or Nonstandard Stovetop): Minutes to Cook	Pressure	Release Method	Cooking Method
Romano Beans	3	3	High	Normal	Steam, Braise
Rutabagas	3	5	High	Normal	Boil, Steam, Braise
Spinach, fresh	1	1	High	Normal	Boil, Braise
Squash, Acorn, halved	7	7	High	Natural, Normal	Steam, Braise
Squash, Banana, cubed	3	3	High	Natural, Normal	Steam, Braise
Squash, Butternut, halved	6	6	High	Natural, Normal	Steam, Braise
Squash, Butternut, large chunks	4	4	High	Natural, Normal	Steam, Braise
Squash, Spaghetti, halved	5	5	High	Natural, Normal	Steam
Squash, Summer (see Zucchini)					
Sweet Potato	5	8	High	Natural, Normal	Steam, Braise
Swiss Chard	2	2	High	Normal	Braise
Tomato Sauce	5	5	High	Natural	Boil, Braise
Tomatoes, sliced	3	3	High	Normal	Boil, Braise
Turnips, sliced	3	3	High	Normal	Braise
Turnips, whole	5	5	High	Normal	Steam
Yams (see Sweet Potato)			High		
Zucchini	5	5	High	Normal	Boil, Steam, Braise

Steam most vegetables and keep the cooking liquid to use in other recipes.

Acknowledgments

My husband, Roberto, and children, Adriana and Vittorio, for eating every recipe in this book—sometimes for an entire week—until it was perfected.

Laura Del Rosso, Franco Ruggeri, Jill Terry, Ramiro Salas, Katherine and Jennifer, for their careful recipe testing and thoughtful feedback. Andrea S. Somberg, for her marketing, negotiation, and bottomless patience. Carol Spier and her wordcrafting that turned what I was trying to say into what should be said.

BJ Berti at St. Martin's Press, for taking a chance on pressure cooking.

Phillip Shima and Sigrid Trombely, for their sharp eyes and knives.

Most of all, I would like to acknowledge the readers of the *hip* pressure cooking website (www.hippressurecooking.com), for their enthusiastic support from the very beginning.

Thank you!

Index

283

About the Author

LAURA D. A. PAZZAGLIA picked up her first pressure cooker after seeing a friend make dinner in ten minutes flat. She quickly realized that the flavor of pressure cooked food is like tasting food in high definition! Three years ago Laura launched www.hippressurecooking.com to share her discoveries, recipes, reviews, and tips. Today Laura is considered one of the world's top experts. She lives in Italy, near Rome, and travels frequently to the United States and Europe to share her passion for pressure cooking.